The Craft of La Fontaine

The Craft of La Fontaine

MAYA SLATER

THE ATHLONE PRESS
LONDON

MADISON ● TEANECK
FAIRLEIGH DICKINSON UNIVERSITY PRESS

First published in 2000 by
THE ATHLONE PRESS
A Continuum imprint
The Tower Building, 11 York Road, London SE1 7NX

U.S. edition published 2001 by
Associated University Presses, 440 Forsgate Drive, Cranbury,
NJ 08512 USA

British Library Cataloguing in Publication Data
*A catalogue record for this book is available
from the British Library*

ISBN 0 485 11567 0 HB

Library of Congress Cataloging-in-Publication Data

Slater, Maya.
    The Craft of La Fontaine / Maya Slater.
       p. cm.
    Includes bibliographical references and index.
    ISBN 0-8386-3920-8 (alk. paper)
       1. La Fontaine, Jean de, 1621-1695. Fables. 2. La Fontaine, Jean de,
    1621-1695--Technique. I. Title.

PQ1808 .S53 2001
841'.4--dc21   00-053552

Typeset by Columns Design Ltd, Reading
Printed and bound in Great Britain by
MPG Books Ltd, Bodmin, Cornwall

Contents

V CREATING A WORLD

NOTE ON THE TRANSLATIONS

Since many of the points I make depend on close textual readings, I have translated the French of La Fontaine as closely and as literally as possible. I have made no attempt to convey the poetic feel of the originals, which would require a much freer translation. I have also refrained from imitating La Fontaine's rhythms and rhymes. For a recent verse translation of most of the fables I mention, see La Fontaine, *Selected Fables*, translated by Christopher Wood, Oxford World's Classics , 1995.

ACKNOWLEDGMENTS

My grateful thanks are due to Professor Jean-Pierre Collinet, who has read and advised me on earlier drafts of this book, and to Professor Terence Cave for his advice and encouragement. Finally, I would like to thank my husband, without whose support I could not have written this book, and Queen Mary and Westfield College for sabbatical leave in which to write it.

Introduction

This book is a defence of detail. In it the *Fables* are closely scrutinized, and the results minutely explored. This approach, which evolved during the years I was working on the *Fables*, is the result of a constant process of frustration, as I strove to incorporate in my analysis of an elusive writer everything I felt he was telling his reader. La Fontaine's poetry is onion-like. Try to peel him to get at the heart: every layer removed reveals another beneath. But that analogy fails to do justice to one of his most striking features, diversity: La Fontaine's poetry is perhaps more like a sackful of presents. Open it, and the items inside, all destined for our delight, are as varied as they are brightly-coloured. It could be argued that this is true of poetry in general, that the art of poetry is that of suggestion, every word evoking multiple meanings. But no poet is more suggestive than La Fontaine. It is impossible to get the point of his poems without subjecting them to close scrutiny – the impression given on a rapid reading is simply misleading.

Indeed, the very existence of La Fontaine's subtleties can easily be overlooked altogether. This is obvious from the response of Francophones who have learnt a few fables as children. They regard La Fontaine as simple enough for a child to understand; and in a sense, that is quite true. But his appeal is more complex than this. As Renée Kohn puts it, 'Les *Fables* conviennent aux adultes aussi bien qu'aux enfants, c'est un des rares livres qui vieillissent avec le lecteur' (p.143) *[The Fables are for adults as well as children, it is one of the few books to grow up with the reader]*. Part of his charm is to be accessible on a number of different levels at once. My process of discovery has often involved reading a poem naively, without afterthought or suspicion, realizing that the text contains an ambiguity, exploring that ambiguity, and arriving step by astonished step at completely unexpected conclusions. At times, I have come to realize that he is telling us the opposite of what I thought at first; or, thinking I had grasped his full message, I have become aware that he is actually conveying two opposite messages at once.

What, in any case, does 'La Fontaine's message' mean? He himself laid no claim to original thought in the *Fables* – he was merely the translator into verse of earlier fabulists like Aesop, Phaedrus or Pilpay. It is clearly important not to attribute to La Fontaine ideas and effects already present in the original fabulists from whom he derived the ideas for his poems. Often, indeed, the message of a La Fontaine fable and its presentation seem at first sight unoriginal, entirely borrowed from his source material. Here again it is essential to explore the poems in detail, perhaps comparing them with their sources, if we are to realize that he is saying much more than his predecessors, and saying it very differently.

I do not see La Fontaine as an easy poet: so much will be clear from the first pages of this book. His difficulty provides an added incentive to view his poetry in depth – the text can actually mislead us if we are inattentive. But even with a careful, in-depth reading, one is probably missing a great deal. During the composition of this book, I repeatedly had to revise my material to incorporate new insights, some of which dawned on me after reading a text a hundred times, while others were suggested by colleagues, friends and students.

In this study, I have attempted to be not only a close reader, but also a flexible one. Throughout, I have striven to adopt two specific approaches as reader. First, I have tried to be open to input of all kinds. No aspect of the poet's craft must be ignored, from his adaptation of his sources to the shape of his poem on the page. In my endeavour to be receptive to anything relevant I constantly came up against problems. One difficulty is the paucity of source material for the *Fables*. As Terence Allott explains, very few of the poems exist either in manuscript or in earlier versions, which could otherwise have offered some clue as to the development of the poet's thought.[1] We can only regret the general absence of a research tool that would undoubtedly often have proved invaluable. On the rare occasions where such material does exist, I have found it can greatly modify a reading of a poem, as will be apparent from my analysis of 'Le Renard, les Mouches et le Hérisson' *[The Fox, the Flies and the Hedgehog]*.

It is impossible to appreciate every nuance of a seventeenth-century French text like the *Fables*. In La Fontaine's poetry can be found veiled satirical attacks, recondite linguistic details, and allusions to forgotten works of literature or obscure currents of thought. As far as possible, I have taken account of this difficulty where it affects my close readings of the text. But it is not the purpose of my study to concentrate on this aspect, which has been admirably investigated by other writers.

My second principle as reader was to aim for rigour in my approach to the *Fables*. This might seem a straightforward endeavour, but La Fontaine can be very difficult to read accurately. The problem often rests with our initial assumptions. It is only too easy to assume that the meaning is obvious, without noticing that we are altering it to suit our preconceptions. If we empty our minds of such preformed notions we can find surprises in his poetry. In this book, I repeatedly try to show what happens if one looks at the actual words on the page – they turn out to have a rather different meaning from the one we were assuming. This method of reading can seem unsophisticated, as we laboriously pore over a line that at first view seems self-evident. But at worst, it has the merit of being honest, and prevents us from warping the text. At best, it enables us to disentangle hidden meanings, snarled up as they are in the web of our preconceived ideas, and to bring them to the light.

La Fontaine himself composed his work with immense care, rewriting his verse extensively, setting great store by getting every detail right. He states this clearly in comments throughout his career as a writer, and reveals it too if we read between the lines of his correspondence.[2] Such painstaking writing deserves equally careful reading.

Whatever the intrinsic merits or drawbacks of this approach, its justification must depend on its results. Throughout this book, I have tried to explore the wider implications of the unexpected discoveries the text has to offer: even when small, they can be significant. A hidden nuance that emerges on close analysis may reveal a new interpretation of a fable. This new perspective may then alter our perception of the way we classify that fable, which, in turn, may force us to re-evaluate La Fontaine's attitude to a major theme.

My reading of La Fontaine could be described, then, as both suspicious (since I am reluctant to make assumptions if they are belied by the actual words on the page), and naive (since I try to take his words at face value, and to divest myself of the presuppositions that might often inform a sophisticated reading).

The above considerations about reading the text have largely governed my choice of topics. However, this choice has also been determined by the desire to broaden the scope of my exploration. I have accordingly chosen topics that are varied enough to enable me to test my method. Their diversity also allows me to explore different facets of La Fontaine's art. In addition, I have tackled aspects that illustrate the difficulty of La Fontaine, which remains an underlying preoccupation throughout this book.

* * *

What general conclusions about La Fontaine can be drawn from my study? One of the most paradoxical aspects of La Fontaine's poetry is that it seems simultaneously pessimistic and ebullient. This contradiction can readily be deduced from the apparent incompatibility between the standpoints of critical works on the *Fables*. Some pages on La Fontaine convey the impression that the writer is a grave, thoughtful figure with the most high-minded of philosophical preoccupations; others describe a lively, mischievous, knavish figure, with a trick to play on every occasion. In both, there is much truth.

How can we reconcile these two opposites? In the course of preparing this study, I have repeatedly been struck by the profound difference between the content and the treatment of the *Fables*. When concentrating on the content, I detect an underlying pessimism in the mood. But when I focus on the craft, I always find it full of life and enthusiasm. This is perhaps one of the principal sources of La Fontaine's paradoxical quality – this simultaneous presence of gloom and *brio*. But it is too simple to say that the two moods coexist as equal partners in the *Fables*. The poet's joyful zest for the actual crafting of his poems affects the overall impression conveyed by the poetry. It is undeniable, though puzzling, that he is widely thought of above all as a witty, humorous fabulist – those critics who paint a more sombre picture are well aware of reading between the lines. I call this puzzling because the great majority of his *Fables* tell of death and suffering. Yet the typical La Fontaine fable has a sparkle that seems to be the result of personal preference rather than adherence to tradition: his forerunners, Aesop and Phaedrus, who give him the subjects for so many fables, are far less prone to lighten the gravity of their mood. La Fontaine pays due attention to this seriousness in his predecessors, but clearly needs to find a way round it. When comparing himself and Phaedrus as fabulists, and after paying due tribute to his illustrious mentor, he comments: 'j'ai cru qu'il fallait ...égayer l'ouvrage plus qu'il n'a fait.' *[I thought it necessary to enliven the work more than he did].* His justification is that he is fitting in with modern trends: 'C'est ce qu'on demande aujourd'hui. On veut de la nouveauté et de la gaieté' *[That is what people require these days. They want novelty and gaiety]* (Préface, p.7). This must surely be a specious excuse: he is, after all, writing at the precise time when verse tragedy is reaching its apotheosis with Racine. What he is seeking to justify is an approach that allows him to incorporate this fundamental contradiction in his whole endeavour as a fabulist.

This incompatibility at the heart of the *Fables* may well be responsible for an inner tension that contributes to the poems' vigour and excitement. La Fontaine plays continually on the element of ambivalence, presenting a wealth of variations on this theme, as on the one hand we commiserate with the victims, and on the other we relish the way their sufferings are described. We may lurch from one extreme of mood to another – from amusement at the wolf dressed in a shepherd's smock, wedging the crook between his front paws, to pity when, unable to free himself from these encumbrances, he is powerless to defend himself against his enemies (III 3). Conversely, we may experience a build-up of sympathy which is rapidly dispelled by the matter-of-fact description of the victim's actual death: this is the case with 'Le Loup et l'Agneau' *[The Wolf and the Lamb].* Or we may read a whole fable in a spirit of confusion, uncertain throughout whether to feel amused or sorry, for instance at the story of the capon flying for his life from the cook with his great knife: the poor bird's final desperate minutes are described in a cascade of witty puns and conceits (VIII 21). What all these have in common is that they require us to view the situation from two angles at once: our emotional response is rendered labile by the shifting perspectives.

Accordingly, this book moves from the optimistic to the pessimistic aspects of the *Fables*, as I progress from studying in detail the poet's craft, through his imagery to the presentation of characters, to narrative voice and ultimately to the shape of the whole.

It remains for me to set my approach in the context of recent La Fontaine criticism. Currently, there is a wide variety of approaches to La Fontaine's *Fables*, and a number of studies have been published, in France, the USA and elsewhere, though this is the first book to appear in Britain for many years. They range from examinations of the literary sources and the historical and philosophical background, through biography, to analyses of relevant themes and of different aspects of the poet's philosophy, poetics, and intellectual position. Most recent criticism of the *Fables* contains at least some close textual analysis. Detailed references can be found in my bibliography. I have not approached my material from any of these standpoints. Rather than directing it, I have allowed La Fontaine's text to lead me. But I also owe much to the many illuminating text-based insights in the works of major La Fontaine critics, and to the superb editorial work of Jean-Pierre Collinet and Marc Fumaroli. My debt to my many predecessors will be mentioned where relevant in my text. Their comments and their example have been an inspiration throughout this study.

I
Style

CHAPTER 1

The practical craftsman

In this chapter, I am focusing on La Fontaine at his most practical and down-to-earth, an efficient engineer whose fairy palaces are built on solid foundations. The more ethereal a building appears, the more it must rely on a stable base and accurate workmanship if its towers are not to topple. And La Fontaine is a great craftsman. This is the aspect examined in this chapter.

My method here is to select: an exhaustive account of La Fontaine's stylistic manipulations would be too unwieldy. I have therefore chosen key aspects of the poet's craft, and will discuss them in some detail. This has a particular advantage: it enables us to focus on the wealth of stylistic techniques that the poet brings to any one of the elements that together constitute his craft. We should thus gain some idea of the scope of his craft within a relatively short space – if he can extract such riches from any one aspect, then why not others?

Let us begin then with the opening lines of the poems, which are likely to determine the atmosphere of the fables that they introduce, in addition to being themselves remarkable for their variety and subtlety.

INCIPITS [3]

A poem's opening lines, or *incipits*, steer the reader in a particular direction. In the *Fables*, which tell a story in a limited space, they are especially crucial, since they must perform their determining function swiftly. In particular, they must prepare the reader to enter the world of the fable, a strange, often magical world, in which anything can happen. They tend to be couched in arresting language, demanding an attentive reading, and informing the reader that what is to follow is special, outside ordinary experience. A strong introduction of this type is enough to decide the main thrust of the ensuing poem. Consider the following example:

Mortellement atteint d'une flèche empennée
Un oiseau déplorait sa triste destinée (II 6)

*[Mortally wounded by a feathered arrow,/ A bird was lamenting his
sad destiny]*

The interesting feature of this beginning is just how much direction it gives the reader. As well as establishing a definitive mood of
exalted emotion and lyrical beauty, it also situates the poem to
come in a world where the supernatural is taken for granted. This
effect is achieved as follows: firstly, the poet establishes an archaic
setting with 'empennée' *[feathered]* [4], and evokes solemn themes
(death, destiny) in the language of high tragedy. Next, the bird-
hero is endowed from the start with the special attributes of a character in such a tragedy. He is aware of being singled out by his
'destinée' and sees his own impending death in a grandiose light.
His awareness further marks him out as a character from a different
kind of fiction, a reasoning animal like the protagonist of a fairy
tale. With this first couplet, then, the poet has prepared us for what
follows in the poem: the tragic story of a heroic animal, couched in
dignified language (unusually for La Fontaine, there is no irony).

This *incipit* firmly places the whole poem in a precise fictional
context. Such a strongly directive beginning remains exceptional in
the *Fables*. More frequently the poet begins on a more ambivalent
note, allowing for more development in the ensuing poem. Yet he
may still convey a powerful mood. 'Le Cerf se voyant dans l'eau'
(VI 9) is the story of a vain stag who admires his antlers and
despises his spindly legs. Later, as his legs carry him away from the
hunt, he realizes that he had his priorities wrong. The central part
of the poem shows up the folly of its protagonist, and to a certain
extent conflicts with the impression of tranquil beauty conveyed by
the first two lines:

Dans le cristal d'une fontaine
Un Cerf se mirant autrefois

[In the crystal of a fountain / A Stag was once gazing at himself]

The poem begins in lyrical, pastoral vein, establishing its
conventional poetic credentials with 'cristal', 'fontaine' and 'mirant'
[gazing]. 'Autrefois' evokes a distant, mysterious past. An anthro-

pomorphic reasoning animal is indicated in 'se mirant', since there is an element of narcissism in the stag's wondering gaze. Although La Fontaine has left himself scope to vary the mood later in the poem, he has from the very start established a literary and lyrical tone, placing the events in a wistfully beautiful context which will colour our reading of the whole.

Looking at still sketchier *incipits*, we can see that La Fontaine still manages to coax the reader by means of a range of devices to enter rapidly and almost without noticing into the realms of the imaginary. The most straightforward technique is simply to inform the reader that the diegetic world of the poem is derived not from fact but from fiction. He precedes one account with 'A ce que dit la fable' *[As the fable tells us]*(V 13), inviting us to assign the subsequent information to the world of fable. The same result is more discreetly achieved by incorporating marker-words that evoke a literary context. Starting a poem with 'Du temps que les bêtes parlaient' *[At a time when beasts could talk]* or even with 'Autrefois' (as with the Stag) hints at the desired impression simply because these formulations suggest a distant past as in a fairy tale. Alternatively, specific fictional contexts can be evoked. La Fontaine writes 'J'ai lu dans quelque endroit' *[I read somewhere]* (III 1) or, more precisely, 'Les Levantins en leur légende/ Disent' *[The Levantines in their legend / Say]* (VII 3). Or he presents an account as fiction with 'Voici l'histoire' *[Here is the story]* (IV 16). When La Fontaine mentions Aesop at the beginning of a poem ('Esope conte', *[Aesop tells it]* VI 13), we automatically expect the ensuing poem to be a traditional fable with all that this implies. In IV 18, too, we are informed that the poem we are about to read is told by Aesop: 'Ecoutez là-dessus l'esclave de Phrygie' *[Listen to the Phrygian slave on the subject]*. Elsewhere, a mere mention of Aesop at the beginning suggests a traditional context in *incipits* like 'Si ce qu'on dit d'Esope est vrai,/ C'était l'oracle de la Grèce' *[If what they say of Aesop is true, / he was the oracle of Greece]* (I 20).

These are the self-conscious evocations of other fictional worlds. They are relatively rare. Yet even where the poet seems to be starting a fable without preamble, there may yet be some tiny stylistic trick that slyly alters our perceptions. A particularly subtle technique involves subverting what seems like a matter-of-fact, even banal *incipit* by surreptitiously including an element that suggests fiction simply because it is inappropriate. With 'Les Sages quelque-

fois, ainsi que l'Ecrevisse / Marchent à reculons' *[Sometimes Wise
Men, like Crayfish, walk backwards]* (XII 10) the poet is ostensibly
making a simple comparison: both crayfish and wise men can in
some sense be described as progressing by backward movement,
since wise men use lateral as well as straightforward thinking. But
juxtaposing the two seems so startling, however apt for the context,
that it evokes a world in which anything might happen, and we are
not surprised to meet two talking crayfish later in the poem. With
'Un Loup rempli d'humanité' *[A Wolf filled with humanity]* (X 5)
we meet a character who has suppressed his nature to an unnatural
degree: we know that wolves epitomize cruelty elsewhere in the
Fables (La Fontaine calls them 'scélérats' *[scoundrels]* in 'Les
Compagnons d'Ulysse'*[Ulysses's Companions]*, XII 1 l.96). It is
impossible to predict how this improbably humane wolf will
behave: again we must be prepared for the unexpected and the
strange, and sure enough we learn later that the wolf is contemplat-
ing vegetarianism.[5] With 'Du palais d'un jeune Lapin' *[From the
palace of a young Rabbit]* (VII 15) a society with a rabbit aristocracy
is offered without comment, and the rabbit-hero duly goes on to
invite a weasel to come before a judge over a property matter.

These inappropriate juxtapositions can be subtle in the extreme,
and the fable element may be almost imperceptible, yet it works its
spell notwithstanding. For example, with 'Un Chat contemporain
d'un fort jeune Moineau' *[A Cat, contemporary of a very young
Sparrow]* (XII 2), we are presented with what seems to be a
straightforward introduction to two characters, and are merely
being told that they are the same age. But the world 'contemporain'
subtly subverts the ordinariness of the line. The grand polysyllable
seems out of place for describing a cat and a sparrow. Its connotations are very human, and one would expect it to be used in a serious, dignified context.[6] So one senses from the start that the
animals are likely to be anthropomorphic. And indeed what follows bears this out, since the fable depends on the fact that this
sparrow and this cat are best friends, flying in the face of their natural instincts.

These *incipits* are light-hearted in tone; and the humour
depends on a clash between two incompatible elements forced
together in a sleight of hand. They are particularly appropriate for
paving the way for fable effects because of the sly way in which
they introduce the surreal. We are being encouraged, in a light-

hearted manner, to enter a world where anything could happen; but the important thing is that we are not invited to question the strangeness of the situation: we have become participants almost without noticing how we have been manipulated.

In general, La Fontaine's *incipits* are governed by the fact that the language of poetry tends by its very nature to be the opposite of banal and ordinary.[7] Poetic language, certainly in La Fontaine's time, reads as though it has been spruced up for a special occasion. This enhanced language is designed to convey a correspondingly elevated content. We know that the inelegant trivia of day-to-day life were considered unsuitable subjects for serious poetry: similarly, simplistic, banal language was deemed undesirable. This is perhaps one of the greatest advantages of telling fables in verse: a feeling of specialness, of heightened awareness, is conveyed from the start, which makes the unreal world of the fable acceptable. With the *incipits*, simply by starting a poem in language that is different from the prosaic, the poet gives his verse additional potential. There are numberless instances of arresting language in La Fontaine's *incipits* which convey from the start a feeling of being beyond the normal, starting with vocabulary that is particularly dense or striking in sound. The technique can be almost imperceptible – a line verges on the colloquial but for the fact that there are too many polysyllables, or the vocabulary is too choice to sound like ordinary speech. This is probably the case with 'Un Homme chérissait éperdument sa Chatte' *[A Man dearly cherished his Cat]* (II 18), where the dense clumping of the two striking words 'chérissait éperdument' is too much of a mouthful not to make us pause. With 'Les Loups mangent gloutonnement' *[Wolves feed voraciously]* (III 9) the poet again seems to be rolling the words round his tongue. Alliteration or assonance make the *incipits* seem unusual in 'Une tortue était, à la tête légère' *[A Tortoise there was, light-headed]* (X 2), or 'Avec grand bruit et grand fracas' *[With great noise and great crashing]* (VIII 23), or 'Certain Fou poursuivait à coups de pierre un Sage' *[A certain Madman was pursuing a Wise Man, throwing stones]* (XII 22). The sounds are too repetitive and too insistent for normal speech. In all these cases, the language hints at a rejection of the ordinary, so paving the way for the fable.

We must not forget La Fontaine's repeated insistence on the importance of variety in his writing: 'Diversité c'est ma devise' *[Diversity is my motto]*, he wrote in his *Conte*, 'Pâté d'anguille' *[Eel*

Pâté]. So it is scarcely unexpected to find him also producing the opposite effect to the above: the unusual side of a poem is reserved till later, and he will begin by describing what seems like a normal world. Most of the *Fables* (more than a hundred and ten of them, in fact) begin straightforwardly in this way. Indeed, the most characteristic La Fontaine *incipit* is a terse, banal account of the events leading up to the main action of the poem:

> Un Octogénaire plantait. *[An Octogenarian was putting in plants]* (XI 8)
> Un Homme accumulait. (XII 3) *[A Man was accumulating money]*
> Un Paon muait. (IV 9) *[A Peacock was moulting]*

Three words of explanation are enough to set the scene here, but they give no indication that there is anything unusual to come. And yet, despite their bald beginnings, all these poems will go on to treat extraordinary material, and to introduce an unreal diegetic world. XI 8 ('Le Vieillard et les Trois Jeunes Hommes' *[The Old Man and the three Young Men]*) ends with a coincidence as fateful as it is improbable: the three young men die rapidly in separate accidents, a fitting punishment for their scornful judgment of the old man for embarking on a long-term planting project at an advanced age. The miser of XII 3 lives in a mysterious seaside fortress, his only visible companion being an ape, who spends the day alone in the miser's locked treasure-chamber throwing his precious gold out of the window into the sea. A jay steals the peacock's feathers in IV 9 and dresses up in them. However, all three poems seem normal and banal to start with, and the far-fetched elements are introduced only gradually. The effect of the *incipits* here is that the reader, expecting a literal account, assimilates the narrative almost before realizing how implausible these poems are turning out to be – a sly way of achieving a similar effect to the earlier examples, of putting the reader in the right frame of mind to accept without demur what he is being told.

Fables come in two parts – to use La Fontaine's own terms, 'la fable' and 'la moralité' *[the moral]* (Préface, p.9). So far, we have considered only the poems that start with the narrative or apologue, the 'fable'. But often La Fontaine chooses to state the moral of the fable first. Almost sixty poems begin on a promythium, or moral statement. Often the initial moral is very brief. La Fontaine himself might have suggested that this was to avoid boring the reader with lengthy theoretical moralizing; however, this brevity also has an impact on the rest of the narrative. As a result of the economy with which the promythium is formulated, its exemplification seems to come very suddenly. One is plunged into the action immediately in what can seem like a bewildering change of subject:

> A l'oeuvre on connaît l'artisan.
> Quelques rayons de miel sans maître se trouvèrent ... (I 21)

[By his work a craftsman can be recognized. / Some honeycombs found themselves without an owner ...]

The shift of subject is so abrupt that it makes one lose one's bearings and puts one into a frame of mind where one does not know what next to expect – a receptive mood for a fable.[8]

Sometimes the poet seems to reject the illusion of unreality. A combination of a fairy-tale world and robust realism is apparent in certain *incipits,* in which he first establishes a heightened mood, then appears to subvert it. But even when he does so, the impact of the first lines still lingers, and the overall effect can be not only complex and subtle, but also magical. In 'Le Loup, la Chèvre et le Chevreau' *[The Wolf, the Nanny-Goat and the Kid]* (IV 15) the poet creates a particular atmosphere, only to dissipate it summarily as the narrative gets underway. The poem is a retelling of the well-known tale in which the wolf tries to trick his way into the goat's house by giving the password in a disguised, bleating voice: the content alone is enough to mark this poem out as a retelling of what, despite its Aesopian pedigree, is a traditional folk tale.[9] The fable however begins in pastoral vein:

> La Bique allant remplir sa traînante mamelle
> Et paître l'herbe nouvelle

[The She-goat was filling her heavy udder and grazing on the young grass]

The flowing alexandrine reinforces 'traînante' literally, 'dragging'), and the idyllic rural touches (rustic language,[10] udders heavy with milk, young grass) evoke the context of lyrical nature poetry (Collinet detects a reminiscence of Vergil's *Georgics* here[11]). This mood is shattered by the next line:

Ferma sa porte au loquet *[Shut her door on the latch]*

which transports us without warning from a verdant landscape into a mundane peasant dwelling and another unreal environment, the folk-tale world of anthropomorphic animals.[12] The rest of the poem is couched in the straightforward, simple language that is normally used for this sort of animal tale, and the peasant's hut, so brusquely introduced, now becomes an appropriate setting.

But although the mood of the lyrical incipit is not allowed to persist, it does affect our reading of the whole poem. The lyrical first lines still linger in our minds, setting the fable in the context of adult poetry with classical overtones of Vergil and Horace. The folk tale proper appears childish by contrast, and undermines the beauty of the *incipit*, ironically contrasting the loveliness of the scene from a distance with its banality when one gets closer. Thus we respond to the poem on two levels, and our reaction to La Fontaine's version of the story of the wolf and the goat will be very different from that of a child listening to a straightforward folk-tale rendering of the same subject. This is important, because it is a fable, not a simple tale that we are reading: we expect that there will be a moral; and the *incipit*, by creating an awareness of a more adult side to the tale, prepares us to take this moral seriously. The first two lines, although they do not determine the mood of the poem, modify our final response, making it more complex. We first enter into one fictional world, then are abruptly transported to a completely different one; we may doubt the authenticity of both, but the original mood, though denatured, still persists.

La Fontaine builds on the initial impact of his opening lines as the poems progress. How he does so will next be examined with reference to two techniques, of which the first is conciseness or compression.

COMPRESSION

The conciseness with which the *Fables* are narrated is well-known. In commenting 'Loin d'épuiser une matière, / On n'en doit prendre que la fleur' *[Far from exhausting a subject / One should only select the pick of it]* (VI, Epilogue), La Fontaine is following in the footsteps of earlier poets and fabulists (and, indeed, his remark is almost a translation from Phaedrus[13]). La Fontaine's contemporaries, too, regard the fable genre as an opportunity for extreme brevity. Benserade, for example, produced a series of fables told in the tersest of quatrains.[14] La Fontaine himself extolled brevity as an essential attribute of the fabulist in many of his writings on the subject.[15] Let us examine how economy in story-telling contributes to the atmosphere of of the fable.

La Fontaine's conciseness often takes the following form: the poem begins (as we have seen) with a brisk entry, followed by a characteristically terse account of the plot and characters. This approach is partly dictated by the genre: a fabulist needs to dispose of events quickly so as to place due emphasis on the moral. But this technique also helps to create a powerful impression. It means that too much happens in too short a space, so that the account seems striking, and makes us take notice. In the following lines, perfectly plausible events seem improbable simply because they are described with the utmost terseness and without any explanation:

> Un vieux Renard, mais des plus fins,
> Grand croqueur de Poulets, grand preneur de Lapins,
> Sentant son renard d'une lieue,
> Fut enfin au piège attrapé.
> Par hasard en étant échappé,
> Non pas franc, car pour gage il y laissa sa queue ... (V 5)

[An old Fox, but a very cunning one / A great chicken-cruncher, a great rabbit-catcher, / You could tell he was a fox a mile off, / Was finally caught in a trap. / Having escaped by accident / Not scot-free, for he left his tail behind ...]

The fox's fortunes change four times with bewildering speed in these few lines, in which the poet has considerably modified the original Aesop fable.[16] The initial character-sketch suggests the following rapid steps in the narrative: the fox is first presented as a successful hunter, apparently cunning enough to be invulnerable; contrary to our expectations he is caught; immediately, by what seems like a miraculous chance, he escapes, only for us to learn with brutal suddenness of his mutilation. The effect of this whirl-wind account is to make the activities of the fox seem too frenetic to be real, so that the reader is distanced from them. We have entered a world where anything, it seems, can happen in a split second. Our sense of reality has gone. We are, in fact, in a condition to accept without scepticism the extraordinary outcome of the poem, involving a gathering of foxes even cleverer than our protagonist, which we are suddenly told has convened like a true parliament, and which sits in an orderly formation, facing the speaker of the hour (we know this because they cannot see our hero's tailless condition until they make him turn round).

Elsewhere, conciseness can be so extreme as to produce an impression of supernatural intervention, and imbue the poem with an atmosphere of strangeness and magic, as in the lines:

> [Un] Chien, voyant sa proie en l'eau représentée,
> La quitta pour l'image, et pensa se noyer;
> La rivière devint tout d'un coup agitée (VI 17)

[(A) Dog, seeing his prey reflected in the water, / Dropped it for its reflection, and almost drowned. / The river suddenly became rough.]

Leaving aside the improbability of a dog preferring the reflection of food to the real thing, the actual succession of events is unreal here. La Fontaine invents a magical touch: the smooth-flowing river, with extreme suddenness, becomes a wildly agitated death-trap, as in many fairy tales in which, by supernatural means, water suddenly becomes violently stormy.[17] Again, the reader is removed from ordinary life and plunged by this abrupt narrative technique into a world where anything can happen.

This speeding-up process involves juxtaposing elements that would in reality have come together gradually. A further result of this can be that the components appear to be connected in a most improbable way. Again, this is reminiscent of folk and fairy tales, as in this example:

> Quatre chercheurs de nouveaux mondes,
> Presque nus échappés à la fureur des ondes,
> Un Trafiquant, un Noble, un Pâtre, un Fils de Roi ... (X 15)

[Four seekers for new worlds, / Almost naked after escaping from the fury of the waters, / A Merchant, a Noble, a Shepherd, the Son of a King ...] This formulation is reminiscent of a number of tales in which ill-assorted characters team up.[18] The traditional folk or fairy-tale narrative offers no explanation for the association. La Fontaine too has no time to explain. The reader is required to suspend disbelief, and no concessions are made to the legitimate doubts one might have about how these very different men could have come together. It is interesting to look back at the work from which La Fontaine took this fable: it is apparent from the title alone that the original tale, by Poussines, was not aiming for Lafontainian conciseness. Fumaroli translates this title as follows: 'Ce récit propose, par l'image d'une société, un exemple de fortune conjoignant des hommes de conditions très diverses. Il révèle les soins bénéfiques de la Providence veillant sur les hommes et montre que celle-ci est le meilleur et le plus sûr fondement de la confiance humaine' *[This narrative proposes, using the image of a society, an example of fortune conjoining men of very diverse conditions. It reveals the benevolent efforts of Providence watching over men, and shows that she is the best and surest foundation for human trust.]* (Fumaroli II 395). The surprise element introduced by the rapid juxtaposition of the singularly inappropriate fellow-travellers is entirely missing in Poussines's tale, which Fumaroli describes as 'an interminable account', and in which the four characters are introduced individually during the course of the narrative.[19]

As we can see, the technique makes the characters and their circumstances seem unreal. The impression is enhanced by the fact that they are not described at all. But character portrayal too may steer the reader towards a sense of unreality if it is compressed:

> Entre deux Bourgeois d'une ville
> S'émut jadis un différend.
> L'un était pauvre, mais habile,
> L'autre riche, mais ignorant. (VIII 19)

[Between two Burghers in a town / A quarrel once arose. / One was poor but clever. / The other, rich but ignorant.]

In this rough character-sketch the poet may be describing perfectly plausible differences between the two men; but the pared-down quality brings out these differences as formal and unnaturally balanced. The two bourgeois appear to be complete opposites in every respect, and there is also an implied internal contradiction between the circumstances and qualities of each individual. This again is the stuff of fairy tales, in the course of which beautiful and noble characters frequently endure hardship, while their inferior counterparts are correspondingly overprivileged.[20] By compressing their portrayal, La Fontaine has transformed his two bourgeois into fairy-tale characters.[21]

Often the poet changes the pace of the narrative, speeding it up as we get to the crux. For example, in 'Les deux Chiens et l'Ane mort' *[The two Dogs and the dead Donkey]* (VIII 25) two dogs indulge in a piece of extraordinary behaviour: seeing a dead donkey floating far out at sea, they decide to drink the sea dry to get at the carcass.[22] Their deliberations are rendered relatively briskly in dialogue, but when the real action starts and the dogs begin to drink, the narrative becomes so fast it leaves us, and the protagonists, breathless:

> Voilà mes Chiens à boire; ils perdirent l'haleine,
>   Et puis la vie; ils firent tant
>   Qu'on les vit crever à l'instant.   (l.28–30)

[Now my dogs were drinking. They lost their breath / Then their lives. They went at it so hard / That they were seen to burst straightaway.]

The effect is like a speeded-up film – the characters become caricatures, and any serious implications disappear. And as with fast film, the result is implausible and unnatural. The impression of unreality is built up by a number of techniques. The syntax is highly compressed: 'ils perdirent' *[they lost]* has two direct objects, which seem equivalent, though a great deal must have happened between 'ils perdirent l'haleine' *[They lost their breath]* and 'ils perdirent la vie' *[They lost their lives]*. The vocabulary too conveys an unnatural concertina-like squeezing: 'à l'instant' *[straightaway]* crams the whole process into a moment. The way the reader is brought in with 'on les vit' *[they were seen]*, as passive observer rather than participant, suggests dreamlike detachment (elsewhere in the Fables 'crever' is used exclusively to mean 'to burst' or 'to burst to death', never simply 'to die').[23] This nuance adds a dramatic and unrealistic touch to the dogs' deaths – they seem visibly to explode. The events narrated were ludicrous to start with – no dog would drink sea-water till it burst – but the potentially disturbing implications of this tale of a double suicide have been glossed over by the brevity of the account, to be replaced by a rendering that enhances the surreal quality of the occurrence, allowing neither the reader, nor the victims, time to draw breath and reflect on these happenings.

Characteristically, compression makes events seem mechanical, and deprives them of their power to arouse an emotional response. And yet the events treated in this way may well be desperately serious, brushes with death or even death itself, as in this case. At such moments, the concise narration seems to fulfil an important function. It permits the grim material to be absorbed without our being distracted by any sympathy for the victims of disaster. It does this first by offering us a perfunctory account of cataclysmic events, so that we will find it difficult to feel involved, and will probably adopt the position of detached, even amused observer. Secondly, it makes the events themselves appear strange and unreal, since in real life they would never succeed each other so swiftly, hence we cannot feel any genuine concern. Lastly, it builds up the impression of a particular kind of comically unreal, macabre world in which death lurks around the corner, and living creatures have a fragile hold on life, but nobody seems to care much. We accept these conditions in a La Fontaine fable because we have been prepared by the poem to expect them.

To refine this latter point further, the formulation of La Fontaine's conciseness conveys the feeling that his characters exist in a world of black comedy. As an example, here is the description of the death of a gnat:

> L'Insecte du combat se retire avec gloire:
> Comme il sonna la charge, il sonne la victoire,
> Va partout l'annoncer, et rencontre en chemin
> L'embuscade d'une Araignée:
> Il y rencontre aussi sa fin.
> ('Le Lion et le Moucheron'
> *[The Lion and the Gnat]*, II 9 1.30–4)

[The insect retired from the fray covered in glory. / As he had sounded the charge, so he sounded the victory, / Went everywhere to announce it,

*and on his way / Met with a spider's ambush. / Here he also met his
end.]*

The atmosphere is conveyed through the narrative technique; La
Fontaine takes a rather moralistic passage from Aesop and transforms it into a lively account which wittily thwarts the reader's
expectations through bathos.[24] 'Il ... rencontre en chemin' *[and on
his way (he) met]* leads us to expect that the gnat will come upon an
acquaintance, not a deadly spider's web. The same trick is repeated
in the last line when we learn of his death, again as a 'rencontre'
[meeting]. This formulation conveys an unsurprised acceptance of
the extraordinary which has just the same feeling to it as a fairy tale
in which the hero, rounding a corner, comes across a palace or a
talking horse or a purse full of fairy gold. The difference is that the
unexpected event so blandly conveyed is a death.

Concise narrative often fulfils this kind of dual function, making the narrative appear surreal, and then, as a consequence, making disagreeable or painful material seem acceptable. Although
most instances of concise narrative have a grim underside to them,
the compression underemphasizes this side, and instead produces a
lighthearted impression of unreality.

COINCIDENCE

One technique that amply demonstrates La Fontaine's penchant
for complex effects is coincidence. This is a quintessentially
improbable narrative device, and its presence alone is enough to
make a narrative seem contrived and unreal. La Fontaine uses it in
a number of poems. But often the coincidence is an illusion – we
are in fact witnessing something rather different. In true coincidence, disparate elements come together of their own accord. If the
situation is being manipulated, whether by characters, by supernatural beings, or even by a narrator, then the result is not true coincidence. This 'manipulated coincidence' is more frequent in the
Fables than coincidence proper. An example will make this difference clear. In 'Le Gland et la Citrouille' *[The Acorn and the
Pumpkin]* (IX 4) a peasant named Garo, relaxing beneath an oak
tree, reflects that God should have given to plants fruits appropriate to their size: a nearby pumpkin should have hung from the
majestic oak, while the insignificant acorns should have grown on

the lowly pumpkin plant. At that very instant an acorn falls on his nose.

> Oh, oh, dit-il, je saigne! et que serait-ce donc
> S'il fût tombé de l'arbre une masse plus lourde,
> Et que ce gland eût été gourde?   (1.27–9)

[*'Oh, oh!' Said he, 'I'm bleeding! What would have happened / If a heavier object had fallen from the tree, / And this acorn had been a gourd?'*]

The acorn has dropped at the appropriate moment for Garo to understand the rightness of the status quo, and the poem continues: 'Dieu ne l'a pas voulu: sans doute il eut raison; / J'en vois bien à présent la cause' (1.30–1) [*God didn't want it so. He was undoubtedly right; now I can see why.*]. It seems that the coincidence has had the lucky result of enabling Garo to point the moral. But are we in the presence of true coincidence here? Although coincidence in fiction implies intervention from an outsider with an improbable degree of control over the situation, in true coincidence this influential outsider should be the author, not, as in this case, God. Arguably this is an example of divine intervention rather than of coincidence.[25]

The more extreme manifestations of coincidence in the *Fables* may well be accompanied by similar hints that supernatural forces are at work, a fact which adds to the complexity but detracts from the coincidence. Perhaps the most striking case is that of 'Le Trésor et les Deux Hommes' [*the Treasure and the Two Men*] (IX 16). Rather than face financial ruin, a bankrupt decides to hang himself. In attaching his rope to a rickety wall, he causes it to collapse, revealing a hidden treasure, which he takes. Later, the owner of the money arrives, and finds it gone. However, the bankrupt had left his rope behind, so the man who has been robbed can and does hang himself. The symmetrical interplay of coincidences gives this poem a satisfying shape. Nothing goes to waste: even the rope fulfils its intended function. As La Fontaine puts it, 'Aussi bien que l'argent le licou trouva maître' [*As well as the money, the noose found a master*] (1.28). In the epimythium, however, the poet adds a further dimension when he explains that the goddess Fortune was responsible for these excessive coincidences. He comments: 'Ce

sont là ses traits; elle s'en divertit./ Plus le tour est bizarre, et plus
elle est contente' *[Those are her traits, they keep her amused. / The
more bizarre the twist, the happier she is.]* (1.34–5). What we had
assumed were coincidences are reclassified retrospectively as the
result of Fortune's whim.[26]

In another poem the intervention of supernatural forces, possibly added by La Fontaine to an original story by Gaulmin,[27] is
present from early on, but very subtly suggested. In 'Le Loup et le
Chasseur' *[The Wolf and the Hunter]* (VIII 27), a greedy hunter,
displeased with a perfectly satisfactory kill of two deer, shoots a
boar; then seeing a partridge he bends his crossbow to shoot it too.
At that moment the dying boar charges and kills him. A wolf
appears, and rejoices at finding the dead hunter and his kill. But
before feasting on the bodies, he decides to consume the catgut
bowstring, so as not to waste it. The taut bowstring releases its
arrow, which kills the wolf. A number of allegorical figures seem to
flit inconspicuously in and out of this implausible tale. The greed
that destroys both the hunter and the wolf is addressed as an
ungrateful monster in the introductory peroration: 'Fureur d'accumuler, monstre de qui les yeux/ Regardent comme un point tous
les bienfaits des Dieux' *[Passion to pile up ever more, monster, whose
eyes / Look on all the gods' gifts as mere dots]* (1.1–2): the gods too are
glimpsed here. Later, when the hunter half-kills the boar, the beast's
prolonged death-throes are described in classical terms:

> Autre habitant du Styx: la Parque et ses ciseaux
> Avec peine y mordait: la Déesse infernale
> Reprit à plusieurs fois l'heure au monstre fatale. (1.20–3)

*[Another dweller in the Underworld: Fate and her scissors / Could
scarcely cut the thread: the infernal goddess / Repeated the monster's
hour of death several times.]*

This is more than a conventional account. A goddess is involved,
who delays the boar's death for long enough to enable it to kill the
huntsman before collapsing – this hint of divine intervention takes
away the quality of true coincidence from the fact that the huntsman's death occurs at the precise moment when he has bent his
bow but not yet released his arrow. Finally, when the wolf arrives,
he rejoices at his lucky find as follows: 'O Fortune, dit-il, je te

promets un temple./ Quatre corps étendus! que de biens!' *['Oh, Fortune,' said he, 'I promise you a temple. Four bodies stretched out! What riches!]* (l.36–7). Fickle Fortune has been introduced. In view of her fondness for bizarre situations, described in the previous example, it comes as no surprise when the wolf is shot by the dead huntsman's unmanned arrow. It seems only too appropriate to allow allegorical and godly figures to be glimpsed in the background of this tale, which would seem impossibly far-fetched if told more straightforwardly. In complex poems like these, the poet is juggling with two approaches to organizing the narrative. Interestingly, although La Fontaine does not clearly differentiate between coincidence and divine intervention, ultimately the two are mutually exclusive: if the gods are involved, apparent coincidences cannot possibly be true ones, since they are engineered from above. In the same way Chance (or Fortune) also ceases to be truly chance when she becomes an allegorical figure.

These examples (and there are others like them) lend excitement and magic to stories in which such unbelievable and unexpected circumstances can occur. In addition, they indirectly make an ontological point: the characters are not independent beings, but are governed by external controlling forces, which intervene when they see fit. The nature of these forces too is implied. As is shown by the last example, their participation in the action seems to reflect a gratuitous desire to create a symmetrical outcome, rather than a humane wish to see justice done or help those in need. These priorities are emphatically not those of the protagonists whose lives they are manipulating.

Most Lafontainian coincidences are much simpler. They tighten up the story-line, and also make it seem implausible, but do not explicitly suggest intervention from outside. These are the true coincidences, and in most cases the poet has imported them directly from his source material. Most often coincidence is a question of timing: a pigeon is caught by a vulture, but just as he is about to be devoured an eagle swoops down out of the blue. It attacks the vulture so the pigeon escapes (IX 2). A partridge makes fun of a hare who has been caught by dogs. 'Au moment qu'elle rit,/ Son tour vient' *[At the instant she laughed / Her turn came]* - a hawk dives down at that instant and carries her off (V 17). The same happens to a cock at the very moment of his triumph in a fight with a rival (VII 12). Some people are congratulating themselves over a portrait of a

man who has single-handedly slain a huge lion. Even as they speak, a
live lion chances to pass by and stops to tell them a few home truths
(III 10). This last poem is a rare example of true coincidence added
to the original by La Fontaine. His lion appears in a witty throwaway
line, arriving in a subordinate clause: 'Un Lion en passant rabattit
leur caquet' *[A passing Lion stopped their mouths]*.[28]
   Or there are coincidences of circumstances. In the very complicated poem 'Testament expliqué par Esope' *[Testament explained by
Aesop]* (II 20) the problem is how to honour the will of a dead
father. The outcome depends on the unlikely fact that his three
daughters, one gluttonous, the second frivolous, and the third mer-
cenary, are left an estate which divides into three parts which
exactly match the beneficiaries. The first share consists of 'tout l'at-
tirail de la goinfrerie' *[all the accoutrements of gluttony]*, the second
of 'celui de la coquetterie' *[those of coquettishness]* and the third of a
country estate with money-making potential. The coincidence is
much too neat to be real. Similarly in 'Le Vieillard et les Trois
Jeunes Hommes' *[The Old Man and the three Young Men]* (XI 8) we
have seen how three youths mock an old man who is planting trees
when he must be so near to death; but shortly afterwards all three
die in independent accidents, so the sage outlives them.[29]
   As well as introducing an element of the implausible into the
narrative these examples of coincidence and manipulated coincidence also enliven the narrative and make it amusing, even though
many of them involve death. The light-hearted treatment of such
coincidences can be demonstrated if it is contrasted with the serious love stories told in the long poem 'Les Filles de Minée' *[The
Daughters of Minyas]* (XII 28), published with the *Fables* though far
from being a true fable itself. The most improbable coincidence
here is the death of Telamon and Cloris. These two constant lovers
are kept apart by a series of appalling calamities, enumerated with
heartfelt seriousness. After years of languishing for each other, they
finally win through to their marriage-day.

> Les noces se faisaient à l'ombre d'un ormeau;
> L'enfant d'un voisin vit s'y percher un Corbeau:
> Il fait partir de l'arc une flèche maudite,
> Perce les deux époux d'une atteinte subite …
> Même accident finit leurs précieuses trames;
> Même tombe eut leurs corps, même séjour leurs âmes. (l.440–54)

[The wedding was celebrated in the shade of an elm; / A neighbour's child saw a crow perching in it; / He loosed a cursed arrow from his bow, / Pierced the two lovers with a sudden shaft ... / The same mischance cut short their precious lives; / The same tomb held their bodies, the same dwelling their souls.]

This straight-faced account clashes with the tone of such episodes in the *Fables* proper, and in fact represents a much less appropriate treatment of coincidence. It is difficult to take the situation seriously, and the coincidence which destroys the lovers seems much too contrived. The constantly shifting, self-aware and ironic tone that the narrator adopts to recount coincidences in the rest of the *Fables* is much better suited to the authorial manipulation and mockery implied in this most ambivalent of narrative techniques.

As we have seen, coincidence presupposes the existence of an external presence, which intervenes in the doings of the characters. One senses the presence of a being indifferent to the happiness and welfare of living creatures, who enjoys manipulating them to create pleasing symmetries and patterns at their expense. An underlying nuance of hostility disturbs the superficially sunny atmosphere. We seem to be glimpsing, however fleetingly, the cruel gods of classical tragedy.

* * *

The three narrative techniques, very different in character and scope, illustrate three distinct facets of the poet's craft. The *incipits* show that from the outset he presents us as readers with an appropriate atmosphere for the fable we are about to experience, and makes us accept the mood he has established. The section on compression demonstrates his ability to create telling effects with the slenderest of means. Finally, with coincidence, we see not only his lively sense of the extraordinary but also how much he can reveal if we are prepared to read between the lines – a type of reading that he requires from us on many occasions, as we will see during the course of this study. In addition, certain Lafontainian moods have begun to emerge: our three techniques have several aspects in common. First, they all show a heightened awareness, a feeling that both style and ideas are out of the ordinary. We are being reminded that what we are reading is very much poetry. Secondly, we have been given a strong impression of manipulation and control, on a number of different levels. Fortune controls the characters, the strong control the weak, and, most important, the author controls the reader (even if the latter fails to realize it). The notions of dominance, submission and manipulation are essential to La Fontaine's thinking; that they are present in his craft is already clear. It will become more so in the next chapter.

CHAPTER 2

Conjuring with style

The importance of craft is demonstrated by La Fontaine in 'Le Pouvoir des Fables' [*The Power of Fables*] (VIII 4). Any subject can be fascinating, provided that it is attractively presented. In this fable, an orator succeeds in capturing the interest of a bored crowd, not by stressing the threat of war, but by telling a fragment of an irrelevant fable. In the epimythium the poet ruefully admits that he too would prefer to listen to an entertaining tale than to labour over the moral of his fable. The whole poem demonstrates the power of a well-presented narrative.[30]

The *Fables* themselves are the clearest indication that for La Fontaine the treatment is as important as the topic. His subject-matter in these poems is immensely varied – almost anything seems acceptable: in this chapter alone we will see him writing on a wide range of subjects, from a ship at sea to a duck in a pond, from a mountain to a spider's web. It is the treatment that binds the collection together and makes it into a whole. Subject-matter is not, of course, irrelevant to the discussion, since we are examining techniques for rendering meaning. But the common element in the material discussed here is the manipulation of style, whether it be through use of words or verse forms. The poet handles his verse with the panache and showmanship of a professional magician. The spells he weaves may not be real ones, but he draws the crowd by his conjurer's 'cent tours de passe-passe' [*a hundred conjuring tricks*]. Here, then, we are concerned above all with technique for its own sake.

As in the previous chapter, the poet's expertise is demonstrated by focusing closely on a few techniques. I begin with one of the most self-conscious, the use of paradox.

PARADOX IN SENTENCE STRUCTURE

Often La Fontaine challenges the reader by presenting us with paradoxes: with a pithy phrase, sometimes borrowed and sometimes invented,[31] he reconciles seeming opposites. This technique could aptly be named oxymoronic. The trick is to make the reader do a double-take, as a falsehood turns into a truth. The *Fables* contain many lines of the type:

> 'Bon nombre d'hommes qui sont femmes' *[A good number of men who are women]*
> 'Devenus forts par sa faiblesse' *[Rendered strong by his weakness]*
> 'Ne possédait pas l'or, mais l'or le possédait'[32] *[Did not possess the gold, but the gold possessed him]*

These pithy paradoxes, though they initially seem like impossibilities, in fact encapsulate the message of the poems in which they occur. In one case, indeed, the poet goes further and actually provides not only a summary of the situation in the poem, but a neat definition of the whole fable genre: he describes 'La Montagne qui accouche' *[The Mountain in labour]* (V 10) as a ' ... fable/ Dont le récit est menteur/ Et le sens est véritable' *[a fable with a lying account but a true meaning]*. Such a paradoxical formulation is eminently appropriate for the fable genre, characterized as it is by duality – between apologue and exposition, between protagonist and target, between pleasing and instructing. Hence these paradoxes are much more than obfuscations: they focus on crucial issues. Their challenging wording thrusts them at the reader, forces us to take notice.

However, this approach, which I have characterized as a kind of conjuring, ultimately implies a denial of the paradox. The poet apparently presents us with a neat expression of something impossible; but on further reflection we realize that the situation is not actually impossible at all. We have been tricked into seeing difficulties where none exist. The reality, as we finally realize, is as familiar, rational and normal as ever. However, La Fontaine has also introduced the possibility of a complication here, even if only to deny it. Our initial reaction, in which we think we are being shown a glimpse of something impossibly difficult, is not entirely dispelled by our subsequent realization that it was only a trick.

Since the trick component lies in the formulation rather than the underlying meaning, we must direct our attention to the means La Fontaine uses to create paradox, and examine the craftsmanship behind these seemingly effortless verbal pyrotechnics. What follows is an analysis of the principal techniques employed.

Brevity is essential, since to seem aphoristic such statements must be immediately arresting. Hence a favourite device is to present an apparent contradiction without comment. It is then left to the reader to relate the words to their context, whereupon the paradox disappears, and the illusion of unreality is dispelled. To reconsider a couple of the examples mentioned above, the poet says he is acquainted with 'Bon nombre d'hommes qui sont femmes' *[A good number of men who are women]* (VIII 6 l.4), an extravagant assertion which fleetingly evokes a race of androgynes.[33] On reflection, however, it makes perfect sense in the context of a discussion of the female tendency to indiscretion, which is often shared by men. Or he explains that when the lion is sick the other animals take control, 'Devenus forts par sa faiblesse' *[Rendered strong by his weakness]* (III 14)[34] – again the initial picture, soon dispelled, is the implausible one of weak animals being endowed with supernatural strength like the villagers in *Astérix*. Or, to add another instance, he describes a young widow ripe for remarriage, and comments 'Le deuil enfin sert de parure' *[Mourning finally serves as finery]* (VI 21 l.38): the context explains the curious attitude to her bereavement suggested by the paradoxical line – in the fable, though still technically in mourning, she has got over her grief and is looking for a new husband.[35]

In these examples, there is also an element of deceit, of wilful manipulation of the meaning of words. This is the secret behind this verbal sleight of hand. La Fontaine appears to be using a key word in one sense, when actually it means something slightly different. In the example 'Bon nombre d'hommes qui sont femmes', the word 'femmes' means not 'women' but 'people having a certain feminine characteristic'. In 'Le deuil enfin sert de parure', 'deuil' *[mourning]* is used inaccurately to mean 'attractive black clothes'. In both cases, the true meanings of the ambiguous words, 'women' and 'mourning', momentarily confuse the reader, giving an impression of paradox.

If the key word has two separate accepted meanings, the phrase takes on a punning quality. For example, a pagan idol is described as

... un Dieu de bois,
De ces Dieux qui sont sourds bien qu'ayant des oreilles. (IV 8)

[A god of wood, / One of those gods who are deaf although they have ears.]

In these lines, which echo the Psalms,[36] La Fontaine is playing on the fact that 'oreilles' *[ears]*, placed so close to 'sourds' *[deaf]*, seems to be a metonymy for 'ouïe'*[hearing]*. But from the existence of the statue's carved wooden ears we cannot infer that it has the capacity to hear but is choosing to turn a deaf ear. The fact that 'oreilles' can have two slightly different meanings has momentarily given us this illusion.

A variation on this technique involves repetition. Words with several meanings can be used differently within the same line. An example already mentioned is the description of the obsessive miser in 'L'Avare qui a perdu son trésor' *[The Miser who has lost his treasure]* (IV 20 l.11), who

'Ne possédait pas l'or, mais l'or le possédait.'

[Did not possess the gold, but the gold possessed him][37]

This phrase resembles a palindrome in construction.[38] The symmetrical shape may initially hoodwink the reader into assuming that the repeated words mean the same thing each time they occur, so that the impossible notion is fleetingly conveyed that the gold has come to life and taken control. But we soon realize that the first 'possédait' relates to physical ownership, the second to obsession. In the light of this difference, the two mentions of 'l'or' also take on different meanings. The first gold is real, the second is insubstantial, the notion of riches. And yet the momentary glimpse of living gold conveys an impression of weirdness which colours our view of the miser's obsession.

It can be seen that these aphorisms are carefully constructed and especially meaningful. That they are privileged in the text is clear from the care with which they are incorporated into the poem. A fable can build up to a paradox which occurs as the crux of the whole. In VII 17 'Un Animal dans la Lune' *[An Animal in the Moon]* a pithy phrase comes at the end of a philosophical examination of a subject that is itself paradoxical. The first section of the poem deals with an apparent contradiction between reason and the evidence of the senses, resolved through cognition (that is, the application of reason to the evidence of the senses). La Fontaine sums up the help given by reason to the sense of sight as follows:

Mes yeux, moyennant ce secours,
Ne me *trompent* <u>jamais</u> en me *mentant* <u>toujours</u>. (l.32–3)

[My eyes, with this assistance, / Deceive me <u>never</u>, while lying to me <u>always</u>]

The construction of this second line is complex. The two words in italics are near-synonyms; the words underlined (placed in parallel at the end of the two hemistichs) are opposite in meaning. The two halves of the line seem perfectly balanced, but in fact, the main clause ('ne me trompent jamais') is presented as the truth while the subordinate one ('en me mentant toujours') represents an illusion, and is presented as false. The actual meaning of the line, in its context, is immediately clear to the reader; the paradoxical element is rendered by the construction. Thus the line encapsulates both the clarification and the obfuscation contained in the debate that led up to it. It also closes the debate: the poet now moves on to introduce a new subject.[39]

These paradoxes have a cumulative impact. The technique soon becomes familiar, and one learns to view these aphorisms as keys to the poet's thought. La Fontaine exploits this sense of privilege in a kind of self-parody. He presents us with a dense formulation, incorporating elements of symmetrical repetition and/or opposites. At first sight, all such statements appear preternaturally wise; but that is only until we look more closely at the content. For instance, La Fontaine writes: 'Le sang les avait joints, l'intérêt les sépare' *[Blood had united them. self-interest parted them]* (IV 18 l.37). There is a pair of genuine opposites in the verbs ('joints', 'sépare'), which invite us by extension to regard the nouns ('le sang' and 'l'intérêt') as opposites too. One can see what La Fontaine means by opposing 'le sang' to 'l'intérêt'. But neither is a pair of true opposites. Again, La Fontaine mentions ignorant people who 'parlent de tout et n'ont rien vu' *[talk of everything and have seen nothing]* (IV 7 l.38). Their exaggerated garrulity and ignorance are summed up respectively as 'tout' *[everything]* and 'rien' *[nothing]* in an oversimplification of reality. The reader has no trouble in realizing that the poet actually means that they are prepared to show off on the basis of inadequate knowledge. Balance and opposition give an aphoristic feel even to a banal statement of fact, such as the account of two men quarrelling over a donkey: 'L'un voulait le garder, l'autre le voulait vendre' *[One wanted to keep him, the other wanted to sell him]* (I 13 l.2), not a specially challenging or paradoxical notion, but symmetrically formulated.

The above technique makes ordinary comments seem special. The opposite result can be achieved, and peculiar comments tossed in as though they were banal. This might be called the 'hidden paradox'. Such comments, less common in La Fontaine, create a different sleight-of-hand effect. An example is the first line of 'L'Homme et son image' *[The Man and his image]* (I 11), which introduces the hero as 'Un Homme qui s'aimait sans avoir de rivaux' *[A Man who loved himself without having any rivals]*.[40] The technique here is exactly the same as a modern standup comedian might use – Woody Allen, for instance, when he remarks: 'My wife left me for another woman'. In both examples the sentence initially seems like a cliché. But one word is out of place, so that the more one thinks, the more the sentence comes to seem unusual. In the case of La Fontaine, the guilty word is simply the reflexive 's', and the implication is that the man is paying court to himself in exactly the same manner as a lover might pay court to the beloved.

Both with paradox and 'hidden paradox', the technique obliges the reader to remain attentive. With the paradoxical formulations, we need to respond to a challenge. Conversely, with the throwaway comment of the hidden paradox we may feel that there is more to the remark than we think, so we had better re-examine the text.

Paradoxical phrases stretch the imagination, making connections which seem at once true and false. These are the conjuring tricks of language, and they create their own illusion.

STYLISTIC EXCESS

All the techniques examined so far enhance the poet's writing, making it arresting, striking, out of the ordinary. One of the principal elements that distinguish poetry from prose is precisely this transformation of language into something richer. The reader guesses that he is reading poetry before he even focuses on the content. I have named this use of language stylistic excess. The term is employed, for want of a better one, to mean overdefinition or excess of relevance. When the language reinforces a poem's meaning in more ways than would seem reasonable, the effect is again akin to a conjuring trick. Like a magician pulling endless scarves from his sleeve, the poet slyly draws out further relevant material where there would appear to be no room for more. The reader of poetry is, of course, familiar with this technique, which is constantly employed by poets in a number of accepted ways. For example, the use of alliteration and assonance to create an excess of relevance is a poetic cliché. No reader would be surprised at the way the sound of the open 'a's and liquid 'l's reinforces the meaning, evoking a glutted, languorous atmosphere appropriate for the rat who lolls in his cheese in La Fontaine's 'Le Rat qui s'est retiré du monde' *[The Rat who retired from the world]* (VII 3):

> Les Levantins en leur légende
> Disent qu'un certain Rat las des soins d'ici-bas ...

[The Levantines in their legend/ Tell of a certain Rat, tired of earthly cares ...]

or the way the tripping 't's suggest a brisk and cheerful mood in 'La Laitière et le pot au lait' *[The Milkmaid and the Milk-Jug]* (VII 9):
  Perrette sur sa tête ayant un Pot au lait ... *[Perrette, having a milk-jug on her head]*
These effects, clear examples of stylistic excess, are not unexpected. They are conventional though effective examples.

La Fontaine, however, takes stylistic excess much further than this. It is when the formulation of a thought comes, on close examination, to seem appropriate in an increasing number of respects that the poet takes on the role of conjurer. Here I propose to examine, in the context of stylistic excess, first the versification of the *Fables*, and then some unexpected stylistic effects, all of which contribute to the sleight-of-hand impression of the whole.

VERSIFICATION

La Fontaine's consummate mastery of verse makes it a flexible instrument for expressing nuances of meaning, which echo the sense of the words themselves. In each example, the meaning of the lines determines their metre, and it is the combination of meaning and metre that produces the overall effect.[41] When the poet makes the poem's rhythm, and even its appearance on the page, seem entirely appropriate to its word-content, the sleight-of-hand element is much in evidence. In the *Fables*, however, such effects derive their impact from being set in a context of well-tried verse forms, which give an underlying pattern to the poems as a collection, and lull the reader into a feeling of familiarity. When the stylistic excess occurs, it stands out in contrast to its conventional setting.

Hence La Fontaine constantly exploits the dignity of the alexandrine, the dodecasyllabic line that is the mainstay of serious classical verse (though of course it is also used in comic verse). In addition, he mainly uses for his alexandrines the appropriate conventional language.[42] Unlike those of many of his contemporaries, La Fontaine's alexandrines tend to be relatively refined. In lighter contexts, he generally prefers to use the equally common octosyllabic line, which has a more jogging, pedestrian feel. His metres tend to be regular and his lines for the most part follow each other in accordance with the rules.

La Fontaine's manipulations of verse forms depend on the reader's knowledge of these conventions, and of how the poet habitually uses them. Tampering with rhyme, rhythm or language will make an impact because on one level the reader's expectations are flouted – although on another this variety of effect is scarcely unexpected, since it was a common feature of comic verse at the time. As is well known, even moving the caesura will change the balance of a line, while *enjambement* suggests that the narrative has overstepped the bounds of the line and is running out of control, conveying an impression of breathlessness, impatience or unbridled emotion. While the standard underlying verse pattern maintains a reassuring atmosphere of familiarity, La Fontaine is no stranger to these manipulations, though they are delicate ones. As Kohn puts it, 'Par les coupes inattendues, les enjambements, la pauvreté même de certaines rimes, l'introduction de vers courts, le poète donne à l'alexandrin un naturel' (p.198) *[By unexpected cuts, enjambements, the very poverty of certain rhymes, the introduction of short lines, the poet gives the alexandrine a natural feel]*. Even apparently straightforward alexandrines are subjected to subtle manipulation to render the meaning more fully. Within a single poem, they can imperceptibly change from vehicles for high seriousness to flexible instruments for rendering a variety of other moods. The fact that they are normally quite decorous means that any variation from this norm will seem striking. Sound, vocabulary, balance and register all play a part, as an extract from 'Le Cygne et le Cuisinier' *[The Swan and the Cook]* (III 12) reveals. A swan and a duck live on an estate. The passage (1.8–14) goes as follows:

> Tantôt on les eût vus côte à côte nager,
> Tantôt courir sur l'onde, et tantôt se plonger,   1.9
> Sans pouvoir satisfaire à leurs vaines envies.
> Un jour le Cuisinier, ayant trop bu d'un coup,   1.11
> Prit pour Oison le Cygne, et le tenant au cou,
> Il allait l'égorger, puis le mettre en potage.   1.13
> L'Oiseau, prêt à mourir, se plaint en son ramage.

[One could see them now swimming side by side, / Now skimming over the water, and now diving, / Without managing to satisfy their empty longings. / One day, the Cook, having drunk too much, / Took the Swan for the Duck, and, grabbing him by the neck, / Was about to cut his throat, and put him in the soup. / The bird, on the point of death, sang his lament.]

In the first three lines the register is eminently appropriate to the most dignified of alexandrines: serious, lyrical and classical. The balance of the lines with their regular caesura is reinforced by the measured repetition of 'tantôt' and 'côte'. The language is that of classical lyrical poetry ('onde', 'vaine'). Indeed, there are sustained echoes of Vergil's *Georgics* with the fleeting evocation of the supernatural in 'courir sur l'onde' (as the birds skim the water they are described as running on it); while the mysterious unsatisfied longings briefly mentioned in 1.10 evoke a wistful anthropomorphism.[43]

In the next three lines (11–13), the alexandrines are preserved but the atmosphere changes completely. The tone is crude, with its references to drunkenness, slaughtering poultry, and soup, unacceptable topics for high-register classical verse. The vocabulary is unsophisticated – 'boire un coup' *[to down a drink]* or 'potage' *[soup]*, a low word more at home in Molière's farcical alexandrine 'La femme est en effet le potage de l'homme' *[Woman is in fact the soup of man]* than in the classical lyrical verse of the previous lines. The verbs ('boire', 'prendre', 'tenir', 'égorger', 'mettre' *[to drink, to grab, to hold, to cut a throat, to put]*) indicate rough, basic actions. This triplet seems to come from a cheerful poem with a low register. This is one of the occasions when, as Biard puts it, 'La Fontaine does not hesitate to write many words which were, at the time, excluded from any literature distinct from the *burlesque*' (Biard 1 p.41).

This triplet is immediately followed by one of La Fontaine's most lyrical lines: 'L'Oiseau, prêt à mourir, se plaint en son ramage' (l.14). This flowing line, with its dying hero and its classical poetic vocabulary ('se plaint', 'ramage') lends dignity to the swan, whose song of lament is that of the dying swans of classical mythology.

In this extract the dual technique of intermingling different registers while preserving the verse-form keeps the reader attentive. We cannot assume a consistent level, as the ground is constantly shifting. We are pulled in two opposite directions: the regular metre tends to lull us by its familiarity, while simultaneously the sudden shifts of tone have the impact of surprise. The effect, as Collinet puts it, is 'à la fois poétique et burlesque' *[at once poetic and burlesque]* (1, p.164). What constitutes the sleight of hand is that all this happens in a passage written in regular alexandrines.

Even the internal rhythms and divisions of the alexandrine can contribute to stylistic excess by reinforcing the meaning of the lines. 'Elle bâtit un nid, pond, couve, et fait éclore/ A la hâte' *[she built a nest, laid her eggs, sat on them and hatched them In haste]* (IV 22, l.15–16) reproduces the haste conveyed in the meaning through *enjambement* and brisk monosyllables. 'Il est bon de parler, et meilleur de se taire' *[It is good to talk, and better to keep quiet]* (VIII 10 l.6) enhances this two-part maxim, giving it an epigrammatic feel through the measured symmetry of the two hemistichs. 'Une Vache était là, on l'appelle, elle vient' *[A Cow was there, she was called, she came]* (X 1 l.31) divides the twelve-syllable line into abbreviated segments to describe a series of events in short, straightforward clauses which match the simple actions of this unassuming animal. In V 8, whose protagonist is an unsophisticated wolf, the poet creates an informal narrative to match in which the verse-form reads like prose, by dividing the alexandrines casually and irregularly rather than rigorously into hemistichs: 'Un Loup, dis-je, au sortir des rigueurs de l'hiver' *[A Wolf, I say, emerging from the rigours of winter]* (l.5), or 'Rusons donc. Ainsi dit, il vient à pas comptés' *[Let us be cunning. So saying, he tiptoed up]* (l.11), or 'C'est bien fait (dit le Loup en soi-même fort triste)' *[That's well done (said the Wolf to himself sadly)]* (l.33). In each case, it can be seen that the internal rhythm of the lines is shaped to reinforce the impression carried by the meaning. But La Fontaine does not confine himself to a regular metre. For still more intensity of meaning, alexandrines can be interspersed with other metres, and the irregular result suggests jumbled emotions. This is the case in 'L'Eléphant et le Singe de Jupiter' *[The Elephant and Jupiter's Monkey]* (XII 21), where a self-important elephant is shocked to learn from Jupiter's monkey Gille that the gods are unaware of his existence. This humiliating news is conveyed in alexandrines, his shocked feelings are indicated by an interruption in the flow of the verse when his reaction is given in an octosyllabic line. In this extract the two animals are discussing the name of the elephant kingdom:

> Vraiment je suis ravi d'en apprendre le nom,
> Repartit maître Gille: on ne s'entretient guère
> De semblables sujets dans nos vastes lambris.
>   L'Eléphant honteux et surpris
> Lui dit: Et parmi nous que venez-vous donc faire? (l.31–5).

['I'm really delighted to learn its name', replied Gille. 'Such things are scarcely a subject of conversation in the vast vault of heaven.' The Elephant, surprised and humiliated, said: 'so what have you come to do amongst us?']

The alexandrines then continue till the end of the poem. The momentary change of metre in l.34 conveys a jarring impression which reinforces and enhances the feeling of shock – the elephant's system of priorities has been flouted, and both he and the metre momentarily thrown off balance.

La Fontaine also exploits a number of other metres. If a length of line is unusual, it will as a result have a particular impact, which can greatly enhance the meaning. 'L'Araignée et l'Hirondelle' *[The Spider and the Swallow]* (X 6) begins with a ten-line speech by the spider. This is couched in regular decasyllabic couplets (much less common than other forms in La Fontaine), with identical stresses throughout, which produces as regimented an effect as a meticulously woven web. Once the spider ceases to speak and the swallow takes action, the metre goes haywire to suit the swallow's darting, sporadic flight and the chaotic happenings the poet describes. At this stage the lines vary in length, seemingly at random, between the dodecasyllabic alexandrine and the octosyllabic line. But the decasyllabic line, reserved for the spider's speech, is absent.

Conversely, to enhance surprise effects in the content, La Fontaine resorts to uneven metres, with lines containing three or seven syllables (X 1 or I 9). He also employs shorter verse forms to increase intensity, and goes so far as to end a poem on a disyllabic line for a real shock effect. The poem, 'La Montagne qui accouche' *[The Mountain in labour]* (V 10), is a fable about bathos (a mountain in labour makes a great commotion but gives birth to a mouse). The meaning is much enhanced by a number of manipulations of the metre. The story is told in the first verse in unremarkable octosyllabic lines. A single line stands out because it is decasyllabic. It describes the exaggerated expectations of the observers. This slightly longer line makes the narrative appear to expand, in tune with the grandeur of the anticipated event. When the poet reverts to the shorter line to describe the final birth the metre seems as much of an anticlimax as the event itself:

> Une Montagne en mal d'enfant
> Jetait une clameur si haute,
> Que chacun au bruit accourant
> Crut qu'elle accoucherait, sans faute,
> 5 *D'une cité plus grosse que Paris;*
> Elle accoucha d'une Souris.

[a Mountain in Labour / Was clamouring so loudly / That everyone, running up at the sound,/ Thought that, without doubt, she'd give birth / To a city bigger than Paris. / She gave birth to a mouse.]

As well as sounding more impressive, the longer line (l.5) stands out from the text by the fact that it is differently indented from the others.[44]

This effect might seem accidental but for the fact that it is repeated in the second verse, only much more emphatically:

> Quand je songe à cette fable,
> Dont le récit est menteur

Et le sens est véritable,
10   Je me figure un auteur
Qui dit: Je chanterai la guerre
Que firent les Titans au Maître du tonnerre.
C'est promettre beaucoup; mais qu'en sort-il souvent?
Du vent.

[When I think of this fable, / Whose account is untrue / And whose meaning is true, / I imagine an author / Who says: "I will sing of the war / Waged by the Titans against the Lord of Thunder." / That's promising a lot. But what often emerges? / Wind.]

As the bombastic author-figure speaks, the lines increase in length, moving from heptasyllabic lines to an octosyllabic line (l.11), then into alexandrines in l.12. The flow of the verse is brutally cut short by the poem's final line of only two syllables: the metre exactly reproduces the nullity of the pompous poetry which has been talked up by its author, only to be revealed as worthless when one finally hears it.[45]

A final example containing a range of metres demonstrates the flexibility of La Fontaine's verse in reproducing nuances of meaning. The serious, misanthropic poem 'L'Homme et la Couleuvre' *[The Man and the Grass-snake]* (X 1) is in alexandrines interspersed with the occasional octosyllabic line. It consists of a lengthy debate between a grass-snake and a man, backed up by witnesses, as to which is the most selfish, men or beasts. At the end of the poem (l.79–90), the metre changes, and becomes much more varied. It concludes as follows (the number of syllables is noted by each line):

12   L'Homme trouvant mauvais que l'on l'eût convaincu,
12   Voulut à toute force avoir cause gagnée.   l.80
12   Je suis bien bon, dit-il, d'écouter ces gens-là.
12   Du sac et du Serpent aussitôt il donna
10   Contre les murs, tant qu'il tua la bête.
8   On en use ainsi chez les grands.
12   La raison les offense: ils se mettent en tête   85
12   Que tout est né pour eux, quadrupèdes, et gens,
3   Et serpents.
8   Si quelqu'un desserre les dents,
12   C'est un sot. J'en conviens. Mais que faut-il donc faire?
8   Parler de loin; ou bien se taire.   90

[The Man was not pleased at being made to see reason, / And wanted to win at all costs. / "It's all very well for me to listen to folk like that," said he. / Immediately he hit the sack and the Snake / against a wall until he killed the creature. / This is what great men do. / Reason offends them. They get it into their heads / That everything is born for them – quadrupeds, people and snakes. / If anyone unclenches his teeth, / He's a fool. I admit it. So what should one do? / Speak from a distance; or else keep quiet .

The debate ends brutally with the snake's murder, which is given a ten-syllable line, the only one in this ninety-line poem, so that it stands out as a final, unique event (l.83). The epimythium is introduced hesitantly in a short (octosyllabic) line (l.84), then gets underway with alexandrines (l.85–6). It is pulled up short with the reminder of the snake who has been so cruelly destroyed, commemorated in a trisyllabic line, which like the snake's death-line stands out as unique in the poem (l.87). Again the discussion starts tentatively with an octosyllabic line (l.88) and seems about to get underway with alexandrines (l.89), but then La Fontaine tells us that we should keep silent, and accordingly breaks the poem off on a shorter (octosyllabic), incomplete-seeming line, ending on 'se taire' (l.90). The content has been subtly reinforced by the metre throughout this extract.[46]

Even details such as the stress on a particular syllable can greatly enhance the meaning of a line of verse. Stress can be manipulated with great subtlety to contribute to stylistic excess. Even if the metre appears irreproachably regular, great variation in stress can be taking place, with corresponding impact on the intensity of meaning. This effect is difficult to pin down, as French versification analysis does not fully acknowledge nuances of stress variation within a line of verse. Nevertheless, it exists, and La Fontaine undoubtedly makes use of it, as an example will show. In 'Le Rat de ville et le Rat des champs' *[The town Rat and the country Rat]* (I 9) the metre throughout is a seven-syllable line. When the apologue is spoken aloud, despite the odd number of syllables this metre sounds perfectly symmetrical, lilting and pleasing because of the stress, which is virtually identical in the two lines of each couplet, for example:

> Autrefois le Rat de ville
> Invita le Rat des champs,

D'une façon fort civile,
A des reliefs d'ortolans.

*[Once upon a time the town Rat / Invited the country Rat / In a very
civil manner / To sample leftover buntings.]*

Here if the final voiced syllable in each line is the only one to be
stressed a convincing reading is achieved.

The epimythium, while keeping to the same metre, makes a very
different impression. It is spoken by the country rat, who breaks
out of this regular pattern to tell his companion that his habitual
practice of stealing food from human tables until he is chased away
is unacceptable.

21   C'est assez, dit le Rustique;
           Demain vous viendrez chez moi;
           Ce n'est pas que je me pique
           De tous vos festins de roi.
25   Mais rien ne vient m'interrompre;
           Je mange tout à loisir.
           Adieu donc; fi du plaisir
           Que la crainte peut corrompre.

*['That's enough', said the countryman. / 'Tomorrow you'll come to my
place. / Not that I pride myself / In royal feasts like yours. / But nothing
interrupts me. / I eat at leisure. / So goodbye. Down with pleasure /
That is spoiled by fear'.]*

It is possible to read the country rat's lines identically to the first
verse, with a stress only on the final syllable,[47] e.g.:

           De̲main vo̲us viend<u>rez</u> chez <u>moi</u>
or
           <u>Je</u> mange̲ tout <u>à</u> loi<u>sir</u>
or
           A̲dieu <u>donc</u>, fi <u>du</u> plai<u>sir</u>

However, if one reads these lines in this manner, one achieves a
monotonous effect that sounds as if it is falsifying the speaker's
actual words. Let us instead stress the rat's words in these lines as
they would have sounded if he had spoken them:

De<u>main</u> vous <u>vien</u>drez <u>chez</u> <u>moi</u>

or

        Je <u>mange</u> <u>tout</u> à loi<u>sir</u>

or

        A<u>dieu</u> <u>donc</u>, <u>fi</u> du plai<u>sir</u>

A reader aiming to achieve a convincing effect in reading this poem aloud would, I believe, be obliged to incorporate into his version at least a modified attempt at the rhythms of natural speech as given here. In this 'spoken version' the stress changes and varies so that the regular rhythm disappears, apparently giving way to the multiple stresses of colloquial speech: the country rat is breaking the pattern, refusing to fit into the shape of the poem, speaking with the natural voice of reason. His altered stress reinforces the impression that he is talking good sense, and is much wiser than the town rat. In this case, then, the stress has added a further dimension to the meaning of the poem. The content tells us that the country rat has good sense. But it is the stress that indicates that he is more natural and normal than his companion.

Enjambement, too, contributes greatly to the impression of naturalness and freedom of the verse, thereby enhancing the meaning. Used in direct or indirect speech, the technique cuts across individual lines and breaks the rhyme-scheme so that the speaker's words read like real conversation. In 'Le Cheval et le Loup' *[The Horse and the Wolf]* (V 8) the individual alexandrines are broken up into irregular hemistichs to render the rhythms of natural speech. In this same poem, *enjambement* further undermines the alexandrine and enhances the immediacy of the reported speech:

        [Le Loup dit]
     Qu'il connaît les vertus et les propriétés
       De tous les simples de ces prés;
15   Qu'il sait guérir, sans qu'il se flatte,
   Toutes sortes de maux. Si Dom Coursier voulait
        Ne point céler sa maladie,
        Lui Loup gratis le guérirait.
        Car le voir en cette prairie
20   Paître ainsi sans être lié
  Témoignait quelque mal, selon la médecine.

[The Wolf said / That he knew all the virtues and the properties / Of all the simples in these meadows; That, without flattering himself, he

knew how to cure /All types of ills. If my Lord Charger would agree / Not to hide his illness, / The Wolf would cure him for free. / For to see him in this meadow / Grazing without being tied up / Proved that he had some affliction according to medical science.]

There are three *enjambements* proper here (at the end of lines 13, 16 and 19), and the text runs into the next line in two further, less extreme cases (lines 15 and 20). Making the text repeatedly over-run the allotted metre suggests not only naturalness but also haste. The wolf appears to be gabbling his words – he cannot wait to get his teeth into the horse.

Indeed, the commonest function of *enjambement* is, as here, to indicate not only natural, prosaic language but also haste, since the words appear to break out of the metre and rush headlong into the next line. Looking at a run of poems from Book V one can see this effect repeated again and again. In V 4 'Les Oreilles du Lièvre' *[The Hare's Ears]* the lion has banned horned beasts from his kingdom. This is the hare's response:

> Un Lièvre, apercevant l'ombre de ses oreilles,
> Craignit que quelque Inquisiteur
> N'allât attribuer à cornes leur longueur   (l.9–11)

[A Hare, noticing the shadow of his ears, / Feared that some Inquisitor / Might claim that they were horns because of their length.]

The *enjambement* between lines 10 and 11 makes it seem as if the hypothetical inquisitor is eager to jump to hasty conclusions. The delayed main verb 'craignit' *[feared]* also links lines 9 and 10 with an *enjambement* effect. The hare appears to hesitate during the sub-ordinate clause 'apercevant l'ombre de ses oreilles', but then has a rush of fear underlined by the fact that 'craignit' is the first word in the line.

In 'La Vieille et les deux Servantes' *[The Old Woman and the two Serving Girls]* (V 6), the two girls are brusquely hauled out of bed:

> ... notre Vieille ...
> Allumait une lampe, et courait droit au lit
> Où de tout leur pouvoir, de tout leur appétit,
> Dormaient les deux pauvres Servantes.   (l.12–16)

[Our Old Woman ... / Would light a lamp and rush straight to the bed / Where with all their strength and all their heart / The two poor Servant Girls were sleeping.]

The *enjambement* reinforces the impression that the old woman is rushing to rouse the girls, who for their part are trying their utmost to get in as much sleep as possible in the last few seconds. There is an attenuated effect of *enjambement* too between the last two lines, since the main verb 'dormaient' *[were sleeping]* is held over from the previous line. Only in the last line do we discover that the girls are still clinging on to sleep, so that this delayed verb retrospectively clarifies the previous lines, rather than hastening us on to the next line.

The effects singled out here are not isolated. The poems combine the techniques mentioned here, and yet others, for complex effect and true stylistic excess. In 'Le Pot de terre et le Pot de fer' *[The Earthenware Pot and the Iron Pot]* (V 2), to take one example of many, the verse reproduces the jerky walking motions which one might imagine cooking pots would make (in Chauveau's illustration[48] the pots have three legs, so would have to adopt a rolling gait like drunken sailors. Gutwirth calls their walk 'le rythme sautillant qui convient aux tripodes' *[the jerky rhythm appropriate for those with three legs]*, p.117). Accordingly, the basic metre is the potentially asymmetrical seven-syllable line.[49] At key stages the metre suddenly changes, so that the reader takes particular notice. There are three alexandrines, two to describe the catastrophic moment when the pot smashes (l.26–7), and one to point the epimythium (l.29). In addition, La Fontaine varies the stress in the individual lines, which makes the rhythm jolt. In the following extract, as with 'Le Rat de ville et le Rat des champs' *[The town Rat and the country Rat]*, a performer would probably feel obliged to deviate from the strictly correct unstressed line with the stress on the last voiced syllable:

> Car il lui fallait si peu,
> Si peu, que la moindre chose
> De son débris serait cause.
> Il n'en reviendrait morceau.   (l.6–9)

[For it needed so little, / So little, that the least thing / Would cause him to shatter. / Not a fragment would come home.]

Looking more closely at these four lines, we can note that they start with hesitation, as though the pot were reluctant to move. The effect is the opposite of *enjambement*: reading it aloud, one is forced to take a breath after the end of the first line, and the repetition of 'Si peu' [so little] in l.2 conveys the feeling that the pot is moving backwards to the first line, reluctant to take the step being urged upon him. Lines 2–3 contain *enjambement*, rendering the pot's fear that it will be rushed into a precarious situation. Through their hesitation and overrunning, these first two lines seem to ignore the existence of a versification pattern, as though this humble and ignorant pot cannot speak properly in rhyme. In addition, variety of register within a regular rhyme-scheme (illustrated earlier from 'Le Cygne et le Cuisinier' [*The Swan and the Cook*]) is shown here – the first two lines are tentative and couched in banal, repetitive language, while several words indicate the pot's insignificance as a mere inanimate object ('peu' [*little*], 'moindre' [*least*] and 'chose' [*thing*]). By contrast, the third line is much more abstract and dignified, revolving round the key word 'débris', a powerful and catastrophic word. So these four lines illustrate all the points raised in this section.[50]

Looking back over these examples, we may ask ourselves whether stylistic excess through versification consists in merely reinforcing the overt content of the passage, or in adding a further dimension not explicitly present in the content. La Fontaine tends to present his material in an ironic, multidimensional light; often the stylistic excess consists not in strengthening an already vivid impression, but in adding a new twist. Take the case quoted above of the wolf's attempt to flatter the horse into letting him come close. The verbal content of the indirect speech is mendaciously ingratiating and respectful. Without the *enjambement*, which alone hints at the wolf's greed, there would be no indication of the hidden purpose of the speaker. Hence the *enjambement* in fact undermines the speaker's intended effect, while at the same time increasing the implications and hence the overall impact of the passage for the reader.

MULTIPLE EXCESS – A DETAILED EXAMPLE

To illustrate the fullness and richness of La Fontaine's stylistic excess, this chapter concludes on a (necessarily detailed) analysis of just two lines. My example is the concluding sentence of 'Le Berger et la Mer' *[The Shepherd and the Sea]*, IV 2:

La Mer promet monts et merveilles;
Fiez-vous-y, les vents et les voleurs viendront

[The Sea promises mountains and marvels; / Trust it, and winds and robbers will come.]

These two lines complete the epimythium of a poem about a shepherd who invests in a ship which sinks. They explain what happens if you trust the sea; they need to be memorable as they encapsulate the point of the fable and its many implications.[51] In the first of our two lines, the sea, in a well-known stock phrase,[52] offers as it were trustworthy promises. The second line begins with the sea's victim believing her; he will suffer for it. My analysis has been split into sections to simplify the examination.

Nouns

Although 'promettre monts et merveilles' (whose figurative meaning is 'to promise the earth') is so well-known nowadays as to be a cliché, it has a wealth of implications in this context. The sea's first promise is concrete, 'monts'. Nothing could be more solid. The second promise already incorporates a note of dubiety. Despite the caring image of the sea hidden in 'merveilles' ('la mer veille' *[the sea watches over you]*), the 'merveilles' are by definition implausible. These two incompatible nouns underline the paradoxical nature of these promises. The implied inconsistency between them is underlined by the similar yet contrasting nouns in l.2, which suggest an opposition between the vague and the concrete. 'Vents' *[winds]* are impersonal, impermanent. They destroy, it is true, but only incidentally. But with 'voleurs' *[robbers]* we get deliberate malevolence, focused on the sea's victim. Together the two nouns hint at a dichotomy between the fantasy world of promises and the harsh world of reality.

Verbs

The same disparity between certainty and uncertainty is reinforced by different aspects of the use of verbs. The last verb alone denotes certainty through its tense: 'viendront' *[will come]*. In meaning, 'promet' *[promise]* and 'fiez' *[trust]* presuppose trust (or over-confidence). The mood of 'Fiez-vous-y' reinforces this impression; it implies but does not employ a nuance of the conditional which one would normally expect ('si vous vous y fiez'). This compressed, inaccurate form makes the victim's uncertainties appear unconsidered and trivial – he hastily trusts without condition. The actual form used is the imperative, a dismissive use which seems to abandon the victim to his own folly. The victim may obey his immediate urge, because he lacks foresight. The narrator, however, can see into the future, and categorically predicts the victim's ruin or destruction, with 'viendront'. Again, 'viendront', the last word in the poem, is incomplete – we expect a further complementary verb, such as 'viendront vous dépouiller' *[will come to despoil you]*. The sketchiness of this construction adds a new nuance: the poem ends on a note of unresolved threat, rich in menace.

Metre

The lines incorporate two equal eight-syllable sections:

> La Mer promet monts et merveilles;
> les vents et les voleurs viendront.

They represent two halves of an equation – a promise and its outcome. The two sections are separated by a short interpolation at the beginning of the second line, the pivotal 'Fiez-vous-y', the key moment when the victim makes his ill-considered decision. This interpolation introduces a completely new element to the meaning, brings in a new character, 'vous', and determines the outcome of the promise. Into this interruption is put the most important action in the couplet, the fatal mistake of trusting the sea. Just as it breaks the regular sequence of octosyllables, so it destroys the hopes of the protagonist. Hence the metre emphasizes the fact that trusting the sea is a pivotal act, one which can alter the course of one's life.

Alliteration and Visual Impact

> La <u>M</u>er pro<u>m</u>et <u>m</u>onts et <u>m</u>er<u>v</u>eilles;
> Fiez-<u>v</u>ous-y, les <u>v</u>ents et les <u>v</u>oleurs <u>v</u>iendront

The transformation of the sea's solid promises (rendered by the use of 'm's) into thin air (rendered by the use of 'v's) is encapsulated in the fact that the strong-sounding 'monts' have as their counterpart the weak 'vents'. The transition point is 'merveilles', the last word of line 1, which contains both letters.

Stylistic excess can also be found in the visual appearance of the words. In these lines about the sea, the key letters are visually appropriate for waves: 'm' looks like a pair of peaks, 'v' like a trough between two waves. The sea seems to be undulating through the text with these recurring letters.

Statement and Implication

The compressed structure means that much of the content is suggested rather than explained. In particular, there are several traces of images in the two lines, and also several implied meanings which colour the whole. While some of the implications should not be taken too far, and while we must remember that the reference to mountains and marvels is a stock phrase, the suggestion of their presence nevertheless enlivens the lines. First we have a hint of a personification of the sea as a goddess-figure who has it in her power to grant wishes ('La Mer promet'). Next, we should consider the actual items promised. The first thing she promises is 'monts'. This is too much to offer: the victim is over-credulous if he believes her. Simultaneously, one might have a fleeting mental picture of a goddess waving a proprietorial hand at a distant mountain range which she is offering, to the delight of her gullible victim. The second pledge, of 'merveilles', is coloured by the extravagance of the first, but is too vague to be visualized. The two promises cover the material world ('monts') and the world of the imagination ('merveilles'). Although the second line brings in the victim, there is no indirect object specifying the recipient of the promises – the sea appears to make them indiscriminately. This makes the sea seem impersonal and uncaring, and also increases the folly of the victim, who jumps at promises that have not even been directed at him. A further sinister note is introduced with 'vous': the victim is identified with mankind in general, and more precisely with the reader. This will make the threat that concludes the poem seem more powerful. In the second line, we have seen that the tense indicates that the victim ('vous', i.e. the reader) is only too ready to agree and seal his own fate. Once he has done so, two evils ('vents' and 'voleurs') attack him. Or at least they appear on the scene – again they seem impersonal, since there is no specific *référé* or object. What the winds and robbers do when they come is not explained, and there is room for speculation. But we can guess that the 'voleurs' are up to no good. Here the hidden nuances have built up the sinister implications of the couplet, and have stressed the foolish gullibility of the man who trusts the sea.

Self-Referential Comment

The link between 'monts', promises and 'vents', crucial here, is found in another poem, 'La Montagne qui accouche' *[The Mountain in labour]*, V 10, mentioned earlier in this chapter. It will be remembered that the mountain in labour cries out in pain, and seems to be about to deliver a huge city. Despite her clamouring, however, she gives birth to a mere mouse; similarly, a writer promises great works ('c'est promettre beaucoup'), but produces only 'du vent' *[wind]*. The wind is, however, slightly different in the two poems: in our couplet it is threatening; in 'La Montagne qui accouche' it is empty. Nevertheless, looking at the two fables together may add a further nuance to our couplet. Ostensibly we are being told that believing the sea's grandiose promises will simply destroy us: the 'vents' are tempests which will sink our ships, the 'voleurs' pirates who will despoil us. However, there is a further distinction, suggested by the recollection of 'La Montagne qui accouche', between the solid 'monts' and the 'vents'. Despite their bluster the winds are finally empty air, and the promises of the sea have come to nothing.

Analysing a text in this degree of detail demonstrates how minute nuances of style build up a dense overall effect. The poet subtly reinforces the overt meaning of his text, and also adds different nuances which enrich the whole. I personally feel that the ideal study of La Fontaine, the one that would demonstrate all his shades of meaning, would consist in a commentary at least as detailed as this on every line of each of the *Fables*. The resulting work must remain an impossible dream.

CONCLUSION

Setting aside any serious consideration of the diegetic world of the fable, this chapter has concentrated on the poet as showman. His effects are pure illusion, artfully designed to bamboozle the audience. For its part, the audience good-naturedly pretends to go along with the mystification, but is fully aware that it is all a game, and that the illusionist is the most down-to-earth of entertainers. I have been attempting, so to speak, to work out by what mechanism the woman appears to have been sawn in half, the rabbit created out of an empty top-hat. There seems indeed to be no limit to La Fontaine's skill as a craftsman, as I have tried to show through my analysis of the two lines.

The conjurer's art consists of minute hidden tricks, coloured scarves so fine that they can be hidden till the time comes to reveal them with a flourish. La Fontaine's writing is rather different. It is indeed full of glimpses of hidden colour, but these may never be revealed to the general reader, and instead may become visible only when the strands of the fabric are disentangled. When the threads of illusion are unravelled, though, we are left wondering for whom he chose to weave it in the first place. His sleight of hand, his subtle manipulation is perhaps undertaken as much for his own pleasure as for that of the painstaking reader. That he is juggling with many different elements at once is the one thing that is abundantly clear through the complexities of his magnificently mystifying technique.

II
Imagery

CHAPTER 3

Imagery: the man in the animal

In a later chapter we will see a great variety of approaches to animal portrayal in the *Fables*. Looking at individual fables, however, we discover that the animal portraits tend to be fixed: in each separate fable the characters are endowed with a firm set of attributes, which will not vary within that context – creating clear parameters makes it easier for the fabulist to convey the moral message without ambiguity. Consider the difference between the portrayals of talking donkeys in individual fables. In 'Le Meunier, son Fils et l'Ane' *[The Miller, his Son and the Donkey]* the donkey is a dumb beast without the power of speech; in 'L'Ane et le petit Chien' *[the Donkey and the Little Dog]* the donkey cannot speak to his master, but can reason within his own mind. He exhibits considerable powers of logic, to which the reader is privy. In 'Les Voleurs et l'Ane' *[The Robbers and the Donkey]* the donkey is able to talk to his master, and tartly puts him in his place. A talking donkey does not suddenly become a dumb beast within a single fable, and vice versa.

This inflexibility is at variance with the impression of versatility in the character portraits, often introduced into the separate poems through imagery. Imagery can open unexpected doors, suggesting possibilities which colour the poem's mood. It can broaden the scope of a fable, and do so without 'cheating' – without bending the rules and parameters laid down by the fabulist for the poem in question.

La Fontaine is not particularly renowned for his imagery. The story-line in most of his fables seems clear-cut and simple, devoid of the striking sustained images that characterize many other poets. However, this very simplicity has its own fascination. The interest of his images lies precisely in their apparent modesty – they are conveyed by a passing allusion, sometimes even by a single word. But this very sketchiness is suggestive in its own way, for the poet can include numbers of such brief images within a single poem, each one momentarily evoking a fleeting parallel.

Let us look at some examples from animal fables, to see how the poet creates a whole new network of suggestions and allusions through a multiplicity of rapid images. We will see that, although the images are extremely diverse, their common theme is central to the whole fable genre: the relationship between animals and man. It is, of course, scarcely surprising that a human presence lurks even behind fables in which human beings have no direct part to play, since the point of a fable is to make the moral applicable to human readers. But what is remarkable is the consistency with which La Fontaine alludes to man in non-human poems, weaving him into the very fabric of animal poetry in a way which ensures that he is always present.

My first example is 'Les Deux Chèvres' *[The Two Goats]* (XII 4). On a first reading, this poem strikes one with its sheer banality. It is a simple tale of two goats who meet head-on, crossing a stream from opposite sides on the same plank; neither will give way, so both fall into the water. The event described seems unremarkable; the poet might have witnessed it himself (although the source is probably Pliny the Elder).

On a closer inspection, this poem reveals a number of images. What function do these fulfil in a poem which seems so ordinary? We will note at the outset that the images all involve transforming the goats into human beings and back again. The multiple transformation process is worth examining in detail.

The poet starts by establishing firmly that the goats are animals by referring to their grazing: 'Dès que les chèvres ont brouté' *[As soon as goats have finished grazing]*. Only when their bellies are full will they indulge in the foolish behaviour that forms the subject of the poem.

After the first, establishing line, La Fontaine immediately likens them to women, but adventurous ones, in l.2–3:

> Certain esprit de liberté
> Leur fait chercher fortune; elles vont en voyage …

[A certain spirit of freedom / Makes them seek their fortunes; they go on a journey …]

'Esprit de liberté' indicates their dislike of being confined to their pasture. 'Esprit' in addition implies wit and intelligence. A free and unconventional attitude is also suggested – they are lovers of 'liberté'. And they actually set off on a journey. Meanwhile, La Fontaine preserves the adventuresses' femininity, already indicated, with '*elles* vont en voyage'. The raffish female adventurers glimpsed here will contrast absurdly with the pretension of the 'Dames' later (l.8).

Now comes bathos. The first image is comically rejected and devalued – the goats' 'voyage' is revealed as merely a removal to another part of their pasture:

> ... elles vont en voyage
> Vers les endroits du pâturage
> Les moins fréquentés des humains.

[They go on a journey / To the parts of the pasture / Least frequented by people].

This reminds us that they are not women but animals. The description of the corner of their pasture, though it gives a precise impression, is somewhat pretentiously phrased, a little as though the goats were seeking a romantic wilderness in a spirit of misanthropic gloom, like Molière's Misanthrope.

The depiction of the pasture now becomes fantastic, the quintessence of rugged inaccessibility described in vivid poetic language with classical overtones:

> Là s'il est quelque lieu sans route et sans chemins,
> Un rocher, quelque mont pendant en précipices ... [53]

[There, if there is some roadless, pathless spot, / A rock, some mount with looming cliffs ...]

These two lines draw attention to themselves, are ostentatiously well written, and there is ostentation too in the throwaway repetition of 'quelque' *[some]*, as though this daunting natural landscape was nothing special to the two sophisticated, world-weary protagonists. There is a suggestion of indirect speech, nature viewed through the eyes of two sophisticated ladies acutely aware of its picturesque beauties but at the same time dismissive to indicate their blasé *ennui*. So the image of the goats as society ladies is already present by implication before the poet uses the term 'Dames' in l.8: 'C'est où ces Dames vont promener leurs caprices' *[This is where these Ladies go to walk their fancies]*. L.8 itself definitively transforms them into ladies, but at the same time reminds us that they are goats through the pun in 'caprices' (derived from the Latin for goat, 'caper'). At the same time, 'caprices' hints at their wilfulness and prepares us for the wanton folly that will lead to their discomfiture at the end of the poem.

The next line again transforms them abruptly back into animals with a second effect of bathos: 'Rien ne peut arrêter cet animal grimpant.' *[Nothing can stop this climbing beast]*. Not only do 'dames' become 'animaux', but the human 'promener' is given an undignified caprine equivalent, 'grimper' *[to climb]*.

As the two goats move towards each other, growing steadily bolder ('s'émancipant') (l.10–13), the animal portrait is maintained, with the 'patte blanche' *[white hoof]* that is the distinguishing feature of goathood in the *Fables*[54], and generally in folk-tales:

> Deux Chèvres donc s'émancipant,
> Toutes deux ayant patte blanche,
> Quittèrent les bas prés, chacune de sa part.
> L'une vers l'autre allait pour quelque bon hasard.

[Two goats, then, growing in daring, / Both with white hooves, / Left the low-lying meadows, each on her own side. / By some lucky chance they moved towards each other.]

They reach the stream, described much more simply than the crags of l.7. Everything is scaled down to the size of small animals:

> Un ruisseau se rencontre, et pour pont une planche;
> Deux Belettes à peine auraient passé de front
> Sur ce pont ...

[They came across a stream, with a plank for a bridge; / Two weasels would scarcely have passed each other / On that bridge ...]

The reminder that they are not after all human ladies makes their previous self-importance absurd, and will contrast amusingly with what is to come.

At this point, the goats become 'Amazones'. They expand to human size again; but these are not ordinary women: they are now fabulous mythological beings, single-breasted huntresses of Greek legend whose queen married Theseus. Since the Amazons were renowned for their intrepidity, it is this aspect that is the overt point of the comparison; but the Amazons were also famous riders, so that the goats' balancing feat on the plank is a visual parody of the huntresses' prowess on horseback. We may also note that a famous contemporary of La Fontaine's was known as an 'Amazone' – an aspect that will be discussed shortly.

The human image now takes over completely:
... l'une de ces personnes
Pose un pied sur la planche, et l'autre en fait autant.

[One of these persons / Placed a foot on the plank, and the other did the same.]

The goats are now 'persons', and, far from having 'white hooves', they place 'a foot' on the plank.
The next passage contains the only sustained image in the poem:
Je m'imagine voir avec Louis le Grand
Philippe Quatre qui s'avance
Dans l'île de la Conférence.
Ainsi s'avançaient pas à pas,
Nez à nez nos Aventurières ...

[I imagine I can see, with Louis the Great, / Philip IV advancing / at the Ile de la Conférence. / So they came forward, step by step, / Nose to nose, our Adventuresses ...]

'Voilà bien le comble de l'audace' *[This is boldness itself]*, writes Gutwirth.[55] In this extravagant comparison, the protagonists, already human, become men, and not ordinary men but the kings of France and Spain. The meeting of two goats on a plank is likened to a famous and ceremonial encounter which took place between the two kings in 1660.[56] The meeting at the pavillon de la Conférence on the île des Faisans was to ratify the marriage of Louis XIV to the daughter of Philip IV, Maria Theresa. This com-

parison works on a number of levels. First must be the visual
aspect: the caution of the two animals makes their progress seem
stately in its slowness – the two kings, weighed down by considerations of protocol, advanced with a similarly measured step, pacing
each other so that neither should reach the ceremonial table to sign
the marriage contract first. Next, the seal is set on the goats' self-
importance. The poet has already made them seem pretentious by
comparing them to 'Dames' and 'Amazones': this latest royal parallel takes the pretension to the ultimate limits. Thirdly, there is
probably a satirical subtext to La Fontaine's account. Fumaroli (II
412) and Sweetser (3, p.99) have pointed out that questions of
precedence were rife at the time. More pointedly, the fact that the
goats have just been described as 'Amazones' gives us a hint that a
more precise satirical allusion may be intended: for one of the most
important and colourful personages at court, Mlle de Montpensier,
la Grande Mademoiselle, was known as an 'Amazone de la Fronde',
together with her two friends the Duchesses of Longueville and
Chevreuse. La Grande Mademoiselle created a scandal at the king's
wedding: she insisted on being present on the island, and when
permission was refused, disguised herself as a peasant girl and came
along anyway. Her haughty manners soon betrayed her. La
Fontaine, by 1660 well in with court circles and court gossip,
would surely have known this amusing anecdote. Furthermore, as
Collinet has demonstrated,[57] the poet had mounted a veiled attack
on La Grande Mademoiselle in another fable, 'La Fille' *[The
Maiden]* – clearly, he was not one of her admirers. So there may be
a specific human target to his mockery here.[58] Finally, there is a
possible political dimension to this parallel. Although the relationship between Louis and Philip was cordial enough in 1660, it sub-
sequently deteriorated; by 1691, when 'Les deux Chèvres' first
appeared, the two nations had been confronting each other in the
war of Spanish succession. The reason the goats in our fable are
advancing so slowly and carefully is that there is a river flowing
beneath them: one false step, and they may fall in. Could a dangerous torrent similarly be threatening to engulf the two kings? Is this
one of La Fontaine's several covert attacks on the dangers of the
aggressive foreign policy that was so characteristic of Louis XIV?[59]
Even if we do not accept all the possibilities suggested here, we can
see how richly allusive is this image of the two kings.

　　Next, La Fontaine relates the image to its subject in stages. The two kings were described overtly through a comparison, introduced by 'je m'imagine' *[I imagine]*. We are not supposed to think that this is actually what he saw. The second part of the image, according to the classical pattern, depicts the reality: 'Ainsi s'avançaient ...' *[So they came forward]*. But La Fontaine is misleading us here. When he describes what was actually seen, he still conveys the impression that these are women, not goats, avoiding an over-abrupt transition from kings to animals. The process of coming down to earth is conveyed by the parts of the body that are singled out. First we have 'pas à pas' *[step by step]*, implying human feet rather than cloven hooves, and with a nuance of courtly ceremony. We should not forget that 'le pas', meaning precedence, was an important element of court life, as we will see later in discussing the fable 'La Tête et la Queue du Serpent' *[The Head and the Tail of the Serpent]*.

The 'aventurières' meet in the middle with 'nez à nez' *[nose to nose]*, which as an exclusively human term again preserves their human character. We should note that they have ceased to be kings and become women again before they meet nose to nose, for the nose is a ridiculous organ, not to be readily associated with a king (though Louis's was certainly a very regal one).[60] Instead, as the protagonists seem less grand, so the parallel with Louis XIV recedes. With the words 'nez à nez' the dignified atmosphere is destroyed. The goats' intransigence, when neither will yield to the other, now seems ridiculous, and their self-importance (' ... toutes deux étant fort fières' *[both being very proud]*) is undermined. Before they finally fall into the water, La Fontaine brings together their human and animal attributes: he makes them vaunt their ancient lineage, but the mythological heroines from whom they claim descent in l.31–2 are not women but goats. And it is as goats that they come to grief. The reader is reminded that these are after all not great heroines, not even by caprine standards, by the dismissive way in which their fate is summed up in the line 'toutes deux tombèrent dans l'eau' *[both fell into the water]*. All the build-up comes to nothing, and in the end they are just two ordinary little animals falling off a plank. The poet does not bother to inform us of their subsequent fate, and we assume that they suffered nothing worse than a wetting.

During the course of this poem, we have seen the goats change bewilderingly from raffish adventurers to amazons to ladies to kings and back to goats, with a number of other momentary trans-formations in between. But these transformations are so fleeting that the reader does not feel consciously jolted by their oddity. The final impression is amusing rather than bewildering.

But these images have much more than mere entertainment value. Instead of contributing overtly to the stated moral, which is an attack on inflexibility, they add a new, underlying dimension. In part, they undermine what the poem is saying, for the two hero-ines, who are supposed to be the epitome of fixity of purpose, undergo a bewildering series of transformations during the poem. However, the pattern of the transformations does add a new side to the moral. The poet starts off with animal heroines, turns them into a variety of human beings, but firmly restores them to their original shape before they fall and the poem ends. The implication is that the human parallels were symptomatic of the goats' self-importance, but that when they come to grief they are brought face to face with their own ordinariness ('Gros-Jean comme devant'[61] *[Good old Jean as before]*). And an additional moral is implied: those who entertain exaggerated illusions as to their own worth will learn the truth the hard way.

La Fontaine's approach to this fable has been to present a poten-tially everyday picture, but to make it seem strange and imaginative by the introduction of human imagery. The imagery further enhances both the moral message and its applicability to human beings. Many of the fables operate in this way: we are presented with a situation involving animals, which is perfectly realistic, and whose outcome is utterly believable. By incorporating a human presence through imagery, La Fontaine emphasizes the relevance of the moral to the reader. Another typical example is 'Le Loup et l'Agneau' *[The Wolf and the Lamb]* (I 10), in which a lamb is caught and eaten by a wolf. The outcome is entirely expected, but the wolf is likened to a king ('votre Majesté'), which emphasizes the relevance of the moral to human readers. In 'La Belette entrée dans un grenier' *[The Weasel who got into a Loft]* (III 17), a weasel, having crept through a hole into a well-stocked storeroom, eats so much that she is too fat to squeeze out again – again, the situation seems believable in animal terms; but like the goats, the weasel is compared to a lady in a series of fleeting images, and we perceive a human application to the moral.

In certain fables of this type, the human imagery is so important that the point of the poem would be lost without it. This is the case with 'Le Cheval et le Loup' *[The Horse and the Wolf]* (V 8). Here the human parallel is so strongly present that the protagonist actually thinks of himself as a man. At the start of the poem, the main character, the wolf, is described as a particular type of human being, an unscrupulous and experienced huntsman, with his own larder. When he sees a horse in a field, he addresses it: 'Bonne chasse, dit-il, qui l'aurait à son croc. / Eh! que n'es-tu mouton? car tu me serais hoc' *[That would be good hunting, said he, for the man who could hang it on his meat-hook. Eh! Why are you not a sheep? You would have been just right for me]* (l.8–9). He sizes up his victim with a professional's eye, and refers casually to a butcher's hook or 'croc'.[62] That he thinks of himself in human terms is confirmed by his envy of the lucky hunter who will have this carcass hanging in his larder – implying that the wolf too has his 'croc' to load.

Next, the wolf becomes a trickster. Sizing up his potential victim, he says: 'il faut ruser pour avoir cette proie. / Rusons donc' *[You need to use cunning to catch that prey. / So let us be cunning]* (l.10–11). By means of this 'rusons donc', La Fontaine is enabled to present a further human parallel. The wolf is now compared to a man acting a part. He pretends to be a doctor, and plays the role with gusto, providing us with a lively comic portrait of a Moliéresque quack. He comes mincing up ('il vient à pas comptés', l.11), and makes a long speech, full of medical jargon and flattery, offering to cure the horse for free. The speech is given in free indirect speech. The 'doctor' describes his profession in a pompous circumlocution ('il … se dit écolier d'Hippocrate' *[He said he was a pupil of Hippocrates]*, l.12). He explains his craft in simplistic jargon – the sort of language that a layman might use if trying to impress with medical knowledge: ' … il connaît les vertus et les propriétés / De tous les simples de ces prés' *[He knew the virtues and the properties / of all the simples in these meadows.]* (l.13–14). He now cajoles his prey, addressing him as 'Dom Coursier' (flattering on a number of counts: the horse is ennobled as 'Dom'; the title is Spanish, and Spain was generally accepted as the provenance of superb horses at the time; he is not an ordinary horse, but a war-horse or 'coursier'). And he offers him free treatment, which the horse cannot reasonably refuse.

The horse in reply pretends to be seduced by these blandishments – he agrees that he is ailing, with an abscess in his hoof. So the wolf takes things further. He is by now so involved in the deception that he is described not as 'le loup' but as 'le docteur'. And the poet now quotes him verbatim:

> – Mon fils, dit le docteur, il n'est point de partie
> Susceptible de tant de maux.
> J'ai l'honneur de servir Nosseigneurs les Chevaux,
> Et fais aussi la Chirurgie. (l.24–7)

[My son, said the doctor, No part / Is susceptible to so many ailments. / I have the honour of treating my Lords the Horses / And am also a surgeon.]

The hypocrite is pretending to be a benevolent older man ('mon fils'); he claims to be experienced, having other equine patients and a knowledge of surgery; he again flatters the equine race ('Nosseigneurs').

The good 'doctor's' little speech finished, the poet reminds us that underneath he is still a shameless predator:

> Mon galant ne songeait qu'à bien prendre son temps,
> Afin de happer son malade. (l.28–9)

[My hero was thinking only of biding his time, / So as to catch his patient.]

When the horse kicks him in the teeth as he inspects the non-existent abscess, the wolf tells himself ruefully that he has deserved it: 'Tu veux faire ici l'arboriste, / Et ne fus jamais que boucher' *[You wanted to be a herbalist, / But you were never more than a butcher.]* (l.35–6). Yet again he sees himself in terms of human professions, the herbalist and the butcher, reminding us of the allusion to the butcher's hook at the beginning of the poem. This final line reflects the wolf's awareness of the true situation – but significantly he still thinks of himself as a working man.

The human imagery is essential to this fable. It alone transforms an account of an episode in animal life into a moral tale with a lesson for man. For we would otherwise learn nothing from the mere facts of the case: it is only too natural for a wolf to seek to batten on a horse, and for the horse to defend itself. The human imagery, in which the wolf, playing a human role, tries to trick the horse into surrender, introduces the whole 'trompeur trompé' *[deceiver deceived]* aspect of the fable, which in turn provides the message.

In the two poems we have examined, the human imagery has brought a new dimension to an essentially believable animal experience. This credibility is by no means found in all animal fables. A second group, as common as the first, presents impossibly far-fetched animal situations from the outset. A fox cooks a meal for a stork and serves it in a dish (I 18); a frog ties her leg and a rat's together (IV 11); a cat covers himself in flour as camouflage (III 18), and so on. Human imagery is as important in this group as in the 'plausible' category. So what is its function here?

To answer this question, let us explore one of the most far-fetched fables, 'La Chauve-Souris, le Buisson et le Canard' *[The Bat, the Bush and the Duck]* (XII 7). In it, the three protagonists become business associates, only to go bankrupt.

From the start, it is difficult for the reader to accept the situation uncritically. It is utterly ludicrous for three such disparate beings to be associated at all (though we must remember that Aesop, not La Fontaine, is responsible for the original idea). In La Fontaine's hands, however, the fable becomes a surreal masterpiece. It is written as though the situation described were perfectly normal. To create this semblance of plausibility, La Fontaine links his characters together by means of a constant underlying human parallel: the three protagonists consistently behave as though they were human merchants. We are not invited to question the status of a bush or a bat as businessmen, we are expected to take it on trust, since the poet writes with such confidence and authority of their financial transactions. The underlying human image seems to be making the situation plausible; but paradoxically it simultaneously strains our credulity to the limit. This is humour of extremes: the poet plays on the notion of the suspension of disbelief, demanding it of the reader, yet creating conditions where it is impossible.

We are plunged into the narrative without any preamble:

Le Buisson, le Canard et la Chauve-Souris,
    Voyant tous trois qu'en leur pays
    Ils faisaient petite fortune,
Vont trafiquer au loin, et font bourse commune. (l.1–4)

[The Bush, the Duck and the Bat, / Seeing that in their country all

three / Scraped but a poor living, / Went far afield to trade, and pooled their resources.]

The three protagonists are already established as independent businessmen, with an eye for profit and considerable ambition. We may well ask ourselves at the outset what business can be conducted by three such merchants, but the poet teasingly avoids giving specific information, as though the matter were of no importance and to be taken on trust. Line 4 is particularly odd. In it we are presented with a number of extraordinary facts. First, the three heroes become business associates. Fable readers expect different species of animals to mingle; but for a plant to join in with the animals is fantasy of a different order, and cannot pass unnoticed. We further learn that the three protagonists travel far. The poet does not just state that their business interests are wide-ranging, but explains that they '*vont* trafiquer au loin' *[go far afield to trade]*, they physically move themselves. Again, while there is no problem with the duck and the bat, it is asking a great deal of us as readers to expect us to accept that a bush travels widely in the line of business (plants in the *Fables* normally remain rooted to the spot, even if they can talk).[63] The third oddity is that the three have shared financial arrangements. We are expected to believe not only that they have a 'bourse' *[purse]*, but also that they share it with the others.

The next sentence gives details of their business dealings:

> Ils avaient des comptoirs, des Facteurs, des Agents
> Non moins soigneux qu'intelligents,
> Des registres exacts de mise et de recette. (l.5–7)

[They had counters, factors and agents / Both conscientious and intelligent, / And kept exact records of investments and receipts.]

Their commercial transactions are here described in much more concrete terms. One might previously have imagined that the business was merely a figure of speech. Now it appears that actual trading is in process, and that there is a real business empire here. The equipment owned by the enterprising trio ('counters', 'records') is that of human commerce. Possibly their faithful and reliable employees are also human. However, these details, while making it plain that their business is considerable, leave us completely in the dark as to its actual nature.

In the next sentence, La Fontaine abruptly reduces the size and importance of the business while yet maintaining the merchant parallel:

> Tout allait bien, quand leur emplette,
> En passant par certains endroits
> Remplis d'écueils, et fort étroits,
> Et de trajet très difficile,
> Alla tout emballée au fond des magasins
> Qui du Tartare sont voisins. (l.8–13)

[All was going well, when their shopping / Passing through certain places / Full of dangers and very narrow, / And very difficult to negotiate, / Sank, all wrapped up, down to the storerooms / which are next to Tartarus.]

Like so many merchants in the *Fables*,[64] these three lose their wealth in a shipwreck. And yet there is something odd about this precious merchandise. It is called an 'emplette'. The term suggests a small, trivial purchase – it was most frequently used to mean a purchase of clothing in La Fontaine's time.[65] The purchase is 'tout emballée', parcelled up like a portable package; and it becomes a mere item in a shop in l.13. Admittedly, priceless commodities can be small in size, and the shop is not an ordinary one, but part of a world under the sea related to the classical underworld. Nevertheless, the impression of a large-scale business empire built up in l.5–7 is implicitly undermined here. The whole business venture is thus made comical. Its small scale clashes bathetically with the build-up of the previous lines. Yet simultaneously it seems even more bewildering, since its exact nature and size are made harder to grasp. However, the human element continues to underpin the poem, since the processes of shopping ('emplette') and wrapping the purchase ('emballée') are purely human activities.

The bush, the duck and the bat react to their loss like experienced businessmen. When they attempt to conceal their problems the poet explains that this is for sound financial reasons: 'Le plus petit marchand est savant sur ce point; / Pour sauver son crédit il faut cacher sa perte.' *[The least little merchant is wise about this; / To save your credit you must hide your losses.]* (l.16–7). But they fail: 'le cas fut découvert' *[the facts were discovered]* (l.19). By whom, we are not told; but the impression has already been built up that they are part of a business world in which many participants are involved. Their bankrupt state is described in largely human terms: they are 'sans crédit, sans argent, sans ressource' *[with no credit, no money, no resources]* (l.20) – the lack of 'credit' and 'money' would not matter to an animal or plant, which needs only the 'resources'. They are threatened with 'le bonnet vert' (l.21), the green cap worn by declared bankrupts at the time (the mind boggles at the idea of a bush wearing a cap). Their ensuing problems are human ones – repayment of sums owed (so they deal in money), bailiffs dunning them, lawsuits (so they are part of a society with a legal system), creditors at their door (so they live in a house) (l.23–5).

The final section of the apologue is the oddest of all. It describes the trio's attempts to remedy the situation:

> Le Buisson accrochait les passants à tous coups:
> Messieurs, leur disait-il, de grâce, apprenez-nous   30
> En quel lieu sont les marchandises
> Que certaines gouffres nous ont prises.
> Le Plongeon sous les eaux s'en allait les chercher.
> L'Oiseau Chauve-Souris n'osait plus approcher
> Pendant le jour nulle demeure;   35
> Suivi de Sergents à toute heure,
> En des trous il s'allait cacher.

[The Bush hooked onto passers-by all the time: / Sirs, said he, I beg you, tell us / Where our merchandise can be / Which has been swallowed up by certain depths. / The Diver went to look for them under the water. / The Bat-Bird no longer dared approach / Any dwellings during the day. / He was constantly pursued by bailiffs / And went and hid himself in holes.]

The poet has hitherto systematically ignored the natural attributes of his protagonists, who have been behaving exactly like men. Now, suddenly, he reminds us what they are. In their extremity, they seem to revert to type, each behaving in a manner characteristic of its species. At the same time, their financial ruin continues to preoccupy them, so that we are shown the bush behaving in a bush-like manner to save itself from bankruptcy, using its clinging twigs or thorns to force passers-by to stop and give it information. Likewise, the duck dives underwater to look for the sunken treasure. The bat's reaction varies the pattern. It avoids going out during daylight so as to evade its creditors: La Fontaine is playing on the fact that bats sleep 'en des trous' *[in holes]* and come out at dusk, equating this pattern of behaviour with that of a bankrupt on the run. He also turns the female bat, 'chauve-souris', into a male 'oiseau chauve-souris' or bat-bird, so that he can be a male bankrupt, and link up with the 'grand seigneur' of the epimythium, as we will see.

This last section appears superficially to explain much of the point of the poem. Hitherto it has been unclear, even bewildering, why the fable told of these three particular protagonists. Now we can see the relevance of their distinguishing features to the situation. The introduction of these features also adds an unspoken moral, which undermines the apparent equation of the creatures with men in the earlier part of the poem: the poet seems at this point to be indicating that it is not possible to suppress one's true nature, to change definitively from being a bush to being a merchant. As he says elsewhere,

> Tant le naturel a de force ...
> Quelque chose qu'on puisse faire,
> On ne saurait le réformer. (II 18, l.30–36)

[Nature has such force ... / Whatever one does, / One will never manage to reform it.]

And there is also the suggestion that pride comes before a fall, another frequent La Fontaine theme,[66] in the contrast between the three creatures' worldly success and their ignominious reversal to their original state. However, this section, which concludes the story of the bush, the duck and the bat, makes no attempt to elucidate the circumstances of their excursion into the world of human high finance, which will indeed remain finally unexplained.

In this way, the apologue of this fable gives an unclear account of an attempt to bridge the gap between the world of man and the world of nature. The enigmatic quality of the sustained human metaphor contributes greatly to the poem, making it seem both strange and funny. One might also add that it is essential for the human metaphor to be elusive. Without its ambiguous quality, the trio's double metamorphosis from animal/plant to human being and back again would seem so far-fetched as to be unacceptable. The poem ends on a final transformation and an epimythium. The poet brings himself in to introduce it:

> Je connais maint detteur qui n'est ni Souris-Chauve,
> Ni Buisson, ni Canard, ni dans tel cas tombé,
> Mais simple grand seigneur, qui tous les jours se sauve
> Par un escalier dérobé.

[I know many a debtor who is neither Bat, / Nor Bush, nor Duck, nor fallen into their situation, / But simply a great lord, who every day escapes / By a hidden staircase.]

He claims he has done with his three protagonists, and has moved into the world of man to complete his fable. Accordingly he introduces a new character, an insolvent nobleman, who now takes over to point the explicit moral, a satirical dig at the profligacy of certain aristocrats. However, there is a clear parallel between this particular aristocrat's behaviour and that of the bat – both make a habit of furtive escape. And the nobleman has the same problem as the bat, that is to say importunate creditors. One could imagine him lurking incognito in a concealing black cloak reminiscent of a bat's wings. So in these final lines the animal image underlies the account of human behaviour much more straightforwardly than similar parallels in the earlier part of the poem. Perhaps this is why La Fontaine applies the adjective 'simple' to the 'grand seigneur' (whose status and predicament are of course far from simple). The poem finally slips away from us on a short (octosyllabic) line – the final point is not clearly made, and the last word 'dérobé' *[hidden]* sums up the whole feeling of this poem which has confused and obfuscated the very issues it raised. Far from making sense of this fable, the imagery has surreptitiously complicated the matter. Its contribution has been to make the poem arresting and amusing just because it is outlandish, while also providing the point of the moral.

Does La Fontaine habitually seek for an effect of excess, and does his human imagery serve to enhance such effects? It is worth examining a fable even more extravagant than the previous one, in my opinion the most extraordinary poem in the whole collection. This is 'La Tête et la Queue du Serpent' *[The Head and the Tail of the Serpent]* (VII 16). This strange fable describes the attempt of the snake's tail to precede its head by travelling backwards. The tail makes representations to the gods about the unfairness of always having to bring up the rear. To render the oddness of this situation, the poet creates a style full of paradoxes, puns, double meanings and oxymorons. Simultaneously, he produces a sustained human parallel which is so carefully worked out that it becomes ridiculous through sheer excess. Using the feminine gender of 'la tête' *[the head]* and 'la queue' *[the tail]*, La Fontaine transforms the snake into a pair of quarrelsome human sisters fighting over precedence. An unpleasant atmosphere is created from the start by the pejorative words applied to the sisters: 'ennemies', 'cruelles', 'débats' *[arguments]*.

Although we are told in the preamble which sets the scene that the two ends of the snake quarrel ('il survint entre elles / De grands débats' *[There arose between them / Fierce arguments]*), throughout the poem we witness the speech only of the tail. This perverse situation greatly contributes to the strange atmosphere. The mouth of the animal, the part that should speak, remains silent, while the tail miraculously gives tongue.

We should remember that the whole point of the rivalry between the two ends of the snake depends on a zoological misapprehension of the time. In La Fontaine's day it was believed that a snake carried poison in its tail as well as in its fangs. This is why the tail feels unjustly underprivileged compared with the head: 'Aussi bien qu'elle je porte / Un poison prompt et puissant' *[Just like her, I bear / A quick and potent poison]*. At the outset we are told that both are distinguished exponents of the poisoner's art, they have 'acquis un nom fameux' *[acquired a famous name]*. This is the first instance of the twisted logic which makes this poem so unusual – the impression is fleetingly conveyed that they are distinguished figures. It is dissipated when we learn where they are most appreciated: 'auprès des Parques cruelles' *[among the cruel Fates]* – the poet simply means that they kill people. But the human context of great reputations and distinction is established, preparing us for the reason for their rivalry, 'le pas' (which means both 'a step' and 'precedence').

We have already seen this human term used inappropriately for the two goats. Here it is appropriate on one level, wildly inapposite on another. The two snake halves may seek precedence over each other – but they would be incapable of taking a single 'pas' since they have no feet. However, as they slither along, they are again portrayed in human terms, as the poet explains: 'La tête avait toujours marché avant la queue' *[the head had always walked in front of the tail]*. Again there is a double meaning here. 'Marcher' is ostensibly used to mean 'to progress'; but the secondary meaning of 'to walk' is irresistibly evoked when we remember the lurking footstep, 'le pas': behind the writhing snake, we seem to detect the two angry women walking.

The tail now breaks into speech to complain of her lot to the gods (we have been prepared for a classical context by the reference to the fates, 'les Parques'). The tail comes across as obsessed by the head, and very resentful. She refers to the head disparagingly as 'celle-ci' *[that one there]*. Continuing with the double meanings, the poet makes her use a form of speech that seems a mere convention but is later taken literally: 'Croit-elle que toujours j'en veuille user ainsi? / Je suis son humble servante.' *[Does she think I want to go on like this forever? / I'm her humble servant.]* The second sentence here is just another way of saying 'Certainly not'. But the snake goes on to say: 'On m'a faite, Dieu merci, / Sa soeur et non sa suivante.' *[I was made, thank God, / Her sister, not her servant.]* The 'humble servante' was also to be understood literally, since it is taken up again with 'sa suivante'. But the joke is that 'suivante' too has a double meaning: it means not only 'female attendant' but also 'follower', hence 'tail end', since the tail perforce follows the head.

Next, the tail refers back to her idea that the head as her 'sister'. She explains that they are 'Toutes deux du même sang' *[both of the same blood]*, so should be treated alike. Again this works on two levels – on the human plane, the tail is pointing out that they are members of the same family, so equal in rank. But we also remember that they form a single serpent body, so the same blood flows through them. The expression is literally true as well as being a cliché.

We now come to the tail's request: 'Qu'on me laisse précéder / A mon tour ma soeur la tête.' *[Let me precede / My sister the head in my turn.]* It contains another pun dependent on an earlier line: on the literal level the tail is simply asking for the snake to move backwards so that she has a chance to go first. But on the human level she is asking to take precedence over a relative equal in rank. This would have seemed irresistibly funny to La Fontaine's contemporaries, living at a time when the court was obsessed with questions of rank and precedence. The snake goes on to promise to perform her task well: 'Je la conduirai si bien / Qu'on ne se plaindra de rien.' *[I will lead her so well / That there will be no complaints.]* The double meaning of 'conduirai' relates to the question of precedence: the tail will guide the head both literally and, in the sustained human parallel, by taking the initiative in decisions. Later the tail will be 'la guide' - here the noun becomes feminine to preserve the underlying image of the two sisters.

We now come to three lines in which, describing the response of the gods, La Fontaine presents us with a dazzling series of oxymorons:

> Le Ciel eut pour ces voeux une bonté cruelle.
> Souvent sa complaisance a de méchants effets.
> Il devrait être sourd aux aveugles souhaits.

[Heaven had a cruel kindness in listening to her wishes. / Often its complaisance has evil results. / It should be deaf to blind wishes.]

As well as reflecting the paradoxical, topsy-turvy character of the fable, these lines subtly reinforce the human parallel running through the poem. For this view of the classical gods malevolently granting what humans think they desire is characteristically found in the quintessentially human context of high tragedy. One has only to think of the gods' treacherous half-revelations to Oedipus, or, to mention a contemporary of La Fontaine's, the cruelly ironic way they grant Thésée's wish in Racine's *Phèdre*. Here, the introduction of the gods, and the implied parallel with human heroes, remind us of the snake's self-importance. This context is sustained right up to the snake's death, as the tail leads the head to its end: 'Droit aux ondes du Styx elle mena sa soeur' *[She led her sister straight to the waters of the Styx].* The Styx being the river surrounding the Underworld, dead human beings must cross it, but dead snakes are presumably denied this privilege, so the snake is being seen in human terms. The epimythium briefly applies this tale to misguided countries which allow themselves to be led astray

– a human application which seems perfectly acceptable after the consistent human parallels throughout the poem.

In order to make this fable work, La Fontaine has created a web of intertwined conceits. First, we noted the numbers of puns and plays on words. Many of the words used are acceptable in themselves; it is only when they are viewed in relation to other terms that the double meanings are fully revealed. This approach echoes the backwards and forwards comparison that is constantly being made here between the back and front ends of the snake. So the narrative technique accurately reflects the content. Concurrently, the image of the two quarrelsome sisters has run through the whole poem, often reflected in these puns, and implicit both in the tail's attitude and in the response of the gods to her request. The whole standpoint of the tail has been human. La Fontaine has built up a picture of a contentious, hubristic, arrogant woman: we are made to feel that she has got her comeuppance at the end. In addition, as Rubin points out, there is a satirical dimension to this fable: La Fontaine is attacking the contemporary emphasis on rank, since the poem shows that 'when the bloodline receives first priority, the state can … go straight to hell' (Rubin 1 p.69). The whole effect is a *tour de force*, a contorted, twisted tale utterly appropriate to its convoluted theme.

In all the fables examined here La Fontaine refers to precise human types, giving a clear identity to the human parallel underlying the animal image. We have seen how the goats, despite their frequent transformations, are compared almost exclusively to noble personages, while the wolf's human equivalent remains a working man. In our two more far-fetched fables, the human image is still more invariable, helping to anchor the poems despite their undoubted oddity: the three bankrupts are consistently businessmen, the two halves of the snake remain grand ladies throughout.

All these poems use human imagery both to reinforce and to undercut the animal story. But we have seen that the human parallels actually play opposite parts according to whether the fable is realistic or far-fetched: in 'Les deux Chèvres' and 'Le Cheval et le Loup', they add an imaginative element to an ordinary situation; in 'Le Buisson, le Canard et la Chauve-souris' and 'La Tête et la Queue du Serpent', they play with the pretence that they are lending normality to an outlandish situation. In both types of fable, they bring out the moral and make it seem relevant in a human context. But their most striking function is undoubtedly to increase the density of the fables in which they occur, making them satisfyingly complex.

But sheer difficulty for its own sake is not the point of these human images. The human application of the moral represents their serious side – after all, La Fontaine is writing to 'instruire' *[instruct]*, as he tells us in his Preface. The fact that the human parallels are difficult to tease out is appropriate not only to their subject matter but also to their message. This far-fetched, elusive human imagery shows us that if we are to appreciate the human side of these fables, and so understand the their full meaning, the poems must be studied in depth. In the next chapter, we will dig even deeper.

CHAPTER 4

Hidden images

La Fontaine may have been familiar with a type of painting in which realistic still-lifes or landscapes, on closer scrutiny, reveal the presence of camouflaged human beings cunningly worked into the scene:[67] some of his most curious writing could be described as the verbal equivalent of this painterly technique. The poetry initially seems pellucid; but on closer scrutiny, hidden beings emerge from the seemingly neutral description, like a landscape picture in which gnarled trees reveal themselves to be composed of intertwined bodies, while ruined houses turn out to be giant human heads. The effect can be very subtle – indeed, it seems hitherto to have passed almost unseen.

It had certainly escaped my notice until one such image revealed itself to me unexpectedly as I was reading the poem 'Un Animal dans la lune' *[An Animal in the Moon]* (VII 17), looking for something completely different. The human figure hidden in the poem is revealed by several words which at first appear straightforward, but also carry a second meaning. These are underlined here:

> J'aperçois le Soleil; quelle en est la **figure**?
> Ici-bas ce grand **corps** n'a que trois **pieds** de tour:
> Mais si je le voyais là-haut dans son **séjour**,
> Que serait-ce à mes yeux que **l'oeil** de la nature? (l.15–18)

[I see the Sun; what is its appearance? / Here below this great body is only three feet round: / but if I saw it up there in its dwelling, / what would it be in my eyes but nature's eye?]

The sun is here viewed from two perspectives at once. Using the double meanings of the nouns, the poet portrays it (or 'him') simultaneously as a heavenly body and a man's body. *Figure* meant 'face' as well as 'appearance' in the seventeenth century as now, *corps* means a physical as well as a celestial body, *pieds* suggests not only a unit of measurement but also a man's feet, *séjour* is the sun's position, but also the man's dwelling. A sun-man lurks behind this seemingly straightforward account of the nature of perception. Only in the last line does the reference to the eye clearly evoke an image, though a different one: nature, not the sun, has been anthropomorphized, with the sun as its eye – and the poet and the sun are eyeing one another. Is the sun-man there by accident or design? Consider the context of the concealed image. Obviously it is eminently appropriate to its context. The poet is telling us throughout the poem that our senses mislead us (for example, the sun looks to us as though it were only three feet in circumference). Later in the poem he will point out that our eyes are betrayed by optical illusions, so that we think we see 'Une tête de femme …au corps de la lune' *[a woman's head … in the moon's body]* (l.35). How apt of him to have hidden a man's body in the sun, Apollo to the Diana he will speak of later. But the sun-man has a dual role to play, for the poem is also about Louis XIV. Later in the poem La Fontaine goes on to cast doubt on the value of Louis's much-vaunted military victories. Is he perhaps insinuating a further hidden parallel, and implying that the sun-king's glorious conquests are as indefensible rationally as the illusory sun-man? Such an interpretation would not be unusual for La Fontaine, who repeatedly subjected the monarch to sly attacks elsewhere in his *Fables*, although such assaults are invariably camouflaged[68]. I concluded that the sun-man image was probably a deliberate, and enriching, addition to the poem.[69]

The next step was to discover whether there were other examples of the same sort of treatment elsewhere in the poems – if there were, it would be even more likely to be a deliberate technique. In fact, I swiftly came to realize that anthropomorphic effects of this kind abound in the *Fables*. Even when a poem tells only of animals and plants, a human presence often lurks hidden, man surreptitiously intruding into the world of nature. This seems only too appropriate in view of La Fontaine's preoccupation with man's relationship with nature. His *Fables* are filled with urgent expressions of a desire to escape from man and find solitude in nature, a desire thwarted by his increasing conviction that such an escape is virtually impossible. Nature is not left in peace: somehow man manages to be there, encroaching on the scene, disturbing the animal or inanimate protagonists:

Mais quoi! l'homme découvre enfin toutes retraites.
   Soyez au milieu des déserts,
   Au fond des eaux, en haut des airs,
Vous n'éviterez point ses embûches secrètes. (XII 15 1.58–60)

[But, after all, man eventually finds all hidden spots. / Whether you be in the middle of the wilderness, / In the depths of the waters, or high in the air, / You will never escape his hidden ambushes.]

Indeed, even when all living creatures are excluded, and inanimates dominate the action, La Fontaine's formulation subtly implies the presence of man. This creates rather a different effect from the man in the sun, where the human figure became visible within the astral body. Here, it is more a question of approach – the poet thinks of inanimate objects in human terms, and slips human attributes into their depiction.

Of course, any fable featuring inanimate objects as characters must incorporate such human parallels, for the very fact that inanimates talk or reason must make them seem human. But here we are witnessing a very different process from this routine humanization of inanimates. Concurrently with the technique we have come to expect, we find a mysterious concealment of humans in nature, their presence glimpsed through images.

A good example of what I mean is I 22 'Le Chêne et le Roseau' *[The Oak and the Reed]*.[70] When the oak reproaches the reed with his weakness, he uses the following formulation:

Le moindre vent qui d'aventure
Fait **rider la face** de l'eau,
Vous oblige à **baisser la tête**:
Cependant que mon **front**, au Caucase pareil, …
Brave l'effort de la tempête. (l.4–9)

[The slightest wind that perchance / wrinkles the face of the water, / makes you bow your head: / But my brow, like the Caucasus … / withstands the onslaught of the tempest]

The water has a face that wrinkles, the reed bows its head, while the oak has a human brow. Later the oak will be seen to have other human attributes too, a back in l.23, and a head and feet when he is described as

Celui de qui **la tête** au ciel était voisine,
Et dont **les pieds** touchaient à l'Empire des morts. (l.31–2)

*[He whose <u>head</u> was neighbour to the sky, / and whose <u>feet</u> reached
down to the Empire of the Dead]*

Though the crown of a tree is commonly described as 'la tête', the
roots are not normally called 'les pieds' in the plural: the vocabulary has been distorted to make the tree seem human. Later the
wind which fells the oak is also anthropomorphized, transformed
into an uncontrollable and aggressive delinquent child, brought
into the world by a human birth-process:

> Du bout de l'horizon **accourt avec furie**
> Le plus terrible des **enfants**
> Que le Nord eût **porté** jusque-là **dans ses flancs**. (l.25–7)

*[From far on the horizon there <u>rushed up furiously</u> / The most terrible
of the <u>children</u> / that the North had till then <u>carried in its flanks</u>.]*
Each of the protagonists, though in fact inanimate, is described in
human terms.

An interesting addition to the human theme in this poem is the
recurrent implied mood of oppression and physical violence, again
couched in human terms: man's cruelty to man. The reed, a lowly
individual, is made to carry heavy burdens: 'un pesant fardeau'; and
he is forced to bow ('baisser la tête'). The oak offers his protection
('Je vous défendrais'), but he himself is not immune from punishment. He can get horribly beaten, though he remains defiant, as is
described again in human terms, showing the oak with a back,
being cudgelled:

> Vous avez jusqu'ici
> Contre leurs **coups épouvantables**
> Résisté sans **courber le dos**. (l.21–3)

*[Up till now / Against their <u>terrible blows</u> / You have resisted without
<u>bending your back</u>.]*
In this fable, then, man is not only present but, by implication,
unmasked as a cruel oppressor of his inferiors. Small wonder that

this fable has been seen as a parable on the fall of La Fontaine's adored patron Foucquet at the hands of an implacable king.[71] In this poem La Fontaine's insistence on the omnipresence of man is matched with an equally pervasive misanthropy.

Hidden imagery, then, gives scope for indirect attacks on man. We observed this earlier with the covert attack on Louis XIV, and in this case with the impression of a cruel oppressor victimizing the oak and the reed. Here, though, the attack is relatively discreet. Elsewhere it is much more overt. So the candle-hero of 'Le Cierge' (IX 12) is compared to the philosopher Empedocles, and becomes 'L'Empédocle de cire' *[the Empedocles of wax]*. Unlike the previous fable, this poem contains very little implied visual comparison between the inanimate hero and his human counterpart (though we have all seen pictorial representations of candles with human faces, for instance in Walt Disney's *Beauty and the Beast*). Instead, the comparison is an intellectual one. The reasoning process of the candle, who, having observed that bricks are hardened by baking, decides to throw himself into the fire to harden himself likewise, is compared to the thoughts of the ancient philosopher Empedocles, who, unable to fathom the mysteries of Etna, cast himself in, seemingly through pique.[72] The difference, as La Fontaine himself tells us in a note, was that Empedocles's suicide was a deliberate act of vainglory. By comparing him to a candle the poet removes any dignity from the philosopher's death, leaving him looking absurd. Indeed, he remarks that the candle, who at least was trying to better himself and did not mean to kill himself, 'n'était pas plus fou que l'autre' *[was no madder than the other]* (l.20). The fable is an undisguised attack on Empedocles, and through him on other arrogant intellectuals.[73]

An additional element in many human-inanimate comparisons, illustrated by the story of the philosopher-candle, is the frequent use of humour: men are criticized through mockery. In this respect, La Fontaine differs from the artists I mentioned earlier, his painterly counterparts, whose work seems to me to be characterized not so much by wit as by a surreal strangeness. La Fontaine's witty effects arise when the elements of a comparison mingle appropriateness with incongruity.

This incongruity is often achieved by creating an effect of distortion within the comparison. In particular, when La Fontaine plays on double meanings of words applicable both in a human and an inanimate context, he may use language that is barely appropriate for one aspect. In 'Le Pot de terre et le Pot de fer' *[The Earthenware Pot and the Iron Pot]* (V 2) the two pots are on the whole more human than inanimate.[74] They have skins ('la peau'), like living creatures – but not really like cooking vessels. The earthenware pot does not wish to travel

> Disant qu'il ferait que sage
> De garder le coin du feu (l.4–5)

[Saying that he would be wise / To stay by the fireside]

where 'le coin du feu' (literally the corner of the fireplace) conjures up the picture of a little old man seated by the hearth, rather than that of a cooking-pot, which one would expect rather to be 'on the fire'. When the pots get moving, La Fontaine puns on their method of locomotion in exactly the same way, using words which again have an element of the appropriate for pots, but are really more applicable to men:

> **Mes gens** s'en vont à trois **pieds**,
> Clopin-clopant (l.22–3)

[My people set off on three feet, / Dot and carry one]

Both pots and men have feet, but 'gens' and 'clopin-clopant' suggest a human context. Even the fact that they have 'three feet' makes them seem like old men, as in the riddle of the Sphinx.

The comic effects of making the inanimate human can be sustained at some length, and with extensive use of ambiguous language. This is well demonstrated by what is perhaps the oddest example of the human-inanimate conflation, 'Les Membres et l'Estomac' *[The Members and the Belly]* (III 2). La Fontaine begins by personifying the stomach, to whom he gives the Rabelaisian name of Messer Gaster.[75] The body, like the state, is divided into the stomach, who is the king, and the limbs, who serve him. To make the human parallel convincing, La Fontaine plays on the double meaning of 'membres': the 'limbs' are also 'members' of a group, clearly of men. La Fontaine's technique here is to take the parallel to its furthest limit almost from the start. Only the first line of the story proper concentrates on the ambivalent terminology which has so far been an essential attribute of all my examples. This line is indeed applicable equally to human beings and inanimate objects: 'De travailler pour [l'estomac] les membres se lassant' *[The members, being tired of working for (the belly)]*. By the next line, however, there is no ambiguity: the limbs are behaving (and talking) like men, not body-parts:

> Chacun **résolut** de vivre **en gentilhomme**,
> Sans rien faire, **alléguant l'exemple** de Gaster. (l.7–8)

[Each one <u>resolved</u> to live <u>like a gentleman</u>, / Doing nothing, <u>citing the example</u> of Gaster.]

Already the limbs have become not only sentient, articulate beings, but also pretentious ones with a sense of grievance. They want to become gentry; they do not see why Gaster should enjoy better conditions than they do. In their indignation, they break into direct speech:

> Il faudrait, disaient-ils, sans nous, qu'il vécût d'air.
> Nous suons, nous peinons, comme bêtes de somme. (l.9–10)

[Without us, they said, he would have to live on air. / We sweat and labour like beasts of burden.]

There may be more to the first line of this couplet than meets the eye. Ostensibly, of course, it simply suggests that Gaster would starve without the limbs. But the notion of a mysterious creature living on air is a familiar conceit in baroque literature. It is linked to the chameleon, which, it was believed, nourished itself in this way.[76] In a later fable, La Fontaine turns the idea on its head, and it is not the king but the courtiers (whom, by implication, the 'members' represent) that are chameleons. He rounds on the court, and bitterly attacks them for being a 'peuple caméléon' *[chameleon folk]* ('Les Obsèques de la Lionne' *[The Lioness's Funeral]*, VIII 14 l.21). The 'peuple caméléon', or 'peuple singe du maître' *[people who ape their master]*, are in this later fable given these insulting sobriquets because they imitate their betters. This is equally true of our fable, where the limbs also wish to live like the king Gaster. Without taking these parallels too far, one can detect an echo here of La Fontaine's treatment of courtiers elsewhere in the *Fables*, reinforcing the suggestion that an underlying human parallel is present in his mind.

In the second line of the couplet under discussion, the attitude of the 'members' is revealing indeed. They indignantly compare themselves to beasts of burden. The implication is that they are superior to such beasts. What would be likely to be the subject of such a comparison, made in such a spirit? It would seem weird for the relative superiority of a limb and a beast to be weighed up like this; but for a man to assess his workload in this way is entirely appropriate, and indeed a cliché. So here again, the limbs are being thought of as pre-eminently human.

Next, the 'members' seem to move indoors from toiling in the fields to working in the kitchen, preparing Gaster's meals: 'Notre soin n'aboutit qu'à fournir ses repas' *[Our efforts only serve to provide his meals]* (l.12). However, the expression is sufficiently vague for us to apply it to limbs working to feed a stomach. As a result, the next line comes as a shock: 'Chommons: c'est un métier qu'il veut nous faire apprendre.' *[Let's strike – that is a trade which he wishes us to learn.]* Suddenly, the 'members' are completely, unambiguously, transformed into men, workers (they talk of a 'métier'), intending to down tools.

The process we have witnessed is a dual one of build-up and contrast. The poet has anthropomorphized the members, at first partially, then completely. But interspersed with these human references have been reminders that the limbs are still parts of the body. So the reader is repeatedly confronted with the incongruity between the two meanings of 'membres', to considerable comic effect.

Once this dual effect has been exploited to the full, La Fontaine returns to the story, and the comic ambiguity becomes less striking.[77] The 'membres' become limbs once more:

> Ainsi dit, ainsi fait. Les Mains cessent de prendre,
> Les Bras d'agir, les Jambes de marcher. (l.14–5)

[No sooner said than done. The Hands ceased to grasp, / the Arms to move, the Legs to walk.]

and the poem moves on, with a nod to the recurrent ambiguity, culminating in a serious moral relating to 'la grandeur royale'.

Although the hidden insertions examined so far are subtle, they
are still clearly perceptible once one focuses on them. But there is
another group of hidden additions in which the human element is
so delicately introduced that it is much harder to bring to light.
From the pictorial point of view, I am reminded of those children's
puzzles in which one is presented with what seems like a straightforward picture, and told to find hidden objects lurking within it.
In La Fontaine's *Fables* these elements, though barely perceptible,
nevertheless have a function to fulfil. They may not impinge
directly on the reader's consciousness; but they still impart their
own atmosphere to the poems. And indeed this may be true of
some of the most admired passages in the *Fables:* they are memorable because of their evocative power; might it be precisely because
they contain half-formulated hidden insertions that they are so
suggestive?

I want to examine in detail several such key passages, in which
the hidden threads, though imperceptible in themselves, must
affect our reading.

In one famous passage from 'Le Songe d'un Habitant du Mogol'
[The Dream of the Inhabitant of Mogul Lands] the poet declares his
preference for solitude:

> ... J'inspirerais ici **l'amour** de la retraite;
> **Elle offre à ses amants** des biens sans **embarras**,
> Biens purs, présents du Ciel, qui **naissent** sous les pas.
> Solitude où je trouve **une douceur secrète,**
> Lieux **que j'aimai toujours,** ne pourrai-je jamais
> Loin du monde et du bruit, **goûter** l'ombre et le frais?
>   (XI 4 1.19–24)

*[Here I would inspire <u>the love</u> of retreat; / <u>It (she) offers its (her) lovers</u>
gifts without <u>obligations</u>, / Pure treasures, gifts from Heaven, <u>born</u>
under one's feet. / Solitude which fills me with <u>secret pleasure</u>, / Places <u>I
have always loved</u>, can I never, / Far from crowds and noise, <u>enjoy</u> your
cool shade?]*

Superficially these lines seem entirely spiritual, extolling solitude as
a gift from heaven. But the language is ambiguous. The words
underlined evoke secret pleasures, away from prying eyes. Playing
on the feminine gender of 'la retraite' (or could it be 'l'amour',

which could also be feminine in the seventeenth century – witness La Fontaine's own line: 'Votre amour était pur̲e̲, encor que véhémen̲t̲e̲', XII 28 l.78) the poet tells us that at a secret meeting place 'she' offers her gifts without reservation,[78] and later there is a reference to birth. It is also worth drawing attention to similarities between this passage and the shepherd's description of love in the fable 'Tircis et Amarante' (VIII 13), in a dialogue between those two characters:

> Il n'est bien sous le ciel qui vous parût égal ...
>   – que sent-on?
> – Des peines près de qui le plaisir des Monarques
> Est ennuyeux et fade: on s'oublie, on se plaît
>   Toute seule en une forêt.

[No gift from heaven would strike you as its equal ... / What do you feel? / Suffering compared to which the pleasures of Monarchs / are dull and bland: you forget yourself, you find pleasure / Alone in a forest.]

We find in both passages the 'gifts from heaven' and the love of nature and solitude, together with a rejection of courtly pleasures and ambitions. In other words, in the well-known passage from 'Le Songe d'un Habitant du Mogol', the poet is viewing nature in exactly the same way as a lover does.

So might the power of our passage, its ability to make solitude seem irresistible, lie at least partly in an implied hidden evocation of secret sexual love? The technique is splendidly appropriate for the context: the very passage that describes the attractions of what is concealed from others, itself conceals allusions to a secret pleasure. Yet at the same time the hidden meaning contradicts the ostensible one, since what seems to be spiritual is depicted in the language of physicality; and the panegyric on solitude seems to suggest a hidden partnership. The overall impact is complex and challenging.

The whole point of this technique is that it is extremely delicately conceived. But there are more sustained examples which, I believe, prove that La Fontaine's mind really does work in this way. One such is a fable which, again, is known as one of the most evocative and moving that La Fontaine wrote. And again a subtle concealed dimension is one of the reasons for this fable's power.

'Les Deux Pigeons' *[The Two Pigeons]* tells the story of a pigeon who leaves his devoted companion to travel, but rapidly comes to grief and staggers home more dead than alive. The animal fable is followed by a double epilogue, first an exhortation to lovers to be a world to each other and not seek variety elsewhere; then a wistful evocation of the poet's own past loves. It ends on a question: 'Ai-je passé le temps d'aimer?' *[Have I left behind the time for love?]*

The sexual content of this fable has given pause to many critics. To put it simply, the problem is this: the two birds are both unequivocally male; each addresses the other as his 'brother' (l.6, l.16 and l.24). And yet, the story of the two pigeons seems to suggest sexual love to the poet: for without transition, he passes from their touching reunion (which concludes the story of the fable proper) to a more general exhortation, addressed not to friends of the same sex, but to 'Amants, heureux amants' *[Lovers, happy lovers]* (l.65). And the final section of the poem leaves us in no doubt: the poet-narrator, who we know is male, recalls his early loves, each one an 'aimable et jeune bergère' *[a delightful young shepherdess]* (l.75).

My question here is: how does the poet manage to get away with this seemingly abrupt transition from describing the friendship between two males to related comments on heterosexual love? The answer is suggested by Leo Spitzer: La Fontaine creates an ambiguous hidden subtext in which the idea of heterosexual love is present from the start even if it is not explicitly visible.[79] In my view, however, this subtext is present to a much greater degree than previous critics have acknowledged.

The language of love is already found in the first line: 'Deux pigeons s'aimaient d'amour tendre' *[Two pigeons loved each other with a tender love]*. And in those passages which describe a friendship between males, the language could just as well be that of male-female love. Consider the words of the stay-at-home pigeon, given in direct speech. His turns of phrase are like those of lovers in serious love poetry and in tragedy of the time. Like them, he refers to his beloved as 'cruel' (l.8), and finds that his love brings him a portentous unhappiness, as suggested by 'malheur' *[misfortune]* (l.13) and 'funeste' *[disastrous]* (l.14). Spitzer, Collinet and Vincent point out that there are echoes of Dido's lament for the departing Aeneas in these lines.[80] The speech is a blow to the heart of the would-be traveller: 'Ce discours ébranla le coeur' (l.18) – again the context is one of love rather than friendship. As he speaks, he weeps. His beloved friend pleads: 'ne pleurez point' *[do not weep]* (l.21). However, he too is unable to hold back the tears as they part: 'en pleurant ils se dirent adieu' *[weeping, they bade each other farewell]* (l.30). At this point the two friends separate, and their relationship is virtually forgotten (to be mentioned once more, again ambiguously, when the poet tells us briefly that they are happily reunited: 'Voilà nos gens rejoints; et je laisse à juger / De combien de plaisirs ils payèrent leurs peines' *[Now our people were reunited; I leave you to judge / By how many pleasures they paid for their pains]*). But this is where the hidden subtext comes into its own. For despite the absence of love in the narrative, the language remains that of love poetry. Each of the wandering pigeon's encounters actually adds to the emotional undercurrent. A tree offers itself to him: 'Un seul arbre s'offrit' *[A single tree offered itself]* (l.33); but … 'l'orage / Maltraita le Pigeon' *[the storm / Ill-treated the Pigeon]* – the inanimate objects have come to life, offering themselves or spurning him like lovers. Next, he sees a field scattered with corn, but does not notice a concealed net:

> ce blé couvrait d'un las
> Les menteurs et traîtres appas. (l.39–40)

[The corn covered / The lying and treacherous lure of a net.]

Taken out of context, the 'lying and treacherous lure' would be more appropriate for a betrayed lover's comment on his faithless mistress than for a pigeon snare. The noun 'appas' in the seventeenth century had two meanings: 'bait' (normally used in the singular, 'appât'), or 'a woman's physical charms', normally plural (as here).[81] Hence La Fontaine's net seems like an ensnaring female. This is reinforced by the two adjectives, which imply strictly human qualities: 'lying' and 'treacherous'. This line, then, suggests a woman, and an amorous entanglement.

The pigeon breaks free, and limps away. He is described, in the only explicit image in the fable, as

> … notre malheureux qui, traînant la ficelle
> Et les morceaux du las qui l'avait attrapé,
> Semblait un forçat échappé. (l.45–7)

[... our unfortunate hero, who, dragging the cord / and the shreds of the net that had caught him, / seemed like an escaped prisoner.]

The fact that the net was earlier seen in female terms must affect our reading of this curious image. The pigeon should not be thought of as a thuggish convict; rather, the lines echo a whole series of parallels between rejected lovers and their cold mistresses in the literature of the time. A typical example is Racine's *Andromaque*, where the 'malheureux' *[unfortunate]* Oreste, unrequitedly in love with Hermione, describes himself as condemned to 'Traîner de mers en mers ma chaîne et mes ennuis' *[drag from sea to sea my chains and my distress]* (I 1).

The final blow to the poor pigeon is as violent as it is unexpected:

> ... un fripon d'enfant, cet âge est sans pitié,
> Prit sa fronde, et, du coup, tua plus d'à moitié
> La Volatile malheureuse (l.54–6)

[... a rascal of a child – they have no pity at that age – / Took his sling, and at a blow, more than half-killed / the unfortunate bird.]

If we continue to think along the same lines, the heartless child who wounds the hero when he least expects it, and almost kills him, also exists in the context of love poetry. Later in our poem, we are reminded of his importance, when the poet tells us 'sous le fils de Cythère / Je servis' *[I served under the son of Cythera]* (l.74–5): just as the naughty child attacks the pigeon in the apologue, so Cupid subjugates the lover in the epilogue.

What happens next is a strange emasculation of the pigeon-hero. La Fontaine uses 'la Volatile malheureuse' as a feminine synonym for the pigeon. This causes the pigeon's return home to be described as though he were female: 'Demi-morte et demi-boiteuse ... elle arriva' *[Half dead and half lame ... she arrived]* (l.59–61). One could again find a parallel with Racine's Oreste, whose passivity in love similarly appears to emasculate him when he is described as being 'à l'amour en esclave asservie' *[enslaved (f) by love]*: Oreste's friend Pylade, by using 'votre âme' *[your soul]* as a metonymy for 'vous', is enabled to talk of him in the feminine in this way. When the two birds are reunited, their gender becomes indeterminate: 'gens' *[people]* (l.63). Probably the effect of this shifting of gender is further to blur the transition between the initial masculine protagonists and the final heterosexual conclusion, already helped by the concealed subtext of heterosexual encounters. As a result, there is no feeling of surprise when the poet directly addresses the 'Amants, heureux amants' *[Lovers, happy lovers]*.

The story of the lover yearning for his unyielding mistress, which lurks beneath the surface of this fable, has a further effect on the whole. It adds a dimension of pathos to this tale with its seemingly happy ending. It makes the poet's exhortation to the happy lovers to be all the world to each other seem like an impossible dream – since the lingering impression of the apologue is of unrequited and unhappy love. Indeed, the overt meaning of the poem bears this out – the very first lines, in a different way, deny the possibility of what the poet yearns for in his epilogue:

> Deux Pigeons s'aimaient d'amour tendre.
> L'un d'eux s'ennuyant au logis
> Fut assez fou pour entreprendre
> Un voyage en lointain pays.

[Two Pigeons loved each other with a tender love. / One of them, bored at home / was mad enough to undertake / a journey to a distant land.]

Although he begins his poem by suggesting a requited love, the poet immediately denies this, telling us baldly that one of the partners is bored and wants to leave.

The mournful side to this fable comes across most clearly in the last lines of all, in which the poet talks directly of his own feelings and wonders sadly: 'Ai-je passé le temps d'aimer?' *[Have I left behind the time for love?]* He is tentative about how women would see him, now that he is older. He describes himself as 'inquiet' *[anxious]* and reveals that he does not dare to love ('Ah si mon coeur osait' *[Ah, if my heart only dared]*). The mood of the poem's conclusion has been prepared by the presence of the undercurrent of romantic melancholy that I have brought out here, but which remains invisible in the text until it is explicitly teased out and brought to light.

There are other examples in which the hidden images have the opposite effect of lightening the mood. One such is 'La Chatte métamorphosée en Femme' (II 18) *[The Cat metamorphosed into a Woman]*. What I want to examine here is the presence in the subtext of an additional character, invisible at a straightforward reading. It will be seen that the presence of this character is not merely interesting in itself, but has considerable implications for the moral of the whole fable. On the surface, there are two main characters – the besotted husband and his cat-wife (whom he has caused to be transformed into a woman so that he can marry her), who disturbs the wedding-night by spending it catching mice. The problem comes with the moral, given us in a lengthy epimythium, in which the poet seems to forget about the newly-weds in order to generalize about bad habits:

> Tant le naturel a de force.
> Il se moque de tout, certain âge accompli:
> Le vase est imbibé, l'étoffe a pris son pli.
>   En vain de son train ordinaire
>   On le veut désaccoutumer.
>   Quelque chose qu'on puisse faire,
>   On ne saurait le réformer.
>   Coups de fourche ni d'étrivières
>   Ne lui font changer de manières;
>   Et, fussiez-vous embâtonnés,
>   Jamais vous n'en serez les maîtres.
>   Qu'on lui ferme la porte au nez,
>   Il reviendra par les fenêtres. (l.30–42)

[So great is the force of nature. / He mocks at everything, once he has reached a certain age: / The jar is impregnated, the cloth has acquired its creases. / In vain may you try to make him / Lose his ordinary habits. / Whatever you do, / You will never reform him. / Prod him with a pitchfork or belt him with a stirrup-leather / You won't make him change his ways. / Even with a stick / You will never master him. / Shut the door in his face, / And he will come back in through the windows. (To make my point, I have translated 'il' as 'he', not 'it', throughout).]

La Fontaine's moral appears to be simple: nature will out. So why does he take so long to tell it? The fact is that in this passage La Fontaine does much more than merely state the moral. He also presents a scenario, a sequence of events and a protagonist (and, in so doing, casts new light on the moral itself, as we will see later). The scene is a room with a door and windows. The two images that exemplify the moral in l.32 are also, incidentally, domestic, furnishing the room with a jar and a piece of cloth. The setting is simple and rustic; pitchforks, stirrup-leathers and sticks are mentioned. In this room is a being, 'le naturel'. Unnamed people try in vain to cure this delinquent being by beating him or throwing him out. We learn quite a lot about 'le naturel': his sex (male), his persistence (he insists on climbing back in when shut out), his tendency to scoff ('he mocks at everything'), his indifference to physical punishment (he doesn't care when he is beaten), even the fact that he is not a child ('he has reached a certain age'). There is even a clue to his appearance in that his nose is mentioned, so he is not invisible, he has a human or animal shape. He is clearly a delinquent, since he needs 'reforming'. Could the clue to this mysterious account be a play on the meaning of 'le naturel' here? As well as meaning 'human nature', does it also suggest a creature of nature, untutored and ungovernable?[82]

The presence of this figure, 'le naturel', has a number of implications. First, it has links with the rest of the fable. The instinctive response to this poem is, I think, to concentrate on the cat-heroine: she is the one to whom the moral applies, because she cannot suppress her feline nature when she is transformed into a woman: instead of sleeping with her husband, she gets up to catch mice. This would seem to be a perfect illustration of La Fontaine's moral. However, there is one link between the husband and 'le naturel' which has nothing whatsoever to do with the cat. If we accept that 'le naturel' suggests instinctual, irrational behaviour, we find the poet telling us much the same thing about the husband. In the few lines that describe the husband's actions the idea is remorselessly reiterated: 'Il était plus fou que les fous' *[He was madder than madmen]* (l.4); 'maître sot' *[Master fool]* (l.10); 'Le voilà fou d'amour extrême, /De fou qu'il était d'amitié *[Now he is mad with excessive love / having been mad with fondness]* (l.11–12). He is called a 'hypocondre' (l.16) which according to Richelet means 'bizarre, fou, capricieux' *[bizarre, mad, capricious]*[83]; and his behaviour is summed up as an 'error' (l.19). In short, he is just as ungovernable and irrational as 'le naturel'.[84] The male sex of 'le naturel', too, logically points us towards the husband.[85]

If the moral here, with its male protagonist, subtly relates to the husband more than the wife, the fable becomes more meaningful. The story of the cat-woman is pure fantasy, so like a fairy tale that its moral relevance must seem remote to the reader. If all that the poet is saying is that nature cannot be changed, there is nothing for us as readers to do but to accept the moral with a nod: we can do absolutely nothing about it. The husband, on the other hand, is doing something that we can all recognize: developing a crazy obsession, refusing to give it up, carrying it through to the bitter end. This is surely a much more realistic subject for a fable, in that the reader can see and learn from his folly. And it is the hidden presence of 'le naturel' that has made this interpretation possible.

Such sustained concealed elements as the pigeon/lover and the husband/natural, which affect the mood and even the moral of the fables in which they occur, are exceptional. But apart from these, the poet uses the technique repeatedly in passing, to sketch in a camouflaged presence which creates an evocative atmosphere. Interestingly, this effect frequently occurs when the poet is talking of hidden, secret things. A secluded spot is a 'Lieu respecté des vents, ignoré du Soleil' *[A place respected by he winds, unknown to the sun]* (XII 29 l.35) – the verbs anthropomorphize the wind and sun, implying that they know to treat the place circumspectly as though they were exercising human judgment. A pool is 'Un vivier que nature ... creusa de ses mains' *[A fishpond which nature ... dug with her own hands]* (X 3 l.30): nature momentarily has hands to dig with. A vine which conceals a stag from the hunt is a 'bien-faitrice' *[benefactress]* (V 15), a word which enables us briefly to glimpse a woman in the plant (and indeed, most of La Fontaine's woodland beings are female).

This latter image further evokes a mythological tradition, again much beloved of artists, in which plants are changed from and into beings, often divine. La Fontaine's lyrical descriptions of sylvan scenes frequently recall pictorial representations of Daphne half-way through her transformation into a laurel-tree. In the *Fables* 'L'innocente Forêt' *[The Innocent Forest]*, like the vine, is the wood-cutter's 'bienfaitrice'; she is decorated with 'ornements', perhaps clusters of fruits or berries (XII 16). Other supernatural beings appear fleetingly – 'une nuit libérale en pavots' *[a night liberal in poppies]* (XI 3 l.20) suggests a goddess scattering soporific poppies; nature becomes a bountiful female figure in the lines ' ... la nature/ Excessive à payer ses soins avec usure' *[nature / excessive in repaying care with interest]* (XII 20 l.11–2). The winds deliberately control the sea like the classical wind-gods: ' ... un jour les vents retenant leur haleine/ Laissaient paisiblement aborder les vaisseaux' *[One day the winds, holding their breath / allowed the ships to land peacefully]* (IV 2 l.16–7). These hints are perhaps picked up more readily by the reader as the mythological world they evoke is so familiar.

In La Fontaine's day, such figures were clichés, familiar to all readers of lyric poetry. But sometimes his visual allusions, brief and light (or even present only as a denial) are more unsettling.

For example, there are several curious references to ears, which conjure up the strangest of pictures. The dog in 'Le Chien à qui on a coupé les oreilles' *[The Dog whose Ears were cut]* ends up with 'd'oreille autant que sur ma main' *[as much ear as there is on my hand]* (X 8 l.20) – the idea of an ear growing in the palm of a hand is evoked even as it is denied. A similar effect is achieved with the poet's inclusion of Rabelais's 'ventre affamé n'a point d'oreilles' *[a starving belly has no ears]* (IX 18 l.20) – this time the fleeting picture, immediately denied, is of a stomach with ears. A hare, afraid that his ears will be taken for horns, remarks:

> Mes oreilles enfin seraient cornes aussi;
> Et quand je les aurais plus courtes qu'une Autruche,
> Je craindrais même encor. (V 4 l.14–6)

[My ears would also be horns; / And if they were smaller than an ostrich's / I would still be afraid.]

Two bizarre images succeed one another: a hare with horns instead of ears, and an earless hare with a head like an ostrich.

La Fontaine may attenuate the strangeness of such images by explaining them through their context. But yet again, the formulation which created the odd impression remains arresting in itself, even if it can be explained away. His statement 'Le Réveille-matin eut la gorge coupée' *[The alarm-clock had its throat cut]*, taken in isolation, conveys the impression that an alarm clock has come to life only to be murdered, even if from the context we know that the 'alarm clock' was in fact a crowing cock.[86] Context apart, the formulation still sticks in the mind (V 6 l.21). 'Il plut du sang' *[it rained blood]* paints another surreal picture, with Biblical overtones (a sinister variation on a theme later to be treated by Magritte).

Again, the context explains the wording: vultures are fighting on the wing and bleeding from their wounds. La Fontaine shows his awareness that his formulation is extravagant when he glosses it ironically 'je n'exagère point' *[I'm not exaggerating]* (VII 7 l.11). A more splendid variation of this picture comes when the poet fantasizes: 'Les diadèmes vont sur ma tête pleuvant' *[Diadems are raining down on my head]* (VII 9 l.41).

Extraordinary surreal effects can be achieved by juggling with size; and La Fontaine's world expands with bewildering ease. As most such enlargements are conveyed indirectly and through covert images, they can be accepted by the reader. The indirectness of the effects is crucial: in each case, the point of the parallel is not the difference in size. Let us examine some examples in detail see how their oblique nature alters their impact, enabling the poet to include extravagantly surreal material in passing.

My first example is an oyster as big as a woman.[87] This oyster-woman is camouflaged like the sun-man and the solitude-woman mentioned earlier. The ostensible point of the description is to make the oyster seem appetizing to a greedy rat. But the figure of an odalisque seems to materialize in the words given in bold here:

> Parmi tant d'Huîtres toutes closes,
> Une s'était ouverte, et **bâillant** au soleil,
> Par un doux Zéphyr **réjouie**,
> **Humait l'air, respirait, était épanouie,**
> **Blanche, grasse,** et d'un goût à la voir nompareil.
> (VIII 9 l.21–5)

[Among so many oysters, all closed, / One had opened up, _yawning in the sun_, / _Rejoicing_ in the gentle Zephyr, / _Drew in the air, breathed, lay wide open_ / _White, plump_, and peerlessly tasty to look at.]

The oyster is certainly substantial ('épanouie' *[wide open*, or *beaming]*, 'grasse' *[plump]*); this impression is strengthened by the fact that the human implications of the words stressed here, suggesting a woman rather than a mollusc, evoke a creature far larger than an oyster. In addition, the ambiguous words 'goût' *[taste]* and 'plump' evoke both woman and gastronomy. 'Réjouie' *[rejoicing]* is singularly inappropriate to oysters, which surely do not breathe either; but most of the other terms used are at least ambiguous, such as 'yawning', which could indicate either the languor of a woman relaxing or the open shell of the oyster. We are left with the impression of a being very unlike an ordinary oyster-sized mollusc, but yet retaining oyster-like attributes.[88]

The main point of an image in which a lion is likened to a once-fortified place is to emphasize his weakness once he has allowed his teeth and claws to be drawn:

> Sans dents ni griffes le voilà,
> Comme place démantelée. (IV 1 l.55–6)

[There he was, without teeth or claws, / Like a fortress that has been dismantled.]

The comparison does not purport to be visual at all, but it does have visual potential – the crenellated battlements of a mediaeval fortress are not unlike huge grey teeth or claws. A nuance of surrealism lurks.

A dog is as well-fortified as the lion is disarmed:

> ... Quand on n'a qu'un endroit à défendre,
> On le munit de peur d'esclandre:
> Témoin maître Mouflar armé d'un gorgerin ... (X 8 l.17–19)

[When you have only one point to defend, / You fortify it for fear of misadventure: / As witness Master Mouflar, armed with a spiked collar ...]

The same comparison between an animal and a stronghold is suggested here. Elsewhere, a chicken-run too becomes an embattled citadel, with the fox as the besieging army (XI 3).

Finally, a parallel between a woman's face and a house implies a disparity in size almost as enormous as the last example:

> Les ruines d'une maison
> Se peuvent réparer; que n'est cet avantage
> Pour les ruines du visage! (VII 4 l.69–70)

[The ruins of a house / Can be repaired; if only this advantage / Applied to the ruins of a face!]

Once again, the image is denied even as it is made. There is also an additional comic irony. Because a house is large, its ruin is correspondingly far more substantial than that of a face can ever be. So it seems singularly inappropriate to compare them. And yet, on another level, the parallel is apt. It suggests the importance of her looks to the woman, and indicates the scale of the disaster, as it appears to her, when she loses her beauty.

Although the manipulation of size is merely incidental to the main point of all these examples, the size factor adds a further uncanny quality to the comparison.

In one fable, size, far from being a hidden element, becomes massively prominent. This is 'La Montagne qui accouche' *[The Mountain in Labour]* (V 10), whose versification was discussed in Chapter 2. How does a writer bring out the size of a huge natural phenomenon, and what is the effect? It is interesting to compare the relevant lines of La Fontaine's fable with those of his predecessors. Phaedrus's version (IV 24) is characteristically laconic:

> Mons parturibat, gemitus immanes ciens,
> Eratque in terris maxima exspectatio.
> At ille murem peperit.

[A mountain was in labour, uttering tremendous groans, and there was the greatest expectation in the land. But that mountain gave birth to a mouse].

Atheneus's Greek version, equally uninformative, goes: 'The mountain was in travail, and Jupiter was afraid'. Rabelais writes: 'A son cry et lamentation accourut tout le voisinaige, en expectation de veoir quelcque admirable et monstreux enfantement' *[At her cry and lamentation the whole neighbourhood came running, expecting to see some amazing and monstrous delivery]*. And Boursault, in his play *Les Fables d'Esope*, explains:

> Mais ce colosse affreux, dont l'orgueilleuse tête
> Alloit jusques au ciel défier la tempête ...
> Trompant des spectateurs l'ardeur impatiente,
> Après une longue attente,
> Accoucha d'une Souris.[89]

[But this fearful colossus, whose proud head / went up to the sky to defy the tempest ... / Cheating the ardent impatience of the watchers, / After a long wait, / Gave birth to a mouse.]

All these versions stress the impressive nature of the occasion and the hugeness of the mountain; but none of them give the reader a clear sense of the mountain's actual dimensions. As a result, the revelation that the mouse is born seems more laughable than strange or unnerving. As far as I can see, La Fontaine's version is the only one to bring home to the reader the truly colossal proportions of the mountain, an effect achieved by spelling out the observers' expectations:

> Une Montagne en mal d'enfant
> Jetait une clameur si haute,
> Que chacun au bruit accourant
> Crut qu'elle accoucherait, sans faute,
> D'une cité plus grosse que Paris;
> Elle accoucha d'une Souris. (l.1–6)

[A Mountain in labour / Was making such a clamour / That everyone, running up because of the noise, / Thought that she would not fail to give birth/ To a city bigger than Paris. / She gave birth to a mouse.]

The speculations of the gathering crowd reveal that the mountain is big enough to carry a city the size of seventeenth-century Paris in its flanks. This is quite a precise measurement, and enables us to picture its dimensions. Furthermore, the crowd's speculations update the fable, relating it to a city La Fontaine's readers would have known well, whose size holds no mystery for them. We seem to be sharing an experience with a group of La Fontaine's fellow Frenchmen, whose lives are the opposite of surreal. As a result, the mouse that is actually born seems infinitely strange and infinitely minute by contrast, and the effect is not only comic but bizarre – we have simply been required to leap too abruptly both from the enormous to the tiny, and from the familiar to the weird.

Fables such as this remain the exception. It would be misleading to give the impression that the collection is full of extraordinary and fanciful verbal pictures of the kind discussed above. Many of La Fontaine's images, like those of most of his contemporaries, seem to be included purely for reasons of convention, and lack the power to evoke a picture. Even here, though, his inventiveness comes into play. Some of his most subtle effects can be detected in images that seem at first sight to be entirely conventional, but with a tiny inappropriate detail that alerts us to the fact that all is not as it seems. An example is an apparently inappropriate conventional image contained in a single word in VI 15 'L'Oiseleur, l'Autour et l'Alouette' *[The Bird-catcher, the Hawk and the Lark]*. The bird-catcher is trying to snare the lark using mirrors. The lark escapes, only to be caught by the hawk. The capture is described as follows:

> Aussitôt un Autour planant sur les sillons
> Descend des airs, fond, et se jette
> Sur celle qui chantait, quoique près du tombeau. (l.7–9)

[Straight away, a hawk hovering over the furrows, / Came down from the skies, swooped, and fell upon / Her who was singing, though close to her tomb.]

It is the use of the word 'tombeau' *[tomb]* to describe the bird-snare that creates the picture here. It seems like an obvious case of banal poetic language, more or less relevant because the mirror-trap is, after all, aimed at capturing small birds which will then be killed and eaten. It seems to be an example of an inappropriate word used to raise the poetic register of the line, an indication to the reader that he is supposed to be taking the impending death seriously. But in fact, the use of 'tombeau' is far from imprecise. The word alters the reader's view of the lark by making the little bird seem human. 'Tombeau' suggests a monument of some importance, a place for ceremonial burial. The human scale of this sepulchre is reinforced by the rest of the line. Because of the exclusively human character of 'tombeau' the lark ceases to seem like a bird, becoming instead a female figure, 'celle qui chantait' *[she who was singing]*. Momentarily, we glimpse a singing woman, standing beside the tomb which has already been built for her. 'Celle qui chantait' has come to seem completely unlike the mesmerized lark dazzled by a mirror: the image has altered our view of the bird-hunt and replaced it with a human tragedy in miniature. So 'tombeau', far from being an inaccurate word which passes muster because of its poetic connotations, is in fact the key-word in a fleeting but vivid image.

'Chacun songe en veillant, il n'est rien de plus doux' *[We all have waking dreams, there is nothing sweeter]*, wrote La Fontaine (VII 9 l.34). The material I have been looking at in this chapter is characterized by this dreamlike quality – surreal, evocative, sometimes witty and sometimes sad. With its help, the poet jolts us out of our expectations, and presents us with a new perspective on his world. It may well be here that La Fontaine is at his most original as a poet.

III
Animals

CHAPTER 5
Animal creations

'Petit récit qui cache une moralité sous le voile d'une fiction et dans lequel d'ordinaire les animaux sont les personnages' (Littré) *[Short account which conceals a moral beneath the veil of a fictitious tale, with characters that are as a rule animals]*. This simple dictionary definition of 'fable' highlights the all-importance of animals in the genre. The traditional fables, not only of Europe but also of other cultures like those of Asia or Africa,[91] have talking animals at their heart. In European culture, the highest authority shares this approach, according to La Fontaine: 'Aristote n'admet dans la fable que les animaux' *[Aristotle admits of nothing but animals in the fable]*.[92] But this familiar tradition brings with it a problematic element. How can a 'personnage' be an animal, when the word means 'character' but clearly implies 'person'? We accept the existence of animal characters, through long familiarity, because it is part of our culture. But what we really mean by 'animal' in this context is by no means self-evident. Basing my observations on La Fontaine's *Fables*, I detect a range of animal characters in the fable, from straightforward dumb beasts to various kinds of surrogate humans.

To start with, then, there is the occasional seemingly authentic animal who cannot speak, and takes no moral initiative. These 'real' animals occasionally appear as peripheral figures in poems where what matters is the human protagonists. In 'Le Meunier, son Fils et l'Ane' *[The Miller, his Son and the Donkey]* (III 1), as we have seen in Chapter 3, the active characters are the miller, his son and the passers-by. The donkey remains a dumb beast of burden, the mere butt of onlookers' remarks.

In accordance with fable tradition, however, most of La Fontaine's animals are largely substitutes for men. The poet stresses the fact that his numerous animal characters exist primarily to make points about human beings, not about their own species. He tells us that 'ces fables sont un tableau où chacun de nous se trouve dépeint' *[these fables are paintings in which each of us finds himself depicted]* (Préface, p.9), and in two other key statements in his prefatory writings comments: 'Je me sers d'Animaux pour instruire les Hommes' *[I use Animals to instruct Men]*[93], and 'les Animaux sont les précepteurs des Hommes dans mon Ouvrage' *[Animals are the teachers of men in my book]*.[94] Writing about animals is tantamount to making assertions about men, since 'nous sommes l'abrégé de ce qu'il y a de bon et de mauvais dans les créatures irraisonables' *[we are the summary of all that is good and bad in unreasoning creatures]* (Préface, p.8). Writers on La Fontaine mostly take this human bias to the *Fables* as axiomatic.[95]

Since animals in fables serve merely to make a point about man, their animal attributes are of secondary importance. These 'animals' may be required to speak, to reason, to fulfil other human, not animal, functions. The fabulist may dress them in clothes, give them books to read, countries to rule. In short, they are to mimic the behaviour of human counterparts, so as to provide a clearly perceived parallel to human behaviour, and a vehicle for the moral message. Such animal portraits, then, are *a priori* implausible, endowed as they are with exceptional powers. But the situation should still appear natural and unworrying to the reader.

One further aspect of this anthropomorphism that deserves brief separate mention is its function as a vehicle for satire in the La Fontaine fable. For La Fontaine differs from the traditional fabulists in one respect, which greatly influences his animal portraits. This is the fact that he lived not in ancient Greece or Rome, like his principal sources, but in the France of Louis XIV.[96] Where his fables have a satirical impact, it is preferable for the message to be put across through the intermediary of animal protagonists for reasons of simple caution. Fables attacking the monarchy, in particular, have a new impact in La Fontaine's time: he does not confine their settings to the republics of Greece or Rome under which Aesop or Phaedrus composed their versions. The reader of La Fontaine may well suspect that when the poet reformulates traditional fables about lions, his versions incorporate a strong, thinly disguised allusion to his own monarch. The disingenuous fabulist makes his point indirectly, referring to 'le roi des animaux' *[the king of the beasts]* (II 12, 19, VI 14), 'sa Majesté lionne' *[his leonine Majesty]* (VII 7), 'ce monseigneur du lion-là' *[His lordship the lion there]* (VII 7), paying lip-service to the convention that this is a lion-king and not a human king.

Paradoxically, however, this satirical dimension does not cause

La Fontaine's versions of the poems to be so firmly rooted in their own time as to seem irrelevant to the modern reader. The contemporary element merely adds yet another layer to the already complex animal portraits, and failure to notice a satirical dig does not invalidate the poem in which it occurs.[97] The very fact that the *Fables* continue to be popular today suggests that most of the poems have an impact that is more general than satirical, aimed not at the poet's contemporaries, no matter how important, but at mankind as a whole.

La Fontaine's animals have an additional source of appeal in their distinctive personalities. Many of the anthropomorphic creations are endowed with idiosyncrasies which transform them into individuals in their own right. These features range from true-to-life details observed with the closeness and accuracy of a naturalist to wildly extravagant eccentricities. It is in this category of 'mixed' animal characters that we must classify most of La Fontaine's animal protagonists. René Bray notes the dichotomy in such portrayals when he comments: 'La Fontaine est un naturaliste plein de fantaisie, sans souci de la vérité, acceptant sans remords les plus fortes extravagances. Mais ... c'est un *peintre animalier* de grande valeur.' *[La Fontaine is a naturalist full of fantasy, with no regard for truth, shamelessly accepting the wildest extravagance. But he is an animal painter of great merit.]* (p.69). La Fontaine almost invariably adds a touch of individuality to his animals, often producing a 'mixed' impression as a result. Even the donkey in 'The Miller, his Son and the Donkey', whom I mentioned earlier as an example of a colourless and passive dumb beast, for one brief moment shows a spark of rebellion, and the poet fleetingly allows us a glimpse of his thought processes, turning him into much more of a character: 'L'Ane, qui goûtait fort l'autre façon d'aller, / Se plaint en son patois' *[The Donkey, who greatly enjoyed the other means of transport, / Complained in his own dialect]* (l.40–41). The individuality and the 'mixed' character of almost all the animals in the *Fables*, even the most incidental, will become apparent during the ensuing discussion.

The poet's predilection for bringing out the liveliness and ambiguity in his animal portraits is at odds with their traditional function in the fable. For animals in the ancient fables were surely there to make the message not more complex but simpler, not more individual but more universal. Hence, traditionally, a fable making a point about stupidity benefited from having a donkey as hero, while a tale of devious cunning was best conveyed by a fox protagonist, since every reader knows the convention that these particular characteristics are embodied in these animals when they are portrayed in fiction.

Superficially, La Fontaine's own animal characters are just what we might expect from other animal literature: his fox is cunning, his dove loving, his donkey stupid.[98] He actually banks on this response from the reader, inviting us to associate an animal with the traditional stereotype, when he describes a fox as follows:

> Un vieux Renard, mais des plus fins,
> Grand croqueur de Poulets, grand preneur de Lapins,
> Sentant son Renard d'une lieue ... (V 5 l.1–3)

[An old Fox, but one of the most cunning, / A great cruncher of chickens, a great catcher of rabbits, / You could tell a mile off that he was all fox ...]

The last line tells us that the fox, cunning and greedy, is supposed to be readily recognizable as a result.[99] And we must remember that to recognize this fox, the reader does not need to know how real foxes behave. Familiarity with literary tradition is what is required.

Indeed, conventional animal portraits are frequently inspired by a tradition that has little to do with genuine animal behaviour, and can even at times contradict the observations of the naturalist. La Fontaine tends to follow literature rather than science on such occasions. For example, his pigeon portraits are based on the traditional view of the dove or pigeon as loving, gentle and self-sacrificing, Ovid's 'oiseau de Vénus' *[bird of Venus]* (II 12). There is no attempt to portray real birds.

However, he can and does add to such simple conventional animal portraits, updating them or making them more individual. In the case of the pigeons, for instance, he describes them as 'une nation ... au col changeant, à l'esprit tendre et fidèle' *[a nation ... whose throats are changeable, whose minds are tender and faithful]* (VII 7). giving to the stereotype a contemporary, précieux formulation, in which the contrast between the birds' appearance ('changeable') and character ('faithful') is captured in a sentimental paradox. As Collinet has demonstrated, there is also a complicated network of literary allusion underlying the apparent simplicity of the pigeon portraits in the fable 'Les Deux Pigeons' *[The Two Pigeons]* (IX 2).[100]

La Fontaine seems unconcerned about portraying animal behaviour as consistently realistic, stressing the fictional character of such portraits, making his animals appear now authentic, now farfetched. He complicates the reader's response by sometimes inviting us to view the stereotypes with scepticism, sometimes pretending to accept them without demur. He is ambivalent about Pliny's assertion that dolphins save men from shipwrecks: 'Pline le dit, il le faut croire' *[Pliny says so, we have to believe him]* (IV 7 l.10).[101] Yet he includes without comment the old legend that dying stags shed tears (in IV 21 and V 15),[102] and accepts the classical myth that dying swans sing, making it the point of the Aesopian fable 'Le Cygne et le Cuisinier' *[The Swan and the Cook]* (III 12),[103] and using it in Le Songe de Vaux, where Mme Foucquet goes to the river-bank to hear the song of a dying swan (*OD*, p.98-). These legendary animal traits are strange and fascinating. Although the poet does not invariably endorse them, they always add to the interest of the animal portraits.

Being interesting is in fact the top priority. Animal portraits should provide diversion without obscuring the point: the reader, comfortable with the familiar animal characters and entertained by their vitality and their ambiguity, should feel well-disposed, more open to the moral of the fable than if he had been subjected to an unrelenting didactic discourse. La Fontaine alludes to the importance of this factor in his Preface; it is particularly relevant when the reader is a child, since children need their lessons couched in entertaining form:

Dites à un enfant que Crassus allant contre les Parthes s'engagea dans leur pays ... Dites au même enfant que le Renard et le Bouc descendirent au fond d'un puits ... Je demande lequel de ces deux exemples fera le plus d'impression sur cet enfant. (Préface, p.8) *[Tell a child that Crassus, going to fight the Parthians, entered their territory ... Tell the same child that the Fox and the Goat got down a well ... I ask you, which of the two examples will impress the child most?]*

The poet is telling us that animal characters help sugar the pill of the moral message. Indeed, he implements his own advice in a much more sophisticated manner than this simple pedagogical comment might indicate.

According to La Fontaine, a fable about animals but relevant to human beings will encourage its target audience to pay attention, and see the human implications. La Fontaine makes this point, though with a negative gloss, in a rare attack on the fable genre from 'Le Pouvoir des fables' *[The Power of Fables]* (VIII 4). He tells us that the Athenians, when in mortal danger, refused to listen to a straight account of their peril; they paid attention only when their predicament was fictionalized through a fable with animal and mythological protagonists, featuring an eel, a swallow and the goddess Ceres. He concludes scornfully with the general comment: 'Le monde est vieux, dit-on, je le crois; cependant/ Il le faut amuser encor comme un enfant' *[They say the world is old; I believe it, yet / It has to be kept amused like a child]* (l.69–70). Fables are a puerile genre, and a poor substitute for plain truths.[104] But despite his apparent contempt for the fable in this passage, he has also, by implication, made a point in its favour: a fable will encourage the reader to pay attention, will help to get a vital message across when all other means have proved ineffective. Significantly, too, he has chosen as his example a fable with animal protagonists.

La Fontaine coaxes the reader into attending to his moral. He does not do so by making our task particularly easy. With his preference for the complex, the subtle and the ambiguous, he rarely conveys a single clear message. Sometimes, indeed, the overt *moralité* can actually seem like the opposite of the underlying moral.[105] However, the ambiguity and complexity of his animal portraits demands the reader's close attention. It is every bit as valid an approach as adhering unquestioningly to the traditional simplicity.

So the animal portraits in La Fontaine's *Fables* are a paradoxical blend of conventional simplicity and innovative complexity. While this combination has its problems, it gives the poet great scope for creating interesting characters. One technique here is the use of recurrent animal characters. As a preface, let us remind ourselves that the traditional fabulist presents simplified animal portraits, schematically, sketchily drawn, endowed with a restricted number of traits (probably only one or two, as in the case of the cunning and greedy fox and the stupid and obstinate donkey). Such simplified creatures can illustrate a point with pleasing clarity just because they are less complex than man. Despite its undoubted advantages, this conventional approach is potentially monotonous. However, the fabulist has another card to play, namely self-reference. This is particularly the case with La Fontaine, who after all published his fables in groups, not just as isolated single poems. With the publication of each volume or *Recueil* he presented to the reader a number of poems about certain species, in which a collective personality inevitably emerged for each creature. Minor variations from one fable to another create an impression of individual variety enriching a familiar portrait. But a sleight of hand is in operation: the impression of individuality is an illusion. It is worth examining one or two animal portraits built up in this way to see how the effect is achieved.

Take the example of the monkey. The traditional picture of the monkey is as a mimic: 'singe et copiste, ce n'est qu'un'. *[Monkey and mimic – both are one.]*[106] This trait lends itself to clever manipulation: merely by keeping to it, La Fontaine appears to give a wide variety of personalities to different monkeys, depending on whom they happen to be mimicking. One monkey (who seems to be an original creation of La Fontaine's, as there is no known source for the fable) beats his wife and drinks in the tavern, 'singe en effet d'aucuns maris' *[A monkey (mimic) indeed of certain husbands]* (XII 19). Another, living among the gods, has become grave and godlike himself, 'Singe avec un front sévère' *[Monkey with a stern brow]* (XII 21 l.26) – again the character seems to be La Fontaine's own invention. Yet another is based on the real monkey Fagotin, who performed circus tricks ('des tours de Fagotin' *[Fagotin's tricks]* (VII 6). But monkeys are not the human beings they are copying, and their imitations are not expected to be perfect. The future monkey-king in 'Le Renard, le Singe et les Animaux' *[The Fox, the Monkey and the Animals]* (VI 6) does not know what a royal crown is for, and uses it for monkey-tricks:

> Le Singe
> … par plaisir la tiare essayant,
> … fit autour force grimaceries,
> Tours de souplesse, et mille singeries,
> Passa dedans ainsi qu'en un cerceau.(l.10–14)

[The monkey / Trying on the crown for fun, / Made faces galore, /

Performed acrobatics, a thousand monkey tricks, / Passed through it like a hoop.]

The shipwrecked monkey in 'Le Singe et le Dauphin' *[The monkey and the Dolphin]* (IV 7) thinks he is imitating an urban sophisticate, talking of his position in Athens as follows:

> ... on m'y connaît fort;
> S'il vous y survient quelque affaire,
> Employez-moi; car mes parents
> Y tiennent tous les premiers rangs:
> Un mien cousin est Juge-Maire. (l.22–6)

[I'm well known there. / If you have any problems, / Come to me – all the chief dignitaries / Are my relatives: / A cousin of mine is judge and mayor.]

But he gives himself away when he talks about Piraeus as though this town were a person. A miser's ape copies the way his master handles coins, but then thoughtlessly tosses them into the sea (XII 3).

Here one minor character-trait has become both the key to the whole personality of the animal, and an agent for its repeated transformation. The single quality of mimicry can destroy fortunes, save or lose lives. It is enough in itself to underpin all the simian portraits in the *Fables*.

We have, however, already seen that La Fontaine is generally reluctant to keep things simple. Accordingly, he adds to this brilliant single trait of mimicry a number of additional characteristics, which he varies from poem to poem. The intelligence of the monkey in particular is variable; the monkey who tries on the crown is witless; the shipwrecked monkey is glib but overconfident. In 'Le Lion, le Singe et les deux Anes' *[The Lion, the Monkey and the two Donkeys]*, however, he becomes a sage counsellor (XI 5), referred to as 'Le Singe maître ès arts' *[The Monkey, Master of Arts]* (l.4), or 'le Docteur' (l.22). Overall, these simian portraits well reflect the range of human originals of whom the monkeys are the 'peuple imitateur' *[imitative people]* (XII 19), and the monkey portraits are both entertaining and instructive.

Other animals that recur frequently in the Fables are treated with this combination of stereotyping (simplicity) and variety (complexity). However, depending on which animal is under discussion, La Fontaine will modify his approach. For example, the cat is a Tartuffian hypocrite; like that of the imitative monkey, the stereotype of the hypocrite lends itself to multiformity as he acts a number of parts.[107] But the range of feline characteristics is finally very different from the simian ones, because La Fontaine consistently introduces an underlying element of deliberate cruelty and malevolence into the cat portraits, which is absent from the monkey characters.[108] The fox, too, could be compared to the monkey in that his stereotype invites variety: he is so cunning that he can think of many solutions to any problem. As he puts it, 'J'ai cent ruses au sac' *[I have a hundred tricks up my sleeve]* (IX 14 l.15). But vulpine portraits, however varied, tend to include greed, so are less bewilderingly diverse than the much more random monkey equivalents.

A second technique is to build up the animals' fantastic side, again making them seem complex. If we compare the animals with their real-life prototypes, we see that they do not accurately reflect the characteristics of their biological originals. Real foxes or donkeys are far from La Fontaine's (and other animal writers') straightforward embodiments of cunning or stupidity. This artificiality will probably seem natural and obvious to the reader, steeped in tradition; but there are occasional moments where our zoological knowledge may hamper our ability to suspend disbelief. Animal characters' real-life attributes may well interfere with the credibility of the part they have to play in a fable, and the resulting combination of authentic-seeming and improbable characteristics can be quite difficult to assimilate. An example is 'Le Corbeau voulant imiter l'Aigle' *[The Crow who wanted to copy the Eagle]* (II 16), a traditional Aesopian fable. In this poem, the crow observes the eagle carrying off a sheep. He decides to try to do the same thing, but gets his claws tangled up in the sheep's fleece. The original story of the fable, reproduced by La Fontaine, seems far-fetched because most readers know that crows are skilled and practical scavengers: no real crow would pounce on a living sheep and attempt to fly off with it. The crow's behaviour is implausible, to say the least.

The traditional fabulist would have approached such problems by simplifying and skimping on detail, encouraging the reader to accept that the hero of the poem is only perfunctorily portrayed as a crow. In this particular case, this is what happens. Elsewhere, however, our poet, with his evident preference for many-sided animal portraits, adopts a different solution, and neatly side-steps the issue. In a brilliant twist, he manages to preserve the impression of multi-dimensional animals. He cannot introduce naturalistic details of their behaviour since these would jar with the selected traits which make them suitable as subjects for fables. Instead, he fleshes them out in an unexpected direction. Instead of building up their zoological verisimilitude, he moves in the direction of fantasy. These animals become like characters out of fairy-tales, imbued with what Renée Kohn calls 'on ne sait quel don de magie' (p.140).

Accordingly, La Fontaine's animals lead improbable lives, full of impossible incidents. In 'Le Renard et la Cigogne' *[The Fox and the Stork]*, when the two animals invite each other to dinner, the poet goes into the intricacies of their polite language using conventional human formulae. He also makes a point of commenting on the minutiae of food preparation and serving, by the two animal gourmets, the food being chopped up and cooked for the occasion.[109] In 'Le Chat, la Belette et le petit Lapin' *[The Cat, the Weasel and the little Rabbit]* (VII 15), the rabbit and the weasel dispute the ownership of a house, and take their quarrel before a judge. As J-D Biard says of La Fontaine: 'in his *Fables*, animals behave as they do only in the world of fables, where foxes feed on grapes, and cows, goats and ewes associate with lions to trap stags' (Biard 1, p.93).

It follows that these animals do things that their ordinary counterparts could not attempt to emulate: they are endowed with superior powers. This enables them to fulfil a further essential function in the fable: it creates a spurious impression of equality between animals and human beings, which in turn makes the animal moral seem more applicable to men. In the case of La Fontaine, this impression is particularly striking, for two reasons. First, the emphasis on individuality means that we are constantly aware that these are not just ciphers for men, but imaginative creations in their own right. Secondly, the animal portraits, far from being simple and easily dismissed, are at least equal in complexity to man. If there is one thing that distinguishes La Fontaine from his fellow fabulists in his attitude to animals, it is this quality of respect for them.

La Fontaine describes the function of animals in the *Fables* several times. Let us look back at the most mature of the three formulations that I mentioned at the beginning of this chapter, 'les Animaux sont les précepteurs des Hommes dans mon ouvrage' *[Animals are the teachers of men in my book]*, which comes from the introductory letter to M. le duc de Bourgogne that precedes the last book of 1693. La Fontaine's formulation is significant. He could have claimed that he was using animals to demonstrate a truth to man; but the use of the word 'précepteurs' implies that the animals, as man's teachers, are superior to man, not simply examples to man. This is reinforced by a comment in VI 1 'Le Pâtre et le Lion' *[The Shepherd and the Lion]*: 'Le plus simple animal nous ... tient lieu de Maître' *[The simplest animal serves as our Master]*. The 'simple' nature of animals is admirable: it should serve as an example to sophisticated man, teaching him a lesson in innocence and freedom from corruption. The ambiguous word 'Maître', too, indicates that the animal is regarded as a teacher, but also suggests that animals are superior, lords and masters of men.

The same assumptions underlie what seem to be less approbatory statements about animals. He may not stress their superiority, but he will not allow them to be inferior. Often, indeed, the two seem virtually indistinguishable. He talks of 'l'Animal qu'on appelle Homme' *[The Animal we call Man]* (VI 20 l.4).

This approach underlies the animal poems, and La Fontaine, I believe, assumes that it is axiomatic. This can be shown by a fable in which the poet makes a series of interrelated, implicit comments on animals and their status compared to that of man, assuming that the reader will understand without the message being spelt out. In this poem, 'Le Lion, le Singe et les deux Anes' *[The Lion, the monkey and the two Donkeys]* (XI 5), a wise monkey, discussing self-love with the lion-king, states that his remarks apply to every species, not just his own. Indeed, he seems to deny that animals are of different species, since both his own species and the lion's are equated as 'la nôtre' *[ours]*:

> –Toute espèce, dit le Docteur,
> (Et je commence par la nôtre)
> Toute profession s'estime dans son coeur,
> Traite les autres d'ignorantes ...
> L'amour propre au rebours fait qu'au degré suprême
> On porte ses pareils; car c'est un bon moyen
> De s'élever aussi soi-même. (l.22–30)

['Every species', said the Doctor, / '(Starting with ours), / Every profes-
sion is filled with self-esteem, / Calls others ignorant ... / Their self-
esteem means that they glorify / Their own kind, for this is a good way
/ Of glorifying oneself.']

The implied message (that no one species, not even man, is superior to the others) rests on the unspoken assumption that man is
just another species, not a master-race. The poem becomes more
complicated: the wise monkey illustrates the point with an anecdote comparing men and donkeys, but from the donkeys' point of
view. One donkey says to another:

> Seigneur, trouvez-vous pas bien injuste et bien sot
> L'homme cet animal si parfait? Il profane
>   Notre auguste nom, traitant d'Ane
> Quiconque est ignorant, d'esprit lourd, idiot: ...
> Les humains sont plaisants de prétendre exceller
> Par-dessus nous. (l.39–46)

[My Lord, do you not find man, that so-perfect animal, / Very unjust
and very stupid? He profanes / Our august name, giving the name of
Donkey / To ignorant, dull-witted idiots: ... / Human beings are
ridiculous to claim they are superior / To us.]

The donkeys are ridiculous because they assume that their species
is 'august'. By analogy, the reader is being invited to question his
own assumptions about the human race. La Fontaine, however, is
careful not to spell this out (the recipient of the lesson is, after all, a
king in this fable – though this king is not a human but an animal
monarch). Ostensibly, though it is used to teach man several lessons, the poem remains an animal fable with no overt human content. The wise monkey himself speaks the moral, telling us that the
fable is about 'L'amour propre donnant du ridicule aux gens' *[Self-*
esteem making people ridiculous] (l.69). He is using 'gens' *[people]* to
refer to monkeys and lions, but the word normally applies to
human beings rather than to animals. This fable, then, demonstrates the extent to which La Fontaine tacitly assumes that animals
can be used to teach men lessons.

     More often, however, La Fontaine prefers to be more explicit.
He makes a point of reminding the reader of the relevance of such

lessons to human beings. More characteristic than the tactful use of 'gens' in the above example is his inclusion of the same word in the double poem 'Le Héron/ la Fille' *[The Heron / The Maiden]* (VII 4): here La Fontaine tells the story of a choosy heron who will not eat till he finds the perfect fish, and ends up having to go hungry. The poet then points the moral, making it plain that 'gens' are exclusively human:

> Gardez-vous de rien dédaigner; ...
> Bien des gens y sont pris; ce n'est pas aux Hérons
> Que je parle; écoutez humains, ...
>   Vous verrez que chez vous j'ai puisé
>   ces leçons. (l.30–34)[110]

[Beware of disdaining anything; ... / Many people have been caught in this trap; I'm not / Addressing Herons; listen, people, ... / You will see that I have learnt these lessons from you.]

The implication of all this is not just that La Fontaine is using animals to teach men. There is another inference which is not, I think, generally singled out. It is that the poet suspects that men in their complacency think themselves superior to animals, but rejects this view. He singles out human presumptions and shows them to be no different from those of animals; the two donkeys in the monkey's anecdote are ridiculous, but men are equally so.

Equally, or even more ridiculous? Should we go further, and see La Fontaine in the *Fables* as champion of his animal creations, and critic of man? It seems to me that in almost every case in which the two are juxtaposed the answer has to be 'yes'. This emerges both in passing comments ('un Chien, maudit instrument/ Du plaisir barbare des hommes' *[a Dog, cursed instrument / Of man's barbaric pleasure]*, XII 15 l.63–4) or in cynical asides like his comment 'Le symbole des ingrats / Ce n'est point le Serpent, c'est l'homme' *[The symbol of ingratitude / Is not the Snake but man]*.

This quotation is taken from the bitter poem 'L'Homme et la Couleuvre' *[The Man and the Grass Snake]* (X 1). This fable is the most striking of a series of poems which discuss animals' merits, explicitly comparing them to the shortcomings of man. It also concentrates on the relationship between them, and in particular on the way man treats animals. This is a different type of

animal/human poem from fables like 'Le Lion, le Singe et les deux
Anes' *[The Lion, the Monkey and the two Donkeys]*: here, a man figures as a character, and his interaction with the animals forms the
subject of the poem. The reader can see animals and man face to
face, and draw his own conclusions. In 'L'Homme et la Couleuvre'
the animals are unanimous: man is unforgivable; he exploits and
abuses animals mercilessly. For his part the poet adds sarcastic comments, revealing total disenchantment with the human race: 'l'animal pervers / (C'est le Serpent que je veux dire, / Et non l'Homme,
on pourrait aisément s'y tromper) ... ' *[The perverse animal / (I
mean the Snake, / Not the Man, one could easily get this wrong) ...]*
(1.4–6).[111] Here again, without a doubt, the poet is on the animals'
side.

A more extreme form of this denigration of man and all things
human is glimpsed in those fables in which the civilized world is
repudiated in favour of an environment empty of man. Here the
poet presents the world from the standpoint of one who loves
nature and hates mankind. In 'Le Songe d'un habitant du Mogol'
[The Dream of a Dweller in Mogul lands], indeed, he suggests that
those who seek solitude are rewarded in the after-life, while socia-
ble behaviour, particularly at court, may incur eternal damnation.
This anti-social bias affects his interpretation of animal fables and
myths. In 'Philomèle et Progné' (III 15), La Fontaine, following
Babrius, creates a sequel to the tale of Philomela, transformed into
a nightingale after being raped by her brother-in-law Tereus.
Philomèle, a thousand years after being ravished, still refuses to
leave her solitary life as a woodland bird and move back among
people: the sight of mankind reminds her of the rape. She tells her
sister Procne as much:

> ... c'est le souvenir d'un si cruel outrage
> Qui fait ... que je ne vous suis pas:
> En voyant les hommes, hélas!
> Il m'en souvient bien davantage. (1.21–3)

*[It is the memory of that cruel outrage / That stops me following you: /
When I see men, alas! / I recall it much more vividly.]*

She condemns humanity altogether because of the evil deed of one
man.[112]

La Fontaine's *Fables* are imbued with such misanthropy. To enhance his animal portraits is an excellent technique for conveying this attitude, enabling him to use animals as 'précepteurs de l'homme' *[teachers of man]*, and in so doing to imply criticisms of man, their pupil. The animals are seen as comparable to men: they deserve equal rights because they *are* equal. Like men, they speak, they reason. The relationship between animals and men is falsely weighted to achieve this effect, so that the two appear to be of comparable status. For example, when a fisherman catches a fish, his victim is articulate and logical, able to discuss and debate the situation on equal terms. When it becomes clear that the fisherman has power of life and death over his captive, this seems shocking. It gives one a jolt when, after the fish's reasoned comments, the fisherman says:

> Poisson mon bel ami, qui faites le Prêcheur,
> Vous irez dans la poêle; et vous avez beau dire;
> Dès ce soir on vous fera frire.

[Fish, my fine friend, you are preaching away, / But you're for the pan. Whatever you say, / You'll be fried tonight.]

(V 3 'Le petit Poisson et le Pêcheur'
[The little Fish and the Fisherman], l.21–3)

Interestingly, La Fontaine comes back to this fable much later, and sums up the events I have just described as follows:

> Autrefois Carpillon fretin
> Eut beau prêcher, il eut beau dire;
> On le mit dans la poêle à frire. ...
> Le Pêcheur eut raison; Carpillon n'eut pas tort.
> Chacun dit ce qu'il peut pour défendre sa vie.

[Once upon a time, the little Carp / Preached and talked in vain; / He was put in the frying pan ... / The Fisherman was right, the little Carp was not wrong. / Each of us says what he can to save his life.]

(IX 10 'Le Loup et le Chien maigre' [The Wolf and the thin Dog], l.1–8)

He stresses the equality between the fisherman and the fish, and the balanced nature of their debate.

Yet despite being equal to man, La Fontaine's creatures remain animals. The leopard who touts for customers for his side-show is extraordinary just because, despite his slick fairground patter, he remains a wild cat with spotted fur (IX 3). Such animal creations are at once like and unlike real beasts; and where they are unlike, they are often superior. They are not beasts but superbeasts.

The ensuing discussion of animals analyses this superbeast side to the animals and how it is conveyed in the poems. For the animals in fables can both reason and talk; and these two talents deserve separate examination.[113]

CHAPTER 6

Reasoning animals

La Fontaine endows his animal characters with remarkable powers of reasoning. In his explicit analysis of the intelligence and spiritual status of animals in the 'Discours à Mme de la Sablière' (IX 20) he firmly rejects the view that they are just brainless mechanisms. He supports his case by giving examples of the incredible talents of real animals, using authenticated travellers' and hunters' tales to illustrate his point. Beavers, for example, build better structures than their human neighbours, the ignorant American Indians (l.93–113); partridges pretend to be wounded to distract predators and lure them away from their nests (l.82–91).

But far greater than those real gifts are the reasoning powers enjoyed by the fictitious animal characters in the *Fables*. La Fontaine at one stage explicitly comments on the fact that his reasoning animal characters have left verisimilitude far behind.[114] In a prose gloss to fable XI 9 'Les Souris et le Chat-huant' *[The Mice and the Screech-Owl]*, talking of the 'progrès de raisonnement' *[progress in reasoning]* of the screech-owl, he says that he is not aiming to create lifelike animals, but extra-clever ones, for 'ces exagérations sont permises à la poésie'.

The presence of brilliant animal logicians, veritable superbeasts, enhances the reader's delight in these fables. Their exaggerated capacities make them into entertaining curiosities. And their sharpened intellectual abilities give balance to the poems by providing the human characters with animal counterparts of equal stature. Just how considerable are the mental powers of these superbeasts?

Some of the animals in the first *Recueil* seem particularly gifted. They grasp the situation and assess the implications: the moral of a fable is frequently couched in the form of a sage utterance by an animal. 'Garde-toi, tant que tu vivras, / De juger des gens sur la mine' *[Take care, as long as you live, / Not to judge people by their appearances]*, a mother mouse tells her baby (VI 5 'Le Cochet, le Chat et le Souriceau' *[The Cockerel, the Cat and the Little Mouse]*); 'laissez-moi travailler; / Ni mon grenier, ni mon armoire / Ne se

remplit à babiller' *[let me work / Neither my storeroom nor my larder
/ Are filled by chattering]*, says the ant to the fly (IV 3 'La Mouche
et la Fourmi'*[The Fly and the Ant])*. In making his animals speak
the epimythium, La Fontaine is not being original, since the
anthropomorphic animals of Aesop, Phaedrus and the other pre-
cursors often do the same.[115] But despite their similar foresight and
analytic powers, La Fontaine's animal dialecticians are very different from the surrogate men of the earlier fabulists. With La
Fontaine, a much more complex process occurs in which animal
and human qualities interact in different ways. How La Fontaine
treats these moral observations by animals deserves separate examination for the light that it sheds on the subtle interplay between
animal and human qualities in his animal portraits.

In a La Fontaine fable, at the very moment when an animal
takes over the poem to point the moral, we are likely to be
reminded of its animal characteristics. For example, the outcome of
his version of the Aesopian fable 'Le Lièvre et la Tortue' *[The Hare
and the Tortoise]* (VI 10) is summed up by the tortoise in the last
lines of the poem:

> De quoi vous sert votre vitesse?
> Moi, l'emporter! Et que serait-ce
> Si vous portiez une maison? (l.33–5)

*[What use is your speed? / For me to have won! What would it be like /
If you were carrying a house?]*

Why has the poet waited till this moment to point out for the first
time that the tortoise has a shell? Chamfort (quoted by Collinet,
p.1153) sees this last line as an example of the psychology of
amour-propre: the tortoise cannot resist reminding the hare of her
handicap, since it makes her victory seem the greater. But the mention of the tortoise-shell fulfils a further function. We are made
aware that we are listening to an animal, not a surrogate human
being. The line thrusts the heroine's animality to the fore, prevent-
ing the reader from taking her words at face value, as though they
had been spoken by a human being.

Overall, there are two principal effects of this technique. The
first is a negative one: the creature's qualities are undermined by its
animality – the tenacity of the tortoise is made to seem undignified

because of her ungainly appearance. Bringing out the animal context introduces a note of incongruity and hence of humour, as a second example will show. In 'Le Vieillard et l'Ane' *[The Old Man and the Donkey]* (VI 8)[116] an enemy appears; the old man begs the donkey to run away with him, and the poem closes with the donkey's reply, in which La Fontaine updates Phaedrus's original Latin version, presenting us with an unmistakably French quadruped:

> – Et que m'importe donc, dit l'âne, à qui je sois?
> Sauvez-vous, et me laissez paître.
> Notre ennemi, c'est notre maître:
> Je vous le dis en bon françois." (l.13–6)

['What difference does it make to me whom I belong to?' / Said the donkey. 'Make your escape, and leave me to graze. Our enemy is our master; / I tell you so in good French.']

In this speech reminders of the donkey's animality are juxtaposed to inappropriate human elements to produce an effect of humorous incongruity. The words 'me laissez paître' *[leave me to graze]* remind one that this is a grazing beast, but also resemble 'me laissez en paix' *[leave me in peace]* [117]; they are like an animal parody of a human sentiment. The idea of this forthright donkey speaking 'good French' while grazing also seems incongruous. The overall effect is that the donkey's undoubted good sense is undervalued (perhaps deliberately so in view of the controversial penultimate line). In this poem and others like it the straightforward seriousness of the traditional epimythium becomes something much more ambiguous, even tongue-in-cheek. The way is paved for the consistent ambiguity and undermining that characterize the *moralités* of La Fontaine's fables.

The second result of having an animal speak the epimythium while yet remaining definitely an animal is very different, indeed opposite: the beast's words invite an implied unflattering comparison with man, who, despite being the higher species, lacks the wisdom of the speaker. In this case, far from being undermined by being placed in an animal's mouth, the words may actually gain in weight. Such is the case with 'Les deux Mulets' *[The two Mules]* (I 4). In this fable, an arrogant mule glories in carrying a load of money; robbers kill him to get at it. His humble companion, who carried only oats, concludes the poem:

> – Ami, lui dit son camarade,
> Il n'est pas toujours bon d'avoir un haut emploi.
> Si tu n'avais servi qu'un meunier, comme moi,
> Tu ne serais pas si malade." (l.16–9)

['Friend', said his comrade, / 'It is not always a good idea to hold high office. / If you had served a miller, like me, / You would not be in such a pass.']

People who believe that high office automatically exalts the holder are targeted here; but no human example could match the impact of giving as an instance of a 'high office' the job of pack-mule. The folly of the arrogant mule passes all bounds; by contrast, the right-thinking mule who speaks the epimythium seems correspondingly wiser than would a human counterpart (and this is not the case in the Phaedrus fable on which La Fontaine is said to have based his version[118]). It seems, then, that there is no overt consistency in the poet's approach to the animals as revealed in their own words of wisdom, the effect of the technique being now to enhance, now to undermine the speakers. Nevertheless, these animal epimythiums do have one thing in common: they cannot be taken at face value. Some add humour, some dignity to the animal portraits; overall they create implied parallels with man; and they make the talking animals more complex, more interesting and above all more ambiguous.

We must next consider how La Fontaine views animal reasoners throughout the poems, not just in the words they may speak at the end. We must bear in mind that we are dealing with two concepts when discussing reasoning animals. La Fontaine builds on the duality inherent in juxtaposing 'animal' with 'reasoner', and brings out the complexities of the equation.

In particular, he seizes many opportunities to build up the mental capacities of the small animals who figure in a number of traditional fables. His treatment of them seems to show a clear preference for piquant contrast by endowing the smallest, most potentially insignificant animals with the most impressive minds. These little creatures grasp the situation and apply their powers of induction with daunting intelligence, and each time there is a disparity between the powerful logic and the diminutive size of the minute animal thinker. For instance, when a frog sees two bulls fighting, she is heartbroken because she foresees dire consequences in the long term: whichever bull is vanquished will be exiled from the meadows and will wander over the marshes, squashing frogs underfoot ('Les deux Taureaux et une Grenouille', *[The two Bulls and a Frog]* II 4). The wisdom of this far-sighted frog must be set against her tiny size: the bulls are not even aware that she exists. Though the frog's logic is flawless, she can be crushed without the bulls even noticing. The effect is one of comic incongruity: the frog is inappropriately philosophical, articulate and far-seeing for such a tiny creature. But there is also an undercurrent that is potentially both moving and frightening in the frog's vulnerability. Whether our sympathies are with the actual amphibian heroine or with the implied human protagonists, the ordinary, weak people caught up in the titanic struggles between great men, is debatable. Again we see a demonstration of the poet's main preoccupations here: the entertainment factor and the equivocal message.

Other examples of tiny animals with finely-honed powers of reasoning are the ant who wants to save his friend the dove when a hunter has crept up on her; he waits till the hunter draws his bow, then bites him in the heel. The hunter turns his head, the dove flies off, the ant has triumphed ('La Colombe et la Fourmi' *[The Dove and the Ant]* , II 12). Another is the lark who reads human nature so well that she can tell exactly when the farmer's assertions that he is about to reap his corn are true ('L'Alouette et ses petits, avec le Maître d'un champ', IV 22). Again, there is the stag-beetle of 'L'Aigle et l'Escarbot' *[The Eagle and the Stag-Beetle]* (II 8) who defeats the eagle and makes Jupiter her dupe. She plans to destroy the eagle's eggs, so the eagle makes her nest in Jupiter's robe, knowing that the beetle will not dare to come and break the eggs under the god's very nose. Instead, the crafty beetle deposits a dropping on the robe; the god shakes it off in disgust, and the eggs tumble out and break: a humble insect has outwitted the queen of the birds and the king of the gods.

Larger animals tend to be treated rather differently. They are endowed with reasoning power, indeed, but this is made to seem scarcely adequate. And it is further compromised by naivety. Despite their best efforts to assess the situation, their ratiocinations lead to disaster. In addition to their ineptitude, their animality provides an incongruous contrast with their attempts to think clearly. The resulting entertainment is often highly fantastical. The most enjoyable effects result from the combination in the bulky logician of limited intellectual powers and recognizable animal characteristics.

Take the example of the donkey in 'L'Ane et le petit Chien' *[The Donkey and the little Dog]* (IV 5), a character built up in this way by La Fontaine from a much drier Aesopian original.[119] This donkey witnesses his master's evident appreciation of a cute little dog who sits on his knee, holding up a paw to be clasped. He deduces that the dog has found the way to his master's heart: 'S'il en faut faire autant afin qu'on me flatte, / Cela n'est pas bien malaisé' *[If I have to do likewise for him to caress me, / That's not very difficult]* (l.18–9). But when La Fontaine goes on to describe how the donkey implements his plan, he makes a point at that stage of including the poet's assessment of the animal's physical characteristics, emphasizing their gracelessness (underlined here). La Fontaine intersperses this with reminders of how the donkey views his own actions (shown in italics here):

> Dans cette *admirable* pensée,
> Voyant son Maître en joie, il s'en vient <u>lourdement</u>,
> Lève une <u>corne toute usée</u>,
> La lui porte au menton *fort amoureusement,*
> Non sans accompagner *pour plus grand ornement*
> De son *chant gracieux* cette action <u>hardie</u>. (l.20–5)

[With this admirable *thought, / Seeing his master in a good mood, he came* <u>lumbering</u> *up, / Raised his* <u>scuffed, horny hoof</u>, */ And chucked him* lovingly *under the chin, / Not without enhancing this* <u>bold</u> *act / By accompanying it with his* pretty song.*]*

Here the donkey's self-flattery clashes with the poet's unglamourized view of his movements, and the double perspective that underlies the treatment of all these reasoning animals is particularly clearly demonstrated. Interestingly the passage ends on an ambiguous note, since 'bold' can imply either approval or disapproval.

The situation becomes much more complex when several animals are involved. One animal (or group of animals) is likely to be better able to assess the situation than others, and will come out of it better: a good number of traditional fables tell of animals outwitting each other. The exception is a poem like 'Les deux Chèvres' *[The two Goats]* (XII 4) in which the two goats are equally stupid, obstinate and headstrong, and both come to grief at exactly the same moment.[120] A more typical Aesopian case is that of the fox who has lost his tail ('Le Renard ayant la queue coupée', *[The Fox whose tail was cut off]* V 5). He tries to persuade the other foxes that tails are heavy, dirty, useless appendages. The foxes are not deceived, and simply jeer at him. La Fontaine describes the arguments of the tailless fox in more detail than the others' answers – here the animal whose logic fails to convince is the interesting one. (Significantly, La Fontaine has altered the bias of the original Aesopian fable, in which far more weight is given to the other foxes' self-righteous rejection of their mutilated companion).[121] In many other fables, the opposite happens, and the more cunning animal provides the interest. Some of the most famous, like 'Le Renard et la Cigogne' *[The Fox and the Stork]* (I 18), or 'Le Corbeau et le Renard' *[The Crow and the Fox]* (I 2), are of this type.

Demonstrating how animals trick each other is one of the mainstays of the traditional fable. Many fables on this theme, taken directly from earlier fabulists, are built up by La Fontaine to emphasize the reasoning processes of the animal protagonists. One example is his version of the Aesopian fable in which one of a group of foxes, cannily inspecting the footprints leading to a sick lion's cave, employs techniques of detection similar to those of Voltaire's Zadig, or indeed to Sherlock Holmes. They refuse to visit the lion:

> Un d'eux en dit cette raison:
>> Les pas empreints sur la poussière
> Par ceux qui s'en vont faire au malade leur cour,
> Tous, sans exception, regardent sa tanière;
>> Pas un ne marque de retour.
>> Cela nous met en méfiance
>>> … dans cet antre
>> Je vois fort bien comme l'on entre,
>> Et ne vois pas comme on en sort.

[One of them gave this reason: / The footprints made in the dust / By those going to pay court to the invalid / All, without exception, point

*towards his den. / Not one points outwards. / That makes us suspicious
... I can see very clearly / How to enter that cave, / But not how to get
out.]*

('Le Lion malade et le Renard' *[The sick Lion and the
Fox]* VI 14, l. 14–24).[122]

In another poem taken from Aesop a bat demonstrates quick
thinking when she escapes from a mouse-hating weasel by maintaining that she is a bird because of her wings, and from a bird-hat-
ing weasel by claiming to be a mouse because of her fur ('La
Chauve-souris et les deux Belettes', *[The Bat and the two Weasels]* II
5). A comparison between the earlier fable and La Fontaine's own
version demonstrates what happens to an animal's powers of reasoning in his poems. In Nevelet's Latin version,[123] the story goes as
follows:

> Une chauve-souris, tombée à terre et faite prisonnière par une
> belette, allait à la mort et demandait grâce. La belette lui
> répliqua qu'il lui était impossible de lui rendre la liberté, car
> elle était, par sa race, ennemie de tous les oiseaux. "Mais je ne
> suis pas oiseau, repartit l'autre, je suis souris." Et elle obtint
> ainsi la liberté. Plus tard, ayant fait une seconde chute et de
> nouveau captive d'une belette, elle suppliait celle-ci de ne pas
> la dévorer. La belette lui objectant qu'elle avait pour ennemies
> toutes les souris, la chauve-souris lui répondit en affirmant
> qu'elle n'était pas une souris, mais oiseau de nuit: elle obtint
> derechef la liberté.

> *[A bat, fallen to the ground and imprisoned by a weasel, was
> condemned to death and begged for mercy. The weasel replied
> that she could not set her free, for her race was an enemy to all
> birds. 'But I'm not a bird,' said the other, 'I'm a mouse.' And she
> won her freedom. Later, having fallen again and been caught by
> another weasel, she begged her not to devour her. The weasel
> objected that she was the enemy of all mice; the bat in reply
> affirmed that she was not a mouse but a night bird. Thereupon,
> she was set free.]*

Compare this bald account with the two speeches made by
La Fontaine's bat. To the mouse-hating weasel she protests:

Pardonnez-moi, dit la pauvrette,
Ce n'est pas ma profession.
Moi, souris! Des méchants vous ont dit ces nouvelles.
   Grâce à l'auteur de l'univers,
   Je suis oiseau: voyez mes ailes:
   Vive la gent qui fend les airs! (l.9–14)

['Pardon me', said the poor little thing, / 'That isn't my profession. /
Me, a mouse! Wicked people have told you that. / Thanks to the creator
of the universe, / I am a bird: see my wings! / Long live the creatures
that cleave the air!']

To the bird hater she exclaims:

   'Moi, pour telle passer? Vous n'y regardez pas.
   Qui fait l'oiseau? c'est le plumage.
   Je suis souris: vivent les rats!
   Jupiter confonde les chats!' (l.25–8)

['Me, pass for a bird? You're not seeing straight. / What makes a bird?
Its plumage. / I'm a mouse. Long live rats! / May Jupiter confound all
cats!']

and the poet expresses approval of her 'adroite répartie' *[skilful*
repartee] (l.29). To argue her way out of these scrapes, La Fontaine's
bat adopts a number of tones. Yet the two speeches remain similar
in approach, incorporating outraged, exaggerated expostulation
('Moi, souris!' *[Me, a mouse?]* and 'Moi, pour telle passer?' *['Me,*
pass for a bird?]), appeals to the powers that be, and expressions of
enthusiasm for both of the bat's adopted species ('Vive la gent qui
fend les airs!' 'vivent les rats!'). Both times the bat produces a sub-
stantive argument, involving an implied physical action: in the first
speech she unfolds her wings to show them with 'voyez mes ailes'.
In the second, she invites the weasel to look: 'Vous n'y regardez
pas', then presumably shows off her body to demonstrate her lack
of feathers. In both speeches, the combination of rhetorical questions and interjections gives an impression of high excitement, so
that though the content of the speeches is dishonest, the underlying emotion is convincing. This formulation, with parallels
between the two episodes, demonstrates the point of the poem,

which is that those gifted with 'skilful repartee' can talk themselves out of anything. The bat's speeches are further enhanced by amusing touches which add not to the point but to the entertainment when she describes being a mouse as a 'profession', and implies that she is the butt of malicious gossip. There is far more to the reasoning of the La Fontaine animal than to its predecessor, the creation of Nevelet.

In some of the few poems which appear to be less strongly inspired by earlier fabulists, and hence are more likely to represent the poet's own bent, La Fontaine creates more far-fetched portraits of extravagantly inventive animals. Take the imaginative fox in 'Le Loup et le Renard' *[The Wolf and the Fox]* (XI 6).[124] (He is stuck in a bucket at the bottom of a well where water is drawn by means of a counterweight system of buckets. The fox persuades the wolf to get into the empty bucket at the top by explaining that the reflection of the old moon down in the well is a delicious round cheese. 'Descendez dans un seau que j'ai mis là exprès' *[Come down in the bucket I've put there for the purpose]* (l.39), he tells his victim. The wolf falls for the trick: 'Il descend, et son poids, emportant l'autre part, / Reguinde en haut maître Renard' *[He came down, and his bulk, weighing down the other side, / Raised Master Fox to the top]* (l. 42–3)). This fox is exceptionally clever, even for a trickster in a fable. Here, where La Fontaine can take the initiative, he tends towards the complex. The elaborate character of this fox's subterfuge is of a piece with the emphasis on subtle, ambivalent psychology that at once fogs the issues and makes them more fascinating in the animal portraits.

La Fontaine is here building on a tradition of implausibility. The mental powers of the original animals from which his characters are derived are already unreal and extravagant. In his source material, a wolf may dress himself up as a shepherd (III 3), or a donkey disguise himself in a lion's skin (V 21). As we have seen, however, La Fontaine's innovation is to build on these existing powers, to increase them and make them much more complex.

The impact of this exuberance is highly ambiguous when one reflects on the contexts in which the animals are required to exercise their powers of reasoning. For only too frequently the original fable gives an impression of a hostile world in which confrontations occur constantly, and it is essential to use one's wits to survive. The animals' reasoning power may well mean the difference between life and death. La Fontaine in his versions may seem to be indulging on behalf of his protagonists in elaborate flights of fancy in the most perilous of circumstances. This tendency would certainly fit with his declared aim of 'égayer' *[enlivening]* the fable genre.[125] But it also leaves one with an impression of cynicism, even pessimism in the way the story unfolds: for despite their inspirational logic, these animals too often come to grief.

CHAPTER 7

The presentation of talking animals

In fables it is taken for granted that animals can talk. This far from straightforward assumption rests on a series of half-conscious and often contradictory expectations which most readers have assimilated since early childhood. We are conditioned, for example, to accept that in one story a talking beast may astonish its hearers, while in another tale the animal's ability to speak will be received without comment or demur. In addition, the logistics of the process are taken for granted: we do not seek even the sketchiest of explanations of how the words sound or who has taught it speech. Talking animals are so well accepted as a narrative convention that such inconsistencies present no problems.

La Fontaine does not share this unquestioning attitude; nor does he pass over the concept of talking beasts without comment. On the contrary, he hints that the whole topic is extremely important, and, giving his own more positive version of a rather self-deprecating comment by Phaedrus on his own work,[126] goes so far as to assert that the way he makes animals (and indeed inanimate objects) talk is his most striking innovation:

> ... jusqu'ici d'un langage nouveau
> J'ai fait parler le Loup et répondre l'Agneau.
> J'ai passé plus avant; les Arbres et les Plantes
> Sont devenus chez moi créatures parlantes.
> Qui ne prendrait ceci pour un enchantement? (II 1 1.9–13)

[up till now I have made / The Wolf talk and the Lamb reply in a new language. / I have gone still further: Trees and Plants / Have become talking creatures in my work. / Who would not take this for an enchantment?]

It is curious that La Fontaine should insist that his presentation of talking animals is innovative, since they have been the mainstay of the traditional fable from Aesop onwards – although it is true that the Aesopian fables are 'très peu dialoguées' *[very thin on dialogue]*, as Roger Zuber puts it (p.49). La Fontaine's innovation lies, not in the fact of the animals' speaking, but in the manner of their speech. Hence my emphasis on the techniques used to present animal speech, which forms the basis of this chapter. The other curious element here is La Fontaine's remark that his talking animals will seem like 'un enchantement'. Far from taking talking animals for granted, as mere ciphers for human equivalents, the poet is focusing our attention on the extraordinariness of the fact that they can talk, and on the unreality of their speech.

This statement of La Fontaine's is more emphatic than his diffident suggestion on another occasion that what makes these portraits new is merely the fact that they are put into rhyme, ' ... nous rimerons/ Ce que disent entre eux les Loups et les Moutons' *[we will put into rhyme / What Wolves and Sheep say to each other]* (VIII 13 l.28–9). This comment seems like false modesty. For it is undeniable, as we shall see, that there is much more to his animals' speech than the fact that it is in verse.[127] If one looks at examples of how talking beasts are presented in the *Fables*, one can detect, first, a varied and subtle exploitation of the convention's potential which contrasts with the earlier fabulists' simpler approach; and secondly, a systematic deepening and enriching of the poems both in language and in character-portrayal.

Dialogue is a two-way process. With talking animals the impact is different according to whether the creatures speak to each other, or instead address people. In general, cross-species conversations between animals and man take on an added significance in the fable genre, in which, as we have seen, animal portraits are aimed at informing or instructing man. But such cross-species conversations are also intrinsically more problematic. We can scarcely be expected to believe that animals can address human beings, whereas we can readily accept that they can communicate with each other. The animal/human dialogues will be discussed first, since they are both more controversial and more central to the fabulist's approach.

In his most literal mood, La Fontaine rejects the pretence that animals can speak to man, and writes from a strictly realistic point of view. Such denials call into question the whole convention. This frame of mind underlies the traditional tale which, in La Fontaine's version, becomes 'Le Rieur et les Poissons' *[The Prankster and the*

Fish] (VIII 8), and whose point depends precisely on the awareness that in real life fish do *not* talk. A prankster lets it be understood that he wants bigger fish to eat than the ones on his plate, by claiming that he has been questioning these little fish but that they are too immature to answer his questions. The poet calls this speech a 'plaisanterie' *[joke]*.[128] There is no pretence that the cooked fish on the plate can really talk. A similar scepticism inspires 'Le Charlatan'(VI 19), which, like 'le Rieur', La Fontaine took from Abstemius. Here a man claims to the king that he can turn a donkey into an orator in ten years. If he fails, he is willing to forfeit his life. In private, he explains that his chances of paying this penalty are minimal: in ten years either he, the donkey or the king will probably be dead. Who believes that animals can talk in this fable? Probably not even the king, who, by insisting that he will inflict a horrible death on the charlatan if unsuccessful, seems to be sadistically earmarking a victim for future torment. In these examples, the convention of the talking beast is tainted with a whiff of human corruption, becoming a false belief cynically maintained for personal gain. The tradition of talking animals is undermined, but only temporarily. The poet expects the reader not to suspend disbelief in general, but instead to view the proceedings, for the moment, with robust commonsense.

A more subtle approach involves quoting animals' speech while yet casting doubt on its factual basis. Again the effect (though less blatant here) is to undermine the convention. La Fontaine writes from a sceptical standpoint, but without explicitly denying at least the possibility of animal speech. 'L'Ours et les deux Compagnons' *[The Bear and the two Companions]* (V 20) provides a case in point. Two hunters are surprised by a bear, and one of them has time only to lie down and pretend to be dead. The bear sniffs him closely:

> C'est', dit-il, 'un cadavre; Otons-nous, car il sent.'
> A ces mots, l'Ours s'en va dans la forêt prochaine. (l. 28–9)

['It's a corpse', said he. 'I must be off, for it stinks.' / At these words, the Bear went off into the nearby forest.]

The bear is talking to himself, possibly not out loud (significantly, La Fontaine's is the first version of the story in which the bear's thoughts are rendered in speech).[129] His words read like the formulation of a thought that any real bear could plausibly have had (if 'thought' is the word for what goes on in a bear's head), since these animals are known to desist from attacking a victim who shams dead.[130] The hunter next tells his companion that the bear said something completely different, and La Fontaine makes the hunter speak the moral. The companion asks:

> Mais que t'a-t-il dit à l'oreille?
> Car il s'approchait de bien près,
> Te retournant avec sa serre.
> – Il m'a dit qu'il ne faut jamais
> Vendre la peau de l'Ours qu'on ne l'ait mis par terre. (l.34–8)[131]

['What did he say in your ear? / For he came very close, / Turning you over with his claw.' / 'He said that you must never sell a bear's skin without first bringing him down.']

The hunter's words put into the bear's mouth an ironic comment on the situation; they make more sense if one assumes that he did not hear the bear actually speaking into his ear, since his account is entirely different from the bear's words as reported by the author. So the reader is left in doubt as to whether or not this is really a talking bear. We could conclude that the poet is describing a perfectly convincing real-life encounter, making his point clear by incorporating two different verbalizations of what the animal might plausibly have thought.[132] Apparently, it is up to us to decide.

In another group of poems, talking beasts are incorporated into a human context in a rather more traditional manner, as the poet focuses on the broader issues implicit in the moral. The character of the talking animals becomes subordinate to their significance as illustrations of a point. The animals speak to man indeed, but the conversation appears as a rationalization, a neat formulation, of the relationship between the two species. The effect is of a parable, in which the animal/man relationship is made to seem more balanced by endowing the animal with speech. In such cases, it seems inappropriate for the reader to respond to the fact that the beast can talk, since its words are more a universal comment on its predicament than an example of ordinary conversation. In both 'L'Homme et la Couleuvre' *[The Man and the Grass Snake]* (X 1) and 'Le Cheval s'étant voulu venger du Cerf' *[The Horse who wanted to take revenge against the Stag]* (IV 13), animals are representatives of their species. The one horse who just once, long ago, in a bid for revenge, allowed man on its back, and never again shook him off, stands for the whole equine race. The cow and the ox who expose man's cruelty and ingratitude in 'L'Homme et la Couleuvre' serve a similar purpose. The words of these animals are not perceived as ordinary speech,[133] and suspension of disbelief seems irrelevant. Even if the conversation is less overtly portentous, it can include an element of such rationalization. In 'Le Cochon, la Chèvre et le Mouton' *[The Pig, the Goat and the Sheep]* (VIII 12), the three animals are in a cart going to market. The goat and sheep are relatively quiet, but the pig is squealing its head off. Endowed with speech, the pig gives an excellent reason for this difference: the other two may be sold for their wool and their milk, but pigs are wanted only for meat, and this means certain death.[134] The pig's words, in short, neatly encapsulate the way man exploits his livestock; the pithy comment is more than the mere verbalization of one character's predicament.

The cumulative effect of these poems is to convey the impression that when animals converse with man, there are serious issues at stake despite the light-hearted presentation. The reader is invited to approach the poem in a spirit of sophistication and scepticism. It is made difficult to take the conversations at face value: the poet is undermining the illusion that his animals can talk.

A number of poems focus on another type of difficulty, namely the problems inherent in the mechanics of making animals address man. It is only too plain that such problems exist, and obvious questions suggest themselves. How do the speech-sounds emanate from a feral larynx? Do they sound similar to the animal's real-life noises? If the creature can talk, can it still make its other noises? An author may of course choose to ignore these questions; but La Fontaine sometimes draws our attention to them. Several times he implies that an animal who can use words is a weird creature, hard to imagine.

First, how does the sound come out? La Fontaine tantalizes us here by suggesting rather than explaining. He repeatedly implies that creatures find it difficult to talk, and have to force the words out as best they can.[135] Indeed, when it comes to communicating with man, it may take a life-threatening crisis to induce them to break silence. A little carp, about to be popped in the pan, finally finds a voice to speak to the fisherman: 'Le pauvre Carpillon lui fit en sa manière' *[The poor little Carp spoke to him in his own way]* (V 3 l.11). A captured snake manages to address his human tormentor, and ' ... en sa langue/ Reprit du mieux qu'il put' *[in his tongue / Replied as best he could]* (X 1 l.14–15). A goshawk, caught in a hunter's net, pleads with him 'en son langage' *[in his language]* (VI 15 l.15). We are given no clue to the mechanics of the process. Yet we must imagine clearly identifiable words emerging from the throats of the bird, the snake and the fish in the three examples, since in each case the human interlocutor hears and understands.

This impression of strained communication, hinted at in numerous poems, corresponds to a definite idiosyncrasy of La Fontaine's, since it is absent from the earlier fabulists' versions. It has a cumulative impact which, despite the wit and vitality of the dialogue, reinforces the familiar pessimistic moral message underlying most of the fables discussed in this section. We have noted that in most of them the poet implies that animals are unfairly victimized by man. If in an attempt to right their wrongs they break through the barrier of silence which excludes them from the human race, even this supreme effort is useless: man remains implacable. When animals manage to talk to man they demonstrate the hopelessness of the struggle of the weak against the strong.

I might be accused of overemphasizing the negative side of the animal/human dialogue in the *Fables*. It is certainly true that there are many examples of witty and light-hearted dialogue. But the *Fables* are more than a random series of individual and unrelated poems; and if one reads them with the overall impact of the collection in mind, then the poems mentioned here will cast a small but cumulative shadow over even the most sparkling conversations between animals and men. The 'enchantment' of animals which can talk has become a means for a disenchanted poet to vent his spleen against mankind.

*   *   *

The *Fables* also include many conversations between animals, in which man plays no part. Talk between beasts draws on a completely different set of narrative conventions. The poet makes no attempt to explain how an animal makes itself understood, as he does when he makes animals talk to men. Instead, he draws our attention to communication between animals in a matter-of-fact way: 'Le Loup en langue des Dieux / Parle au Chien dans mes ouvrages' *[In my work the Wolf talks to the Dog /In the language of the Gods]* (IX 1 1.5–6).[136]

Nevertheless, a problem remains. While normal animal sounds are unintelligible to a human ear, the exchanges between animals in fables are reproduced in human language. The reader must guess whether these are magical animals addressing one another in words, or whether we are being given a translation by the omniscient author.

La Fontaine, then, leaves it unclear whether the actual sounds made by his animals when talking to one another are inarticulate cries or human words. When a frog speaks to a rat, we are told she does so 'en sa langue' *[in her language]* – presumably a series of croaks ('La Grenouille et le Rat' *[The Frog and the Rat]*, IV 11 1.9). However, the content of her civilized and conventional speech seems unlike an animal's. The summary of her discourse takes eight lines, so she must have given a sustained oration. But did she employ what we would recognize as language? It is up to the reader to decide. This question could be posed for any of the large number of animal poems in which beasts address each other.

Occasionally, we are given more of an idea of the quality of the animal sounds, which are not like speech though reported using words. The animal courtiers at the lion's court are said to 'rugir en leur patois' when they speak ('Les Obsèques de la Lionne', VIII 14 1.16). 'Rugir' *[to roar]* tells us that their conversation sounds like animals roaring, and 'patois' *[dialect]* conveys a rustic, crude impression. The wolf, too, gives tongue, in a unique example of an animal consciously attempting to emulate human speech ('Le Loup devenu Berger' *[The Wolf who has become a Shepherd]*, III 3). His vocal chords are unsuited to the exercise. Instead, he lets out a howl which echoes through the woods:

> Il ne put du Pasteur contrefaire la voix.
> Le ton dont il parla fit retentir les bois. (1.23–4)

[He could not imitate the Shepherd's voice. / The sound of his speech echoed through the woods]

For the purposes of this fable, it is assumed that an animal's cry is the only sound he is capable of making.[137] Elsewhere, the rules change, though only up to a point. Another wolf is more of a mimic, and utters what he thinks is a bleat just like the nanny-goat's:

> ... il contrefait son ton,
> Et d'une voix papelarde
> Il demande qu'on ouvre ...

> *[He imitated her voice, / And in a quavering tone / Asked for the door to be opened ...]*
> ('Le Loup, la Chèvre et le Chevreau' *[The Wolf, the Goat and the Kid]* , IV 15, l.15–17)

However, the baby kid is suspicious at the sounds the wolf makes and will not let him in without further proof that he is indeed the nanny-goat, so presumably his imitation is less than convincing.

The impression built up by such examples is that the animal's 'speaking' voice resembles its real-life cry. In some poems, La Fontaine reinforces this by the imagery he uses for animal speech. In a mock-heroic passage inspired by Aesop,[138] a gnat's voice is likened to a victorious trumpet-call, a sound clearly recognizable as an inflated version of the insect's high-pitched whine ('Comme il sonna la charge, il sonne la victoire', *[As he sounded the charge, so he sounded the victory]* II 9 l.31). Onomatopoeia too can convey the impression of how a voice sounds. In several poems the lion's speech is so rich in 'r's that it sounds like a full-throated roar. And the lamb in 'Le Loup et l'Agneau' *[The Wolf and the Lamb]* frequently uses the sound 'è' ([ˇe]) in conversation, which makes his words sound like the baa-ing of sheep: ' ... que Votre Majesté / Ne se *mette* pas en col*ère* / Mais plutôt qu'*elle* consid*ère* / ... je *tette* encore ma m*ère*.' *[Let your Majesty / Not be angry, / But instead consider / ... that I am still drinking my mother's milk.]*[139]

In one traditional fable, 'Le Lion et l'Ane chassant' *[The Lion and the Donkey out hunting]* (II 19), the story distinguishes between an animal's speech and its non-verbal noises. The donkey's bray, which makes 'un bruit épouvantable' *[an appalling noise]* (l.14), serves to frighten the lion's prey out of hiding. But afterwards, the lion and the donkey have a conversation about the hunt which proves that the donkey can not only bray but also speak. Does his speech sound like attenuated braying? Certainly it is quieter and more measured than his call, since there is no suggestion that it grates on the lion's ears. This goes counter to the donkeys' own verdict on their speech in another fable, in which one donkey complains to another about man that 'il traite notre rire, et nos discours de braire' *[he calls our laughter and conversation braying]* (XI 5 l.44) – here their braying and their speech are seen as one.[140]

The uncertainty about what exactly is meant by 'animal speech' in these poems appeals unobtrusively to the imagination, and insinuates a sly hint of mystery. Some of the demands made on the reader would be preposterous if taken to their logical conclusion – we cannot really be required to picture in detail or to make sense of a frog discoursing elegantly to a rat or a wolf bleating like a goat. These are 'badineries', playful glimpses,[141] hinting at curious possibilities.

Though preoccupations with the mechanics of how creatures can talk to each other underlie many of the *Fables*, La Fontaine, like his predecessors, does not focus on them too obviously. In the bulk of the poems, indeed, he leaves the phenomenon of the animals' speech entirely to the reader's imagination and concentrates on how this speech reflects the personality and preoccupations of the speaker. He makes good use of the incongruity inherent in endowing a dumb beast with what appears to be human speech, and through this dichotomy creates comic, magical or satirical effects.

Some of his animals are made to talk very simply, using country terms, so that their vernacular gives a vague illusion of reflecting an animal's interests and environment. There are many examples, like the sensible, homely wisdom, untainted by sophistication, of the mother lark in 'L'Alouette et ses Petits, avec le Maître d'un champ' *[The Lark and her Babies, with the Owner of a Meadow]* (IV 22). When her fledglings tell her the farmer is threatening to get his friends to help reap his corn,

> S'il n'a dit que cela, repartit l'Alouette,
> Rien ne nous presse encor de changer de retraite;
> Mais c'est demain qu'il faut tout de bon écouter.
> Cependant, soyez gais; voilà de quoi manger. (l.36–9)

[If that is all he said, replied the Lark, / There is as yet no hurry for us to change our refuge. / But tomorrow you must listen carefully. / Meanwhile, cheer up! Here is some food for you.]

The simple vocabulary and the reference to food which give the passage its rustic flavour are Lafontainian innovations.[142]

At times the animals' speech has an authentic feel to it because it resembles the language of the people who share the environment of the animal protagonists. A cat addresses a sow as 'Ma bonne amie et ma voisine' *[My good friend and neighbour]* (III 6); a dog describes his behaviour at a wedding: 'étant de noce, il faut … que j'engraisse' *[since I'm a guest, I'm … bound to get fat]* (IX 10). The hare insults the tortoise by suggesting she take a folk cure for madness: 'Ma Commère, il vous faut purger/ Avec quatre grains d'ellébore' *[neighbour, you should take a purge / Of four grains of hellebore]* (VI 10). A donkey describes his behaviour when carrying a load of vegetables to market: if his master looked the other way, 'J'attrapais … / Quelque morceau de chou qui ne me coûtait rien' *[I used to snatch a piece of cabbage which cost me nothing]* (VI 11). These creatures speak like country folk.[143]

At their most sophisticated, however, La Fontaine's animals make of speech a civilized art, indulged in for its own sake. As Zuber says, some of them are 'd'une virtuosité brillante' in their use of language (p.50). But then the poet reminds us that it is after all animals which we are observing. The protagonists of 'Le Chat et le Renard' *[The Cat and the Fox]* (IX 14) may enjoy an abstract discussion to while away the time ('Le chemin était long, et partant ennuyeux, / Pour l'accourcir ils disputèrent' *[The road was long and moreover dull. To make it seem shorter, they debated]*, l.7–8), but this does not stop them from behaving in a manner characteristic of their species when under stress ('sur un arbre il [le chat] grimpa bel et bien. / L'autre fit cent tours' *[(The cat) climbed up a tree, and no nonsense. / The other made a hundred twists and turns]*, l.24–5). The contrast is between their civilized, 'human' conversation (which Fumaroli calls 'la parodie de la *disputatio* scolastique' (II 372)) and their undignified, 'animal' scramble to escape from the hounds.

Indeed, La Fontaine's most frequent treatment of talking beasts is to establish such a contrast between the elegance of their pronouncements and the brutishness of their behaviour. This disparity corresponds to a similar distinction between their idea of themselves and how they seem from outside. They think of themselves as civilized, even elegant; but to us they seem instinctual, even bestial. Their self-delusion further involves self-importance, probably the most common characteristic of La Fontaine's animal protagonists in the *Fables*. In many cases, animal arrogance, expressed through speech, results in a hubris which gives comic tension to the poems. An example would be the affected ecstasies of the young rat in 'Le Rat et l'Huître' *[The Rat and the Oyster]* (VIII 9), as he wanders through the landscape commenting rapturously: 'Que le monde est grand et spacieux!' *[How big and spacious the world is!]* He is so intoxicated with his own rhetoric, and suffers so from what Odette de Mourgues calls his 'inepte arrogance intellectuelle' (1, p.177–8), that he is oblivious of danger. And sure enough, this rat does not live long.[144]

La Fontaine tends to portray animals whose self-importance, expressed through their speech, contrasts with their lack of intrinsic dignity. Implicit in such portraits is a corresponding lack of humour in the self-glorifying speaker. However, some of La Fontaine's animals, even pretentious ones, do indulge in puns and word-plays.[145] We have seen how the pompous snake's tail in 'La Tête et la Queue du Serpent' *[The Head and the Tail of the Serpent]* in saying of the snake's head 'On m'a faite, Dieu merci,/ Sa sœur, et non sa suivante' *[Thank God, I was created / Her sister, not her follower]* (VII 16 l.16–7) is punning on the double meaning of 'suivante', servant and follower (since the tail follows behind the head).[146] An equally self-important fly imitates Mlle de Scudéry's 'Les Mouches galantes aux Mouches volantes' *[The amorous Flies to the flying Flies]*[147] to pun on her name, since 'mouche' can also mean a patch:

> Je rehausse d'un teint la blancheur naturelle;
> Et la dernière main que met à sa beauté
> Une femme allant en conquête,
> C'est un ajustement aux mouches emprunté.

[I enhance the natural whiteness of a complexion; / And the last touch that a woman makes to her beauty / Before she goes out to conquer / Is an embellishment borrowed from flies.]
(IV 3 'La Mouche et la Fourmi' *[The Fly and the Ant]*, l.16–8)

Her rival the ant, not to be outdone, replies by playing on other meanings of 'mouche':

> Nomme-t-on pas aussi Mouches les Parasites? …
>   Les Mouches de cour sont chassées;
> Les Mouchards sont pendus. (l.36–40)

[Are not Parasites also called Flies? / Flies are chased from court; / Informers are hanged.]

One could add numerous examples of unconscious witticisms put into the mouths of animals, so that the poet and the reader share a joke at the speaker's expense. A typical example is the exclamation of the stupid billy-goat in 'Le Renard et le Bouc' *[The Fox and the Goat]* (III 5). When he cries 'par ma barbe' *[by my beard]* (l.17), he is employing a 'formule de serment des romans de chevalerie' *[a form of oath from the romances of chivalry]*[148] to demonstrate noble masculinity. If he had been a man, his words would have achieved their desired effect. But as he is a goat, they instead evoke a silly, bearded goat-face and merely reinforce this character's animality.[149]

All these animal speakers are using words for effect, to demonstrate their learning and intelligence or to enhance their self-importance. Such speech put into the mouths of animals fulfils a further function. It enables the poet to satirize through parody, casting light not only on the animal speakers but also on the human speakers whom they appear to be emulating. An obvious example is the series of lion portaits, in which the lion speaks like a human king, his grandiloquent pronouncements appearing incongruous simply because, instead of issuing from a kingly mouth, they are emerging from a roaring muzzle. La Fontaine's lion-king says contemptuously to his victim: 'Nous n'appliquerons point sur tes membres profanes / Nos sacrés ongles' *[We will not apply our sacred nails / To your profane limbs]* (VIII 14 l.35–6). He is stressing his regality (using the royal 'we' and describing himself as sacred), and also portraying himself as a man, with 'ongles' *[nails]* rather than 'griffes' *[claws]*. Another lion issues an edict couched in the precise language of a human monarch:

> De par le Roi des Animaux
> Qui dans son antre était malade,

>Fut fait savoir à ses Vassaux
>Que chaque espèce en ambassade
>Envoyât gens le visiter ... (VI 14 l.1–5)

[In the name of the King of the Beasts, / Who was ill in his cave, / It was made known to his Vassals / That each species should send an embassy / To visit him ...]

A few key words ('Beasts', 'cave', 'species') betray the fact that this announcement is not made by the monarch whom La Fontaine's contemporaries knew: but apart from them it matches perfectly. Such passages slyly mock the grandeur of the animal protagonists' royal pomp – mere beasts have no business to be so self-important. But they also poke fun at the dignity of the human king by portraying him by implication, in all his hauteur, as a self-important lion.

In La Fontaine's poetry, then, such pretension in talking animals tends to ridicule not only the actual speakers, but also the fabulist's human targets. The extent to which this is true is clearly demonstrated if we consider the range and scope of his pompous animal speakers. Even within the seemingly narrow confines of the animal court, La Fontaine includes a wide range of courtiers, with a corresponding variety of styles of ostentatious speech. These animal courtiers vary from pronouncing unctuous discourses redolent of hypocrisy: 'Sire, dit le Renard, vous êtes trop bon Roi;/ Vos scrupules font voir trop de délicatesse' *['Sire,' said the Fox, 'you are too good a King; / Your scruples show too much delicacy.']*(VII 1 l.3–5) [150] to telling the king home truths: 'Comme vous êtes Roi, vous ne considérez/ Ni qui ni quoi' *[As you are the King, you don't consider / The whys and wherefores]*(V 18 l.9–10). Each of these speakers is parodying a human counterpart. And a particular animal character can vary from poem to poem. King Lion, while frequently behaving uncannily like a human monarch, nevertheless changes style from one fable to the next. Always in control while he retains his strength, always reminiscent of a human king, he yet varies his mood, conveying an additional unpredictability. Sometimes he speaks with regal grandeur, as in the examples mentioned above. At other times he uses simple, straightforward speech: 'Point du tout, dit le Roi, je les veux employer. / Notre troupe sans eux ne serait pas complète' *['Not at all', said the King, 'I want to employ them. /*

Our troop would be incomplete without them.'](V 19 l.13–4). Elsewhere his language can seem violent and brutal. The lion of 'Le Lion et le Moucheron' *[The Lion and the Gnat]* (II 9) roars at the gnat, calling him the 'excrément de la terre' *[excrement of the earth]*. Equally hostile but more sinister is the lion of 'La Génisse, la Chèvre et la Brebis, en société avec le Lion' *[The Heifer, the Goat and the Ewe, in association with the Lion]*(I 6) whose technique is to pretend to reason with his victims, confronting them with the unanswerable logic of brutality as he shares out the four animals' booty:

> [La première part] doit être à moi, dit-il, et la raison
> C'est que je m'appelle Lion:
> A cela l'on a rien à dire.
> La seconde par droit me doit échoir encor:
> Ce droit, vous le savez, c'est le droit du plus fort.
> Comme le plus vaillant je prétends la troisième.
> Si quelqu'une de vous touche à la quatrième
> Je l'étranglerai tout d'abord. (l.11–18)

['(The first share) should be for me,' said he, 'And the reason / Is that my name is Lion: / Nobody can say anything against that. / The second should be mine by right as well: / That right is the right of the strongest, as you know. / I lay claim to the third as I'm the bravest. / If any one of you touches the fourth, / I'll strangle them at once.']

Here the lion's speech has the bullying nastiness of a thug. He cynically pretends to justify his action, knowing full well that the other three animals are too weak to oppose him. The pretence disappears with the last, violent line. Collectively, these speeches of the lion build up an impression of a many-faceted, unpredictable, hence dangerous, king. The only feature which remains constant is his power. The implications for the human monarch are clear. So this animal's speech contributes greatly to the satirical impact of the fables in which he figures.

The lion speaks to good effect, always succeeding in intimidating his inferiors. But animal speech may produce a different impression from what the speaker intends. La Fontaine can play the part of a psychologist, hinting at the personalities of the characters through their use of language, implying truths about them which they are unaware of betraying, and would probably prefer to conceal. Take the exchange between the heroes of 'Le Chat et le Rat' (VIII 22). The cat, caught in a net and trying to persuade the rat to gnaw him free, uses a dignified verse form, mostly consisting of alexandrines; the resulting lines could have come straight out of a classical tragedy:

> C'est à bon droit
> Que seul entre les tiens par amour singulière
> Je t'ai toujours choyé, t'aimant comme mes yeux.
> Je n'en ai point regret, et j'en rends grâce aux Dieux. ...
> Ce réseau me retient; ma vie est en tes mains:
> Viens dissoudre ces noeuds ... ' (l.18–25)

[I had good reason / To cherish you, alone of all your kin, for love of you, / For I loved you like my own eyes. / I have no regrets, for which I give thanks to the Gods ... / This net has trapped me: my life is in your hands: / Come and release these knots]

The reader will be sceptical of the cat's insistence that he has always loved the rat, and on the lookout for confirmation that this is a lie. Confirmation comes in the form of literary artifice. The cat's speech alludes to a variety of literary registers: *précieux* hyperbole ('choyé' *[cherished]*), Biblical simplicity ('t'aimant comme mes yeux' *[I loved you like my own eyes]*[151]), Tartuffian pseudo-religious fervour ('j'en rends grâce aux Dieux' *[I give thanks to the Gods]*), and an interesting adaptation of the accepted figurative vocabulary of classical tragedy with 'réseau' *[net]* and 'noeuds' *[knots]*, but used literally since the cat is snarled up in a net ('Viens dissoudre ces noeuds' *[Come and release these knots]* echoes a Racinian formulation[152]). The resulting speech seems highly artificial, and is enough to warn us that the cat is a hypocrite.

This impression is reinforced by another technique frequently used by La Fontaine to render animal speech. He incorporates a number of different styles of animal conversation within a single poem. The contrast between two speakers can tell us much about them both. In this case, the artifice of the cat is contrasted with the rat's forthright style of speech:

> Le Rat dit: Idiot!
> Moi ton libérateur? Je ne suis pas si sot. (l.33–4)[153]

[The Rat said: 'Some idiot! / Me, free you? I'm not such a fool.']

The rat's crude vocabulary, unacceptable for an elegant speaker ('idiot', 'fool') cuts right through the conventional speech of the cat. The juxtaposition of the two speakers' registers tells us all we need to know about the clash of their personalities: the ostensibly civilized but duplicitous cat confronted by the down-to-earth rat. There are numerous other examples of fables where the contrasting registers of the interlocutors show each other up, for instance 'Le Loup et l'Agneau' *[The Wolf and the Lamb]*, where the respectful correctness of the lamb's speech contrasts sharply with the brutality of the wolf's replies (I 10).[154]

If clashing registers occur within the speech of a single animal, the speaker appears to be prey to conflicting emotions. For example, in 'L'Araignée et l'Hirondelle' *[The Spider and the Swallow]* (X 6), the spider complains to Jupiter about the swallow who steals all the flies:

> Entends ma plainte une fois en ta vie.
> Progné me vient enlever les morceaux:
> Caracolant, frisant l'air et les eaux,
> Elle me prend mes mouches à ma porte:
> Miennes je puis les dire; et mon réseau
> En serait plein sans ce maudit Oiseau ... (l.4–9)

[For once in your life, listen to my complaint. Procne comes and takes all the food: / Pirouetting, skimming over the air and the waters, / She catches my flies at my door: / I can call them mine, and my net / Would be full without that cursed bird ...]

The spider's speech is mundane, petty and simply expressed, the metre of the lines as rigid and unvarying as a perfectly-structured spider's web.[155] She is filled with narrow-minded resentment, lives behind closed doors, possessively collecting 'her' pieces of food in the net of her web, and cursing her rival, Progné the swallow. One line, however, stands out: 'Caracolant, frisant l'air et les eaux' *[Pirouetting, skimming over the air and the waters]*. With its verbs of acrobacy and speed, its literary references[156] and its broad strokes ('the waters' is both more poetic and suggests a wider area than 'water') this line lyrically renders the swallow's blithe flight. The spider's language in this one line implies that, trapped as she is in her web, she can, inspite of herself, see and envy the swallow's freedom.

It may however happen that arresting language reveals little about the psychology of the speaker, instead providing an authorial comment on the broader issues of the fables. The leopard's description of his spots in 'Le Singe et le Léopard' *[The Monkey and the Leopard]* (IX 3) is a case in point. He is an enthusiastic manipulator of speech, and uses language in a subtle and allusive manner. His adjectives are lively and vivid, and argue a preoccupation with the niceties of expression: his skin ' … est bigarrée, / Pleine de taches, marquetée, / Et vergetée, et mouchetée' *[is mottled, / Covered in blotches, patched / and spotted, and parti-coloured]* (l.7–9).[157] As for the allusive quality, Fumaroli (II 362) points out that 'bigarrure' *[motley]* is also a technical term to describe the language employed by seventeenth-century fairground orators. Hence the leopard's speech is not only vivid in sound, but also suggestive of the contemporary literary scene. Later in the same poem, the leopard's rival the monkey uses 'tours' *[monkey tricks, or turns of speech]* as opposed to 'bigarrures': another play on a rhetorical technical term.[158] There seems to be an element of mockery at the expense of the human orators or rhetoricians in the way the poet places their technical language inappropriately in the mouths of animals.

More explicit literary allusions are not infrequently made by La Fontaine's animals. They enjoy showing off their book-learning; but their allusions may undermine their attempts to impress, making them seem ridiculous instead. The rat in 'Le Rat et l'Huître' *[The Rat and the Oyster]* (VIII 9) claims he has completed the journey of conquest envisaged by Picrochole in Rabelais's *Gargantua*. As Daniel Bergez puts it, 'Le Rat se souvient même de Rabelais: il pratique l'intertextualité, lui aussi se soumet au principe classique de l'imitation' *[The Rat even remembers Rabelais. He practises intertextuality, and he too submits to the classic principle of imitation]*.[159] The rat says: 'J'ai passé les déserts, mais nous n'y bûmes point' *[I passed through deserts, but we didn't drink there]* (l.16), while Rabelais's Picrochole wonders: 'Que boyrons-nous par ces désers? Car Julian Auguste et tout son oust y moururent de soif' *[What will we drink in these deserts? For Julian Augustus and all his army died of thirst there]*.[160] Unfortunately for the rat's pretensions,

Picrochole's prospective journey is ludicrously extravagant, so impossible that he has agreed to it only because he is half-mad. The wild excesses of the Rabelais source make a mock of the rat's attempts to enhance his credibility by suggesting that his own journey is a parallel to it. Incidentally, whom is the rat trying to impress? The poet does not even hint at interlocutors, though one can assume the rat would not be so ostentatious, or so dishonest, in soliloquy. Does he have an admiring rat audience, or does he address the reader? Whatever the answer, the rat's incompetent attempt to demonstrate his book-learning achieves the opposite of its intended effect, and makes one laugh at his expense.

But not all animal learning ridicules the speaker. Several animals have a talent for epigram and produce pithy aphorisms worthy of La Fontaine's admired La Rochefoucauld. Such animal epigrams may well be included because they were in an earlier version of the fable. For example, a dying lion, too weak to defend himself when even the donkey comes to kick his prostrate form, makes a comment which is not only bitter but strikingly put:

> Ah! c'est trop, lui dit-il, je voulais bien mourir;
> Mais c'est mourir deux fois que souffrir tes atteintes.

['Ah! It's too much,' he said to him. 'I was ready to die; / But to suffer your attack is to die twice.']
('Le Lion devenu vieux' *[The Lion grown old]* III 14 l.11–12)

Here, La Fontaine is copying the Phaedrus version almost word for word, his language echoing not only the thoughts but also the formulation of the earlier writer.[161] So what is the impact of this classical formulation? It gives a literary flavour to the animal's speech, making it seem dignified.

The animals' capacity to encapsulate a reflexion in a neat form (and to allude eloquently to earlier masters!) accompanies the remarkable logical powers already discussed. There are many instances of an elegant train of thought which is further enhanced by sophisticated formulation. Take the fox's comment on the bust of a hero. He realizes that the bust is hollow, and uses the fact to remark pithily (again echoing and expanding an earlier version) on the difference between appearance and reality, and on the human implications of his observation:

> Belle tête, dit-il, mais de cervelle point.
> Combien de grands Seigneurs sont Bustes en ce point!

['It's a fine head,' said he, 'But no brains. / How many great lords are busts in this respect!']

('Le Renard et le Buste' *[The Fox and the Bust]*
IV 14 l.11–12)[162]

The same is true of the bird in 'L'oiseau blessé d'une flèche' *[The Bird wounded by an arrow]* (II 6). Though mortally wounded, the bird is able to comment epigrammatically though without levity on the ironic fact that birds themselves provide the means for their own destruction by growing the feathers which give arrows flight:

> Faut-il contribuer à son propre malheur!
> Cruels humains, vous tirez de nos ailes
> De quoi faire voler ces machines mortelles. (l.4–6)[163]

[Must we contribute to our own misfortune! / Cruel man, you take from our wings / The means to make these deadly weapons fly]

Other animals demonstrate a capacity for sustained discourse, following a train of thought through to a logical conclusion. We have seen how the cat and the fox while away the hours of their journey in debate ('Le Chat et le Renard' *[The Cat and the Fox]*, IX 14). In the case of the philosophical hare of 'Le Lièvre et les Grenouilles' *[The Hare and the Frogs]* (II 14), we witness the protagonist's reflections on the topic of fear and its implications for various species. The hare uses rhetorical tricks: he states a general truth, then comments on its particular relevance in his case; he debates with an imaginary interlocutor, or uses antithesis (see line 8, 'jamais ... toujours' *[never ... always]*):

> Les gens de naturel peureux
> Sont, disait-il, bien malheureux:
> Ils ne sauraient manger morceau qui leur profite.

Jamais un plaisir pur; toujours assauts divers.
Voilà comme je vis: cette crainte maudite
M'empêche de dormir, sinon les yeux ouverts.
Corrigez-vous, dira quelque sage cervelle.
Et la peur se corrige-t-elle?
Je crois même qu'en bonne foi
Les hommes ont peur comme moi. (l.5–14)

['People who are naturally timid / Are very unhappy,' said he. / 'They can't get the benefit from a morsel that they eat. / Never a pure pleasure; always a range of assaults. / That is how I live: that cursed dread / Stops me sleeping, or keeps my eyes open. / "Put it right", says someone wise. / Can you put right fear? / I honestly think / That even men are afraid as I am'.]

Eighteen of the thirty-three lines of the poem reproduce the hare's introspections. He also speaks the epimythium. The narrator several times draws our attention to the reflective tendencies of the hare by means of authorial comments: 'Un Lièvre … songeait' *[a Hare … was thinking]* (l.1); ' … rêvant à cette matière' *[reflecting on this subject]* (l.20); 'Ainsi raisonnait notre Lièvre' *[Thus reasoned our Hare]* (l.15). This poem, which contains one of the lengthiest animal verbalizations in the collection, shows how far the reasoning capacities which we have already observed can be demonstrated through an animal's speech.[164]

Such poems present such a convincing picture of an anthropomorphic animal's capacity to verbalize its thoughts, that these talents may come to seem like the norm. A portrait of an inadequately articulate talking animal may be affected by this assumption. For example, the highly verbal, rational hare is given a diametrical opposite by La Fontaine when he transforms a rather anodyne character from Pilpay[165] into the laconic bear of 'L'Ours et l'Amateur des jardins' *[The Bear and the Garden-Lover]* (VIII 10). Despite his affection for his human companion, this bear is 'très mauvais complimenteur' *[very bad at paying compliments]* (l.30), and 'en un jour ne disait pas deux mots' *[never said two words all day long]* (l.41). The poet comments that he is a 'mauvais raisonneur' *[a poor reasoner]* (l.55). Here the poet is writing as though he expects his animals to be competent speakers, so that the bear has been found wanting. However, it is interesting to note that in the case of La Fontaine's hare the animal speaker is at this stage not addressing man or even an animal interlocutor but is alone, talking to himself. In contrast the bear is like the protagonists of the poems mentioned earlier in which the animals, confronting man, find the power of speech only in exceptional circumstances, and then only to a limited extent.

* * *

So far, we have been looking at the intrinsic qualities of animal speech. We must next consider its role in the plot of the fable. Normally, animal speech contributes little to the outcome of a poem. If the animals had been dumb it would have been the same: the wolf would still have eaten the lamb who had the misfortune to drink from the same stream (I 10). At times, indeed, the speech seems independent of or even contradicts the action of a poem. This is the case with 'Le Coq et le Renard' (II 15). In this fable, the two old adversaries behave in time-honoured fashion: the fox tries to lure the cock from his perch, while the cock refuses to come down. But their conversation tells a very different story: it is full of brotherly love, peace and joy. The fox explains that all the animals have signed a treaty of peace, and that he is their emissary. The cock replies that he is only waiting for the hounds to arrive so that they can all embrace: he can see them coming in the distance. At this, the fox runs away, explaining that he is in a hurry to spread the glad news, and will come back later. Neither interlocutor abandons the pretence for a second.[166] The animals' ability to deceive through language makes the poem much more complex and it also gives rise to the epimythium: 'c'est double plaisir de tromper le trompeur' (l.32); but it does not change the physical actions of the protagonists until the very end when the fox runs away because he can't be sure that the hounds are nothing but the cock's invention. Animal speech in this case enriches the poem throughout but transforms it only at the end.

Where the verbal blandishments of the animal speaker are successful, however, it seems that language has definitely contributed to the outcome. In some of the court fables, skilful animals consolidate their position and manipulate a powerful monarch with fair words. In 'Le Renard, le Singe et les Animaux' *[The Fox, the Monkey and the Animals]* (VI 6) La Fontaine elaborates on an

Aesop fable.[167] Having made his fox courtier set a trap for the king, he shows how he entices him into it with words by using direct speech:

> Le Renard ...
> Sans toutefois montrer son sentiment
> Quand il eut fait son petit compliment,
> Il dit au Roi:
> ... tout trésor par droit de royauté
> Appartient, Sire, à Votre Majesté.
> ... C'était un piège. (l.17–26)

[The Fox ... , / Without however revealing his feelings, / When he had paid his little compliment, / Said to the king: / ... 'All treasure belongs to your Majesty / By royal right.' / It was a trap.]

In a more sinister example, Raminagrobis, the cat-judge, successfully lures his potential victims to their deaths with words: 'Mes enfants, approchez,/ Approchez, je suis sourd, les ans en sont la cause' *[My children, come closer, come closer, / I'm deaf, it's because of my age.]* ('Le Chat, la Belette et le Petit Lapin' *[The Cat, the Weasel and the Little Rabbit]*, VII 15, l.39–40). In a single manipulative sentence, he simulates paternal affection ('my children'), hints that he is harmless because he is old, and justifies his request that they come within reach ('I'm deaf'). The sound of the words is hypnotic, run through with soothing 's's, many of which are liaisons which make the speech flow smoothly. The very blandness and flow of the words make them sinister.

Language is not absolutely essential to the outcome of these poems (a different predator lures his victims to their deaths by simple movements, without the aid of Raminagrobis's hypocritical language, in 'Le Renard et les Poulets d'Inde' *[The Fox and the Guinea-Fowl]*). However, in another group of poems the plot and outcome depend entirely on the fact that the animals can talk. An extreme example is the case of a vain tortoise, whose ability to speak, combined with the complacency which most often accompanies this talent in the *Fables*, results in her downfall (X 2 'La Tortue et les deux Canards' *[The Tortoise and the Two Ducks]*). She is carried through the air by two ducks, hanging on to a stick by her mouth; she cannot resist agreeing with admiring passers-by that she is the queen of the tortoises.

... Elle eût beaucoup mieux fait
De passer son chemin sans dire aucune chose;
Car lâchant le bâton en desserrant les dents,
Elle tombe, elle crève aux pieds des regardants. (l. 28–31)

[She'd have done much better / To go her ways without speaking; / For in unclenching her teeth and letting go of the stick, / She fell, she burst at the watchers' feet]

The destruction of this remarkable tortoise is due to her exercising her powers of speech: it is the actual physical process of opening her mouth to speak which destroys her. Danner comments that the moral 'amusingly demonstrates the proposition 'Si quelqu'un desserre les dents/ C'est un sot' *[If anyone unclenches his teeth, he's a fool]*', which ends the previous fable (Danner 1 p.97). Fumaroli (II 382–3) further points out that speech is implicated in the 'moralité' of the poem. The ostensible moral is that vanity leads to destruction. But, as Fumaroli puts it, 'C'est la parole, celle qui trompe et celle qui est prononcée *en trop* qui perd, et qui même tue' *[It is speech, misleading and superfluous speech, which destroys and even kills]*: the implicit moral is that superfluous speech can destroy.[168]

More commonly, speech becomes essential to the plot because it enables animals to respond in a sophisticated, complex manner. Take 'Les Poissons et le Cormoran' *[The Fish and the Cormorant]* (X 3), interestingly placed next to 'La Tortue et les deux Canards' by La Fontaine, reinforcing the message that language is dangerous.[169] In this poem, the cormorant persuades the fish that they are in danger of being fished out of existence at some future date; he talks them into letting him carry them in his beak to a safer pond. What concerns us here is the extraordinary response of the fish, who accept the cormorant's argument and cooperate accordingly. The conversation leads to their destruction, since the cormorant carries them one by one to a shallow pool where he can later catch and eat them. Similarly, the frogs in 'Les Grenouilles qui demandent un Roi' *[The Frogs who demand a King]* (III 4), which La Fontaine took from Phaedrus, would have saved themselves from mass destruction if they had not had the gift of speech: it is through language that they importune Jupiter for a king, only to be given a frog-eating crane. They, and many other animals in the

Fables, would have fared better if they had obeyed the poet's advice to 'se taire' *[keep quiet]* (X 1 l.90).

* * *

Summing up the overall impact of the animal/human conversations in the *Fables*, I concluded earlier that they had a dual effect. Their presentation was lively and pleasing, while the implications of the content were disturbing: the power of speech simply reinforced the animals' helplessness and vulnerability. Looking back over the whole of this discussion of animals' speech, what conclusions suggest themselves? Again the effect is a dual one. The conversations themselves are lively and light-hearted; but if one focuses on the content of the poems, the impression of vulnerability persists. The conversations (whether between animals or man and animals) tend to express an underlying menace. The context is frequently life-threatening, and most of the weaker characters singled out in this chapter are due to meet their deaths. Speech can rarely save the talking beasts[170]; indeed, it is much more likely to hurt them, often by drawing attention to them when they would have been safer lying low. Many of La Fontaine's poems deal with the relationship between the strong and the weak, the great and the small. Almost always, he focuses on the frailty of the weak, crushed by the strong. And in these poems about conversation, the reader tends to be placed in the position of siding with the weaker interlocutor, only to witness his discomfiture. Despite the wit, the imagination, the 'badineries', La Fontaine's talking animals ultimately leave one with an aftertaste of sadness. Through them, the antisocial message of his final fable 'Le Juge arbitre, l'Hospitalier et le Solitaire' *[The Arbitrator, the Hospital Visitor and the Hermit]* (XII 29) comes across, more playfully put but more negative in implication. Communication, deceptively attractive, is harmful: salvation can ultimately lie only in the silence of solitude: 'il est bon de parler, et meilleur de se taire.' *[It is good to talk, and better to keep quiet.]*[171]

IV
Characters

CHAPTER 8

Neglected protagonists

The outcome of a fable and the implications of its moral are likely to be different for each of its protagonists. Most commonly, there are two groups of characters, and these probably play opposing roles in the action. One may be the predator, the other the victim ('Le Loup et l'Agneau' *[The Wolf and the Lamb]*); one foolish, the other wise ('Le Singe et le Dauphin' *[The Monkey and the Dolphin]*); one insignificant, the other important ('Le Bûcheron et Mercure' *[The Woodcutter and Mercury]*), and so on. This is a practical shape for a didactic form: the outcome will favour one character at the expense of the other, so that the moral shows up clearly. If we look at the titles of the *Fables*, we find that most of the poems follow this rule, and name two protagonists, or groups of protagonists, as in the examples I have just given. Hence the very titles tend to reinforce the duality of the fable form.

Even if there are more than two main characters, we will commonly find that they can be grouped into two opposing camps. For example, in 'L'Aigle, la Laie et la Chatte' *[The Eagle, the Sow and the Cat]* (III 6), the cat is a trickster, while the sow and the eagle are both her dupes, and suffer similar fates. In 'Les deux Perroquets, le Roi et son fils' *[The two Parrots, the King and his son]* (X 11), the parrots are on one side, the men on the other, and the experiences of the two birds demonstrate that one should not trust those in power, as represented by the king and his son. Alternatively, in a fable which names many protagonists in the title, there is still a duality of structure: minor eponymous characters may serve as a mere audience to the two central figures, as in 'Le Renard, le Singe et les Animaux' *[The Fox, the Monkey and the Animals]* (VI 6), in which the other animals look on as the fox outsmarts the monkey.

If the title names only one protagonist, there will still be an element of duality or opposition. Single eponymous protagonists such as the Taper of IX 12 and the Scythian Philosopher of XII 20 try to outdo a rival whom they are ill-qualified to emulate. In 'Le Mal Marié' *[The Man who married badly]* (VII 2) the husband, as he tries to solve the problem of an unhappy marriage, is offset against his nagging wife.

However tempting it may be to look at a fable from a single point of view, taking the explicit moral as our guide, and picking out as our focus of attention the protagonist to whom the moral seems most obviously to apply, it is a mistake to ignore this element of duality. In a number of fables, the central figure attracts so much interest that it is only too easy to overlook the function of other eponymous protagonists. We do not waste time thinking about the moral of 'Le Pot de terre et le Pot de fer' *[The earthenware Pot and the iron Pot]* (V 2) from the point of view of the iron pot: the events of the fable are so catastrophic for the earthenware pot, who is broken into pieces when he bumps into his iron friend, that we are effectively forced to concentrate on him. But viewing such fables from a single angle may result in an incomplete reading.

To give a simple example, in the very first fable, 'La Cigale et la Fourmi' *[The Cicada and the Ant]*, the focus is on the cicada, and the poem's obvious message is an attack on her improvidence. But if we focus on the ant, the poem reveals a new side, and becomes in addition an attack on the unprepossessing combination of complacency and lack of charity epitomized by that insect personage.

This example suggests that focusing on all the elements in the title of a fable can greatly enhance our reading. Why then do we tend instinctively to overlook some of them? Partly, I think, because the surface meaning, indicated to us by the explicit moral, is so convincing that it seems unnecessary and indeed almost perverse to look for other strata beneath it. But such perversity can bring rewards. This chapter demonstrates how approaching the *Fables* from a dual standpoint, giving each of the characters his proper importance, can enrich our reading of the poems. I shall try to show that the underemphasized characters in certain fables, those on whom we do not instinctively focus, may be of considerable interest in themselves, and, more importantly, may add a further dimension to the principal moral.

This process is clearly demonstrated if we look afresh at a fable in which La Fontaine directs us firmly towards one of the eponymous characters, keeping the others in the background. My example here is 'La Tortue et les deux Canards' *[The Tortoise and the two Ducks]* (X 2). This fable has been seen as one of La Fontaine's most cruelly punitive: I have already discussed the harsh judgment on the tortoise for her garrulity.[172] It tells the story of a tortoise who longs to travel.[173] She talks of this to two ducks, who arrange to carry her through the air: 'Dans la gueule en travers on lui passe un bâton' *[They passed a stick sideways through her mouth]*. But as she flies through the air, she cannot resist calling out to sceptical observers that she is the queen of tortoises, and, in opening her mouth to do so, lets go of the stick and falls to her death. These dramatic events ensure that the tortoise-heroine occupies the centre stage. As a result, the other two eponymous characters, the ducks, seem to be purely incidental, introduced simply as the means whereby the tortoise gets her come-uppance.

If we focus on these ducks instead, we discover that they have very particular features, strong personalities of their own, and a different moral function from that of the heroine.[174] Let us re-examine the events of the fable, singling out the ducks.

The moment they learn of the tortoise's ambition to travel, they offer to help. This is how they put it to her:

> Voyez-vous ce large chemin?
> Nous vous voiturerons par l'air en Amérique.
> Vous verrez mainte République,
> Maint Royaume, maint peuple; et vous profiterez
> Des différentes moeurs que vous remarquerez.
> Ulysse en fit autant.   (l.8–13)

[Do you see that broad pathway? / We will convey you by air to America. / You will see many a Republic, / Many a Kingdom, many a people; and you will benefit / From the different customs you will observe. / Ulysses did the same]

The ducks are not simply agreeing to do what the tortoise wants, but are strongly urging her on. To help persuade her, they paint a rosy and unrealistic picture of the pleasures in store for her. The practical problems of the journey are glossed over. The sky becomes a broad, comfortable road. The method of locomotion too seems attractive. With 'voiturerons' the ducks seem to be offering a comfortable carriage or 'voiture', and in addition the word, a précieux coinage mocked at by Molière,[175] is affected and pretentious: the tortoise will travel in elegant comfort and impress her friends. The outlandish suggestion that she can travel by air (a means of loco-motion strictly reserved for birds and science-fiction characters in La Fontaine's time) is casually slipped in as though it were perfectly natural. The tortoise's journey is equally fanciful: not only is she to travel as far as America, but she is to do so by way of a considerable number of different countries ('mainte République, maint Royaume'). She will see the world and derive intellectual profit from her observations. The ducks finish off their patter with a ref-erence to Ulysses. That the tortoise should be comparable to a Homeric hero is ludicrous enough; but there are other unfortunate connotations to the comparison. Ulysses was an unwilling traveller, who endured appalling hardship on his ten-year journey; moreover he was the epitome of wisdom and cleverness, as different as possi-ble from the impulsive, gullible tortoise. Indeed, the poet inter-venes at this stage to cast doubt on the reference: 'On ne s'attendait guère / De voir Ulysse en cette affaire' *[One was scarcely expecting / To see Ulysses in this affair]* (1.13–4), implicitly criticizing the ducks for mentioning him.

In this speech the ducks have played a series of dishonest tricks on their victim, exactly like a pair of dubious confidence tricksters. As Gutwirth puts it (1 p.104), 'ils ont toute la faconde, tout l'em-pressement de ces bonimenteurs d'un siècle encore à venir: MM les commis voyageurs'. *[They have the gift of the gab and the pushiness of those masters of claptrap of a later century, commercial travellers.]* They are trying, by making extravagant claims, to sell something not worth having. The ducks are advocating the trip to the tor-toise, not the other way round; this is confirmed by the next line: 'La Tortue écouta la proposition' *[The Tortoise listened to the propo-sition].* The word 'proposition' suggests a business transaction, and that such a transaction takes place is confirmed by the text, which next presents us with a fait accompli, 'Marché fait' (1.16): a bargain has been struck. There is no need to interpret these words any way but literally, as meaning an actual deal: the ducks would not have so exaggerated the advantages of what they had to offer unless there was something in it for them – presumably they are to receive pay-ment. Significantly, the agreement is completed before we have noticed what is happening: again the impression is of sharp prac-tice, with the crafty ducks clinching the deal rapidly, without allowing their victim time to think it over.

The ducks' tricks are not yet over. They next have to get the tortoise's means of transport ready. We are told 'les canards forgent une machine' *[The ducks forged a machine]* (l.16). This sounds like the ducks' own description of what they are up to, expressed in indirect speech, for it exaggerates and misrepresents what is actually happening. In fact the ducks are looking for a suitable stick; but 'forged' suggests they are working metal, and 'machine' invokes an elaborate contraption, and is certainly an inappropriate word to use for a 'stick'. The tortoise has by now become very much the victim of the affair. She is called 'la pèlerine', possibly again by the ducks or possibly by the narrator. Either way, there is a nuance of contempt in the use of the word, which properly belongs to the burlesque.[176] She commands no respect or sympathy, only ridicule.

The ducks' main contribution to the fable ends with the preparation for the flight:

> Dans la gueule en travers on lui passe un bâton.
> "Serrez bien, dirent-ils; gardez de lâcher prise."
> Puis chaque Canard prend ce bâton par le bout. (l.18–20)

[They passed a stick sideways through her mouth. / 'Hold tight!' they said. 'Be careful not to let go.' / Then each duck took one end of the stick.]

The tone and mood change abruptly here as the ducks get down to business. Both the narrative and their speech become crude, simple and straightforward. All the hyperbole disappears. The tortoise is no longer a *précieuse* on a culture trip round the world, she is an animal with a 'gueule' (literally a 'muzzle'); the 'machine' has become a simple 'stick'; instead of the comfortable trip in a 'voiture' she has been promised, she is told grimly to hang on for her life. The fairy tale is over, and reality has taken its place. The image of the ducks as confidence tricksters is complete when we see how far the reality of what they have to offer falls short of the yarns they were spinning when setting up the deal.

Focusing on the ducks adds a new dimension to this fable in a number of ways. First, it reveals a poem richer in character portraits than first appears. Secondly, it makes the moral more complex. The tortoise's fault, for which she is horribly punished when she falls from the sky, seems at first sight to be vanity: opening her mouth to show off, she lets go of the stick and falls. But in her earlier exchanges with the ducks she has also committed a number of other blunders, and listening to the far-fetched blandishments of the ducks is one of the worst. La Fontaine himself does not restrict the moral to the final vanity of the tortoise. He also derives explicit lessons from her response to the ducks. He makes this plain when he lists the weaknesses that have contributed to her destruction as 'indiscrétion ... / Imprudence, babil, et sotte vanité, / Et vaine curiosité' *[indiscretion, imprudence, prattle, stupid vanity and idle curiosity]* (l.32–4). Some of these faults could be seen as referring both to her final, fatal mistake and to her earlier acceptance of the ducks' proposition. Her 'indiscretion' and 'imprudence' are self-evident. Her 'prattle' is demonstrated not only when she speaks and so falls but when she initially gossips to the ducks. Her 'vanity' can be seen not only in her readiness to agree that she is a queen (which prompts her final, fatal words), but also in her eagerness to be thought of as a new Ulysses, or a cultured *précieuse* on a world tour. But one of her faults, her 'vain curiosity' does not apply to the events immediately preceding her fall, but does apply to her desire to see the world, fired up by the cunning ducks. In addition, focusing on the ducks obliges us to add yet another moral, unspoken but nevertheless present, to the several that the poet has put forward: don't be gullible, or you will come to grief.

One reason why these ducks tend to be overlooked is that the fable makes sense without singling them out for attention. Their portrait seems to be a perfect example of the gratuitous 'enrichments' which La Fontaine sought to include in the fables of his second *Recueil*.[177] Ostensibly, the ducks are enjoyable incidental characters, contributing to the reader's amusement, and helping to make the hideous suddenness of the tortoise's destruction seem comic rather than sinister. It is only after an analysis of their function that it emerges that they too have a contribution to make to the moral message.

The neglected character can have a still more complex effect on the fable, determining its shape, giving it a structure. This is very much the case with the fox in 'Le Fermier, le Chien et le Renard' *[The Farmer, the Dog and the Fox]* (XI 3). This fable tells the story of a farmer and his dog. A fox breaks into the farmyard and kills the chickens. The farmer blames his dog for not raising the alarm, but the moral shows him to be in the wrong for not protecting his own property himself. The fox plays only an incidental part, early in the poem; indeed, the best-known and most striking passage in the poem is a mock-heroic description of the carnage after the fox has been and gone. Describing it, the poet gives free rein to his parodic Homeric muse. The focus and interest of the poem seem clear. It is no wonder that the fox tends to be overlooked as a character in his own right, viewed as a simple instrument of destruction like the two ducks, and forgotten by the end of the fable, when the moral is seen to apply only to the farmer and his dog. And yet, as will be seen, the fox has his own very particular contribution to make to the poem.

If we approach the poem from the standpoint of the fox, there emerges a very interesting example of an underlying pattern of shapes, which as far as I know has not been noticed by other readers, but which gives this part of the fable a definite structure, and the whole fable an extra dimension.

The first part of the fable is about the violation of a safe haven when the fox breaks into the chicken-run and kills the chickens. The action, in which the predator circles and circles until he finds an opening, at which point he pounces, is echoed by a series of subtle allusions to circles, some of which are entirely indirect, but which together build up a clear shape to the poem, giving it an underlying geometry.

The poem begins with a general comment:

> Le Loup et le Renard sont d'étranges voisins:
> Je ne bâtirai point autour de leur demeure.

[The Wolf and the Fox are strange neighbours: / I will not build near their dwelling.]

Ostensibly 'autour' means 'near' here; but the word more properly means 'around'. The notion of the poet building a home which actually encompasses the two predators' is rejected but yet brought into play, and the pattern of one element encircling another is introduced. At the centre of the circle is a pair of animals, one of whom, the wolf, disappears, while the other, the fox, is to be our protagonist.

The focus shifts immediately to this fox. He is no longer at the centre of activity as in the opening lines, but outside it. This is clear from the next sentence: 'Ce dernier guettait à toute heure /

Les poules d'un fermier.' *[This latter kept constant watch / On a farmer's hens.]* He busies himself around the chicken-run. His uncertainty is given a backwards and forwards motion ('je vais, je viens' *[I come, I go]*), which corresponds to his ambivalence: 'D'une part l'appétit, de l'autre le danger' *[On the one hand, appetite, on the other, danger]* (l.6). However, the fox himself also introduces the notion of circularity in his description of his activities. First he says that in his efforts to break in, 'j'imagine cent tours' *[I imagine a hundred tricks]* (l.11). Of course, 'tours' are tricks, here, though the word can also mean 'circles'. But later we will be told 'le voleur tourne tant qu'il entre au lieu guetté' *[the robber goes round so much that he gets into the place he was watching]* (l.26): it was by going round and round that he finally found the way in, so that with hindsight the 'cent tours' do imply not only his clever stratagems, but also his circling movement.[178] Secondly, in a curious image, the fox likens the chickens to coins, resentfully comparing his frustration with the farmer's plenty:

> ... le rustre, en paix chez soi,
> Vous fait l'argent de tout, convertit en monnoie
> Ses chapons, sa poulaille. (l.11–13)

[The lout, comfortable in his home, / Makes money out of everything, converts / His capons, his poultry into cash.]

Again, the overt point of the comment is nothing to do with shape: the fox is simply furious because the farmer is coining money by owning chickens. However, he actually makes the farmer 'convert' the birds into coins ('monnoie'), which thus affords a fleeting picture of them reduced in size to perfect rounds, which will contrast with the much larger circles implied later.

The fox now swears by the gods to outwit the farmer. His oath fits with his predicament: 'je jure les puissances / De l'Olympe et du Styx' *[I swear by the powers / Of Olympus and the Styx]* (l.17–8). Again, the ostensible point of the invocation is clear and even banal; but again there is an underlying reiteration of the pattern already suggested. The gods who can grant his desire are seen in terms of their unattainable home on the top of Mount Olympus, whose central summit is denied to man. In this, Mount Olympus is like a grandiose version of the longed-for chicken-run, round which the fox is circling. The Styx, the river that surrounds the underworld in ancient legend, may seem to be included merely because the fox intends to kill the chickens, and send them down to the underworld. But the river also constitutes a barrier, since the dead must win the right to cross it; it is also, famously, a seven-fold circle. The fox revolves these ideas in his heart (literally, rolls them around – 'Roulant en son coeur ces vengeances' *[Rolling these vengeful ideas round his heart]*, l.19) – even within his mind he makes circles.

Now the scene is set for the drama. Every creature on the farm is asleep, unaware that the farmer has accidentally left the door of the hen-run open. The trusting sleep of the household is dwelt on, and the poet uses a plethora of 'o' sounds here, that are both soothing in sound, and also so many circles suggesting their false sense of being ringed round with security: 'Chacun était plongé dans un profond sommeil ... Poules, poulets, chapons, tout dormait' *[Everyone was plunged into a deep sleep ... Hens, chickens, capons, all were sleeping]* (l.21–3).

The fox gets in and kills all the chickens. At this stage, the chicken-run is compared to a besieged city which has finally been conquered. Clearly it was a walled city – otherwise the parallel with the fenced-in chicken-run would not suggest itself. And since the attacker went round it ('tourne tant', l.26), the wall was circular. Day breaks, and the carnage is so horrific that it almost interrupts the cycle of nature:

> Peu s'en fallut que le Soleil
> Ne rebroussât d'horreur vers le manoir liquide. (l.31–2)

[It almost happened that the horrified Sun / Went back down towards his watery home.]

Instead of completing his daily half-circle through the heavens, the sun almost reverses the circle and turns back, so unnatural was the mass slaughter of the poor chickens.

The combination of siege and sun-god naturally leads into the burlesque evocation of the Trojan war which I mentioned earlier as the most striking image in the poem.[179] The last of the images relevant to our theme occurs during the Trojan passage. In it the fox is compared to the great warrior Ajax, who during one night killed a vast quantity of oxen and sheep, mistaking them in the dark for the troops of a rival commander, again the ubiquitous Ulysses. We note in passing that the chickens have changed in size, from being as small as coins to being as big as oxen, while the fox has become man-size, and indeed hero-size ('Le Renard autre Ajax' *[The Fox, a second Ajax]*, 1.43). But for the circle theme the point to note is that Ajax is described as the central figure, piling the carcases up around his tent:

> Tel ... autour de sa tente
> Ajax à l'âme impatiente,
> De moutons et de boucs fit un vaste débris,
> Croyant tuer en eux son concurrent Ulysse ... (37–40)

[So, ... around his tent, / Ajax of the impatient soul / Made a vast heap of sheep and goats, / Thinking that he was killing his rival Ulysses ...]

The fox, having achieved his aim, has become the centre of the action. No longer circling round the unattainable, he has reached the mid-point of the circle, as suggested by the second use of 'autour' *[around]* in the poem. And thus the poem too has come full circle, as the fox, who was initially introduced as the central figure in 1.1–2, has come back to his original position. The underlying image of circling now disappears with the fox, as he slinks off carrying as many of his victims as he can. It remains for the poet to describe the aftermath of the event and point the moral of the poem.

Not only does this sustained patterning suggest a new dimension to the poem if it is viewed from the angle of the fox. It also contributes a further moral: the fox's patience and tenacity are rewarded with success. This new moral has two distinct implications. First, from the fox's point of view, we are shown that single-minded determination will solve the most intractable problems; secondly, from the farmer's angle, we see that no safeguards will ever prevent a truly determined onslaught on our property. Finally, there is an instructive contrast between the attitudes of the three eponymous characters. The farmer and the dog are marginally half-hearted about defending the hens, so lose them; but the fox is totally determined to get them, and so succeeds.

Giving their due to characters who generally tend to be overlooked can have a still more essential role to play in our understanding of the fables. It may indeed provide the only clue to explaining apparent inconsistencies in a fable, which otherwise may be difficult to interpret. I believe this to be the case with my third example, 'Démocrite et les Abdéritains' *[Democritus and the Abderites]* (VIII 26), which presents the reader with a number of puzzles.[180]

The poem appears at first to be unusually straightforward. It begins with a promythium, in which the poet states the case that is to form the argument of his fable, and in the strongest terms:

> Que j'ai toujours haï les pensers du vulgaire!
> Qu'il me semble profane, injuste, et téméraire;
> Mettant de faux milieux entre la chose et lui,
> Et mesurant par soi ce qu'il voit en autrui! (l.1–4)

[How I have always hated the views of the common people! / How profane, unjust and overbold they seem to me; / They put a false barrier between the world and themselves, / And measure up against themselves what they see in others!]

He goes on to illustrate his point by means of an apologue about Democritus, who was thought mad by the people of Abdera. They called the famous doctor Hippocrates to come and cure him. Hippocrates, having talked to him, realized that Democritus was as sane as ever. This story proves that ordinary people are poor judges, and not to be trusted.

At first sight, there appears to be little scope for alternative readings of this fable. The central figure is Democritus; the problem posed by the apologue is whether or not he is mad. The other characters mentioned in the title, the Abderites (les Abdéritains), serve merely to demonstrate the poet's contempt for ordinary people, and scarcely give us pause. The poet has made his scorn only too plain; it is an attitude that has the most distinguished of poetic credentials, echoing as it does Horace's 'Odi profanum vulgus'. The naive Abderites (who in any case had a reputation for stupidity in the ancient world[181]) are shown up in contrast to Democritus himself, who is far from the madman they think him. La Fontaine sums this up without compromise: 'Ces gens étaient les fous,

Démocrite le sage' *[These people were the mad ones, Democritus the wise one]* (l.8). When we meet Democritus, he is engaged in serious and abstruse research, probing 'les labyrinthes d'un cerveau' *[The labyrinths of a brain]* (l.34).[182] Hippocrates and Democritus reason together 'sur l'homme et sur l'esprit' *[on man and the mind]* (l.41). He is clearly at the height of his intellectual powers. It is tempting to dismiss the Abderites as utter fools, to assume that although they do rate a mention in the poem's title they are without interest apart from their stupidity, and to conclude that La Fontaine has proved his point.

However, if we look again at these events, concentrating this time on what La Fontaine actually says about the Abderites, rather than dismissing them out of hand as fools, the situation looks much more complex. Their view of the condition of Democritus is quoted at some length in their invitation to Hippocrates to come and cure him:

> Notre concitoyen, disaient-ils en pleurant,
> Perd l'esprit: la lecture a gâté Démocrite.
> Nous l'estimerions plus s'il était ignorant.
> Aucun nombre, dit-il, les mondes ne limite:
> > Peut-être même ils sont remplis
> > De Démocrites infinis.
> Non content de ce songe, il y joint les atomes,
> Enfants d'un cerveau creux, invisibles fantômes;
> Et, mesurant les cieux sans bouger d'ici-bas,
> Il connaît l'univers et ne se connaît pas.
> Un temps fut qu'il savait accorder les débats;
> > Maintenant il parle à lui-même.
> Venez, divin mortel; sa folie est extrême. (l.13–25)[183]

['Our fellow-citizen', said they, weeping, / 'Is losing his mind. Too much reading has ruined Democritus. / We would respect him more if he were ignorant. / He says there is no limit to the numbers of worlds: / Perhaps they are filled with infinite numbers of Democrituses. / Not content with this fantasy, he adds atoms, / The progeny of a hollow brain, invisible phantoms; / And, measuring the heavens without moving from here below, / He knows the universe and does not know himself. / There was a time when he knew how to resolve a debate; / Now he talks to himself. / Come, divine mortal, his madness is extreme.']

Judging from this speech, what sort of people are the Abderites? Are they indeed 'mad', as La Fontaine tells us later? Let us look back over their actions and words. From the start of the poem, their distress demonstrates their compassion and concern, and makes them seem endearing rather than ridiculous.[184] Next, their comment that they would feel esteem for Democritus even if he were ignorant (l.15) shows a commendable respect for the man himself, as opposed to the trappings of his scholarship. The assumption that he must have lost his mind is based on sound reasoning: his personality has changed, and he no longer helps to maintain the peace between them. Worse, he now talks to himself (l.23–5). They take the sensible and logical step of inviting the most distinguished doctor of the time to come and treat the patient.

But at the heart of their speech is their account of Democritus's philosophy. And here again they show a clear understanding of the issues raised. Admittedly, they reject his ideas, but they sum them up succinctly, and the logic behind their thinking is flawless. The first theory (l.16–18) is that of the 'pluralité des mondes' *[plurality of worlds]*.[185] The Abderites unerringly focus on the eccentric aspect of Democritus's version of the theory: not only are there an infinite number of other worlds, but they are the same as ours. The Abderites wittily pick out the oddity of Democritus's conclusion (that there must exist an infinite number of other Democrituses since there is an infinite number of other worlds), and express it as a kind of joke, exaggerating the number of Democrituses in each world, so that we have the fleeting picture of numberless planets full of nothing but Democrituses (l.16–18).

The second theory of Democritus to be rejected by the Abderites is that of the existence of atoms. Here there is less right on their side, since modern science, while rejecting the idea of infinitely reproduced identical worlds, wholeheartedly accepts the existence of atoms. However, the Abderites do give a valid reason for their inability to accept Democritus's idea: they find it impossible to accept something for which their senses offer no evidence, 'invisibles fantômes'.

The third idea to be rejected, in l.21, is a more technical matter of the measurement of distances outside the earth, presumably using trigonometry. Here again, the Abderites are relying on common sense, and are unable to appreciate the abstruse reasoning of

Democritus. The Abderites' attitude to both these two points can be compared to La Fontaine's own view, expressed in VII 17 'Un Animal dans la lune' *[An Animal in the moon]*. Here he maintains that the evidence of the senses should be combined with scientific knowledge to give an accurate picture. If nothing else, the Abderites are at least demonstrating logic and common-sense here, and so are half-way to the truth.

The Abderites conclude their verdict on Democritus with a pithy line,[186] which neatly encapsulates their view of him, at the same time allowing his theories the benefit of the doubt: 'Il connaît l'univers et ne se connaît pas' *[He knows the universe and does not know himself]*. Quite apart from its elegant formulation, which itself says much about the Abderites' ability to assess a situation, this seems a fair summary. If Democritus is no longer behaving normally as a social being, he has to some extent lost touch, however well he may know the universe.

There is some sense in the Abderites' speech; but is followed by the meeting between Democritus and Hippocrates, in which it is made clear that far from being mad, Democritus is a genius, and the Abderites totally misguided. La Fontaine concludes his fable with a summary of the main point, which appears to reinforce the general view that the common people's judgment is sadly lacking:

> Le récit précédent suffit
> Pour montrer que le peuple est juge récusable.
> En quel sens est donc véritable
> Ce que j'ai lu dans certain lieu,
> Que sa voix est la voix de Dieu? (l.45–49)

[The foregoing account is enough / To show that the populace is an untrustworthy judge. / In what sense then is it true / – As I have read somewhere – / That its voice is the voice of God?]

This final *envoi* is the source of the puzzlement which I mentioned at the start of this analysis. For the above passage is far from straightforward. No sooner has La Fontaine affirmed the moral in lines 45 and 46 than he casts doubt upon it. In the last line of the poem, he introduces a new and opposite view of the judgments of the common people: they are said to speak with the voice of God. Their opinions are no longer hateful and mad, but divine. La

Fontaine does not say that he agrees with this verdict; yet it seems over-hasty to assume that he rejects it. He asks a simple question, and leaves it to the reader to decide. Commentators are unclear as to the significance of this interrogative ending. Collinet quotes a passage from d'Assoucy, which La Fontaine may well have known: 'Je sais bien que quelque sot me dira que la voix du peuple est la voix de Dieu, mais je sais aussi qu'il y aura quelque sage qui dira que la voix du peuple est la voix des sots' *[I know full well that some fool will tell me that the voice of the people is the voice of God, but I also know that some wise man will tell me that the voice of the people is the voice of fools]* (p.1219). It is tempting to assume that if La Fontaine is remembering this passage, he is alluding to the well-known *vox populi, vox dei* in a spirit of comic irreverence, since this sidesteps the issue of possible ambiguity in the portrayal of the people. However, the early La Fontaine commentator, Chamfort, writes: 'La Fontaine prend l'air du doute par respect pour l'Ecriture, dont ces paroles sont tirées' *[La Fontaine takes on an air of uncertainty through respect for the Scriptures, from where these words are taken]* (*GEF* II 345). Chamfort's facts are incorrect, as the words are from a popular saying, and not from the Scriptures; but, as Michael Vincent points out (p.37–8), Chamfort is right in detecting a feeling of respect behind La Fontaine's words, whatever their inspiration. And, as we have seen, the Abderites have, by their own reported words, proved that common people such as they are not complete fools, but thought-ful, caring and worthy citizens.

Whatever the poet's inner thoughts, the final line itself is reso-nant, powerful and famous, and carries with it its own dignity. Although he ends on a question mark, La Fontaine allows the link between the people and God to remain in our minds in a memo-rable conclusion to his poem. The line resembles other grave and beautiful endings to fables which may have seemed frivolous till that moment.[187] The beauty of the line requires us to take it seri-ously. La Fontaine is asking us whether what to some is a position of ridicule, may not to others be the voice of God himself. Although overtly La Fontaine endorses the negative view of the common people, the poem's final line cannot help but cast a shadow of doubt on the message of the rest. Perhaps the final moral should be that we cannot judge the common people, since there is more to them than meets the eye.

In all my examples, examination of the neglected characters in a fable reveals further morals concealed behind the obvious and explicit one. My final case demonstrates how, by giving all the characters their due, the fabulist can encompass completely different problems in one poem, and produce a variety of morals. An unusual example of a three-sided fable, 'Le Chat, la Belette et le petit Lapin' *[The Cat, the Weasel and the little Rabbit]* is rewarding to examine in this spirit, since here each of the three protagonists is in a very different position from the other two.

The fable tells of a rabbit who leaves his burrow one morning, only to find, on his return, that a weasel squatter has moved in. The latter refuses to budge, and suggests that they go to a cat-judge for arbitration. The cat solves the problem by eating both plaintiff and defendant. The epimythium declares that minor rulers who choose kings as arbiters may suffer the same fate. La Fontaine's overt moral, however, fails to do justice to the individual fates of the three protagonists.

To start with the rabbit, his death demonstrates the extent to which the weak can be victims of injustice, for he is entirely blameless. Let us look first at how La Fontaine brings this implied moral home. The rabbit epitomizes innocence. We are told from the start that he is a youngster, a 'petit Lapin' *[little Rabbit]*, a 'jeune Lapin' *[young Rabbit]*. Describing his morning outing, La Fontaine stresses its harmlessness and charm, and gives it an endearing comic dimension. The outrage occurs

> ... un jour
> Qu'il était allé faire à l'Aurore sa cour,
>   Parmi le thym et la rosée.
> Après qu'il eut brouté, trotté, fait tous ses tours,
> Janot Lapin retourne aux souterrains séjours. (l.5–9)

[One day, / He had gone to pay court to Aurora /Amongst the thyme and the dew. / When he had nibbled the grass, trotted about, run all his errands, / Janot Lapin returned to his subterranean dwelling]

The atmosphere of the classical pastoral eclogue is evoked in the reference to rabbit as a courtier of the goddess Aurora. The mention of thyme and dew gives the lines a conventional prettiness. An ominous glimpse of a darker classical world is conjured up by the description of the burrow as a 'subterranean dwelling', with its echoes of the Vergilian underworld. Juxtaposed with the countrified name of the prince of this underworld, Janot Lapin, this takes on a comic, burlesque quality. The undignified, rabbit-like actions of Janot, chewing grass and trotting about, build up the animal side of the comparison, and contrast amusingly with the higher register of the other elements here.[188] The whole picture makes Janot Lapin seem endearing. Having got the reader on the rabbit's side, the poet recounts Janot's argument with the weasel, in which he produces reasoned and legally unimpeachable arguments:

> Jean Lapin allégua la coutume et l'usage.
> Ce sont, dit-il, leurs lois qui m'ont de ce logis
> Rendu maître et seigneur, et qui de père en fils,
> L'ont de Pierre à Simon, puis à moi Jean transmis. (l.25–8)

[Jean Lapin pleaded custom and usage. / He said: 'It is their laws that have made me lord / And master of this house, and which from father to son, / Have passed it from Pierre to Simon, then to me, Jean.']

So Jean Lapin is not only engaging but also reasonable. And his brutal elimination by the cat-judge, who 'Mit les plaideurs d'accord en croquant l'un et l'autre' (l.45) seems doubly harsh as a result, and proves to the reader that the world is an unfair place.

The weasel is depicted with much less approval. The poem begins:

> Du palais d'un jeune Lapin
> Dame Belette un beau matin
> S'empara; c'est une rusée.

[One fine morning, Lady Weasel / Took possession of a young Rabbit's palace. / She is a crafty creature.]

The poet has already judged her to be a cunning manipulator; he also makes it clear here where justice lies – the palace belongs to the rabbit, and the weasel has seized it unlawfully. When the weasel is challenged by the rabbit, she produces a series of glib but unconvincing arguments to justify her action: first, the burrow is unworthy of all this fuss (l.18–19); next, it seems unacceptable that according to the law, property is normally inherited rather than going to random people (l.20–4). It is the weasel who suggests that the two animals should go to the cat for arbitration (l.30–1).

From the weasel's point of view, La Fontaine's explicit moral does seem relevant: she pays the penalty for seeking justice from one more powerful than herself. La Fontaine comments:

> Ceci ressemble fort aux débats qu'ont parfois
> les petits souverains se rapportants aux Rois. (l.46–7)

[This is very like what sometimes happens / When lesser sovereigns appeal to kings to settle their disputes.]

But there are additional morals here. First, the weasel's fate also demonstrates that wickedness tends not to go unpunished. Next, it shows that one cannot necessarily harm with impunity those weaker than oneself. There is a parallel between the fate of the weasel and the moral of Aesop's version of 'The Frog and the Rat', as told by La Fontaine in his 'Life of Aesop': 'un plus puissant que nous me vengera: je périrai; mais vous périrez aussi' *[A greater power than we will avenge me. I shall perish; but you will perish too]* (Collinet, p.26). The rabbit could have addressed the weasel in Aesop's words. From the weasel's angle, then, the poem becomes one of the numerous 'trompeur trompé' *[deceiver deceived]* fables in the collection.

The third character, the cat, is described by La Fontaine with an unusual wealth of literary allusion. He combines the sanctimonious hypocrisy of Molière's Tartuffe with a more secular brand of insincerity taken from Rabelais and others.[189] The well-known literary references tell us from the start that the cat is not to be trusted, since they remind us of a number of fictional characters, all hypocrites. He is first mentioned by his name, Raminagrobis, which is a traditional name for a prince of cats and also for a hypocrite. *GEF* quotes Noel du Fail: 'on parle peu, avec un haussement d'espaules et yeux sourcilleux et admiratifs, en faisant bien le Raminagrobis ... ' *[one says little, with a shrug of the shoulders and caring, admiring eyes, doing a good imitation of Raminagrobis]*(II 188). Next, he is 'Un chat faisant la chattemite' *[a cat playing the part of 'chattemite']*, the last word being a term employed by Rabelais (Collinet quotes Richelet's dictionary: 'Mot vieux et burlesque, qui signifie hypocrite', *[an old-fashioned, burlesque word meaning a hypocrite]* p.1184). La Fontaine now gives us a brief character-sketch of Raminagrobis in religious terms that echo Molière's descriptions of his Tartuffe: 'un dévot ermite' *[a pious hermit]*, 'Un saint homme de Chat, bien fourré, gros et gras' *[a holy man of a Cat, well stuffed, big and fat]* (Molière's character eats huge meals 'fort dévotement' *[very piously]*, and is 'gros et gras, le teint vermeil' *[big and fat, with a ruddy complexion]*). He also calls the cat 'bien fourré' *[well stuffed]*, in an allusion to Rabelais's predatory 'chats fourrés' *[stuffed cats]*. Before the cat has spoken a single word, the literary references have made the reader aware that he is false and probably dangerous. His claim that he is old, deaf and benevolent ('Mes enfants, approchez, / Approchez, je suis sourd, les ans en sont la cause' *[My children, come closer, / Come closer, I'm deaf, it's because of my age]*) is unconvincing.[190] The cat is an instrument of destruction, and it comes as no surprise when he kills and eats both the weasel and the rabbit.

When we focus on the cat, the moral seems different again. The poet demonstrates that those who are known to be powerful and malevolent will not change their natures, and are not to be trusted, however much they may protest their goodwill. This too is a familiar La Fontaine moral, found in other cat fables.[191]

It can be seen then that giving all three protagonists of the fable the weight that they deserve means that the fable emerges as much richer and more complex than La Fontaine himself indicates in his rather simple epimythium. It incorporates an apparent contradiction: from the weasel's point of view, the fable demonstrates that cunning is not always rewarded, but from the cat's angle it shows that cunning does prevail if backed up by force. However, it is not difficult to reconcile these inconsistencies, and to see a clear message emerging from the whole. Overall, the fable gives us a hierarchical view of the world. Innocent weaklings are everybody's victims. Tricksters can win through guile alone, but unless their cunning is matched by strength, their victory will be only temporary. But those who combine craft with strength and lack of principle will score the final success. This cynical scale of values accords perfectly with the message of other fables.

*   *   *

In examining how the use of multiple perspectives can enrich and sometimes alter our interpretation of a poem, I have so far been focusing on the titles of the *Fables*, selecting for scrutiny those eponymous characters whose fate tends to be overlooked. It could be interesting and productive to take this process further.

First, why are some characters named in the titles, while others are omitted? One might have expected that 'Les Compagnons d'Ulysse' *[Ulysses's Companions]* would be called 'Ulysse et ses Compagnons' *[Ulysses and his Companions]*. By refraining from casting Ulysses in the title role, is La Fontaine inviting us to view the hero's arguments as secondary, focusing the reader's attention firmly on the companions instead? And does this perhaps reinforce the message that the poet ironically pretends to reject at the end of the poem: the companions are in the right to refuse to be men? Another potentially fruitful approach is the order in which the eponymous characters are named. Sometimes the poet appears to be governed by reasons of euphony: in 'Les Souris et le Chat-Huant' *[The Mice and the Screech-Owl]*, for example, the paralysed mice take unjustifiable precedence over their owl-conqueror. In 'Le Chat, la Belette et le petit Lapin' *[The Cat, the Weasel and the little Rabbit]*, however, the order corresponds to the respective power of the characters, with the cat much the strongest, dominating the weasel who in turn browbeats the helpless rabbit.

What of the fables in which the titles make no mention of any characters, but instead emphasize more abstract elements, such as 'Les Souhaits' *[The Wishes]*, 'L'Education' or 'L'Avantage de la Science'? I suspect that we are here being invited to regard the characters as less important. A further line of approach could be to compare the titles used by La Fontaine with those of his sources: for example, Baudoin's fable 'Du Lion, du Renard et du Loup' *[Of the Lion, the Fox and the Wolf]*, in La Fontaine's version, is given the far more sinister, powerful and interesting title of 'Les Animaux malades de la peste' *[The Animals sick of the plague]*.

We can gain insight into La Fontaine's attitude to the relationship of titles, characters and text from the fable 'A Monseigneur le duc de Bourgogne'. La Fontaine was given the title 'Le Chat et la Souris' *[The Cat and the Mouse]* by the king's small grandson, with the request that he write a fable to go with it; he immediately invents a range of characters who could fit the roles, a beautiful girl, a king, Fortune, the young prince himself. Interestingly, he ends up writing about – a simple cat and mouse.

CHAPTER 9

The poet's voice

There is no such thing as unbiased narrative. Every author chooses what to include and what to omit, and this inevitably slants the resulting text. This is true of all writing, from nursery rhymes to obituaries. In the *Fables* we see this process constantly in operation, for instance in the perfunctory treatment of violence and death. Deaths are mostly passed over without explanation or comment: the poet is systematically avoiding confronting the reader with the grim implications of his material. By such means, he infiltrates the text, an invisible yet perceptible presence.

As it is fables that La Fontaine is writing, there is an additional reason for regarding his authorial intervention as inevitable. A fable, being a moral tale traditionally aimed at teaching a lesson, *must* express a clear point of view. The recipient of a fable can expect guidance from the fabulist, an explanation of the significance of his message. For this reason alone, we can look for a narratorial presence in the *Fables*.

La Fontaine appears quite willing to show his hand as narrator. He readily incorporates value-judgments, openly directing the reader towards a particular standpoint. Almost any fable will demonstrate this point. For example, in IX 18 'Le Milan et le Rossignol' (in which a kite catches and kills a nightingale), the poet clearly indicates his opinion of the two protagonists from the start. In the first line, we are told that the kite is a 'manifeste voleur' *[obvious thief]*. When the nightingale lands in his clutches, the event occurs 'par malheur' *[unfortunately]* (l.4): the narrator is definitely on the nightingale's side against the kite. This reinforces the message of the fable and guides the reader towards the conclusion, since the poem proves that the powerful are implacably bent on crushing the weak, and cannot be swayed. For this message to come across, the strong character in the fable must seem inhuman and the weak one endearing; in La Fontaine's treatment, the nastiness and brutality of the dominant character's destructive behaviour hits us with full force. Here, then, the narrator's stance is unequivocal, and reinforces the moral of the fable.

This straightforward alliance between narrator and reader, in which there is no ambivalence about the interpretation of the material, is traditionally regarded as essential to the fable genre. La Fontaine himself implies this in the Preface to the first *Recueil*, in which he tells us, citing Plato, that fables are helpful in educating children, 'car on ne saurait s'accoutumer de trop bonne heure à la sagesse et à la vertu' *[for it is never too early to accustom oneself to wisdom and virtue]*. If the fables are to inculcate these qualities into children, they must convey an unambiguous message. The moral should come across loud and clear; it will then strike the child as more memorable than a straightforward factual account, since a fable is a work 'plus conforme et moins disproportionné ... à la petitesse de son esprit' *[better suited to and less inappropriate for... his immature mind]* (Préface, p.8).

But the reader who assumes that La Fontaine's motives are honestly explained in his Preface, and, on reading through the poems, concludes that in each fable the narrator offers an unequivocal message, is profoundly misguided. Such artlessness from a writer like La Fontaine, that master of subtlety and nuance, would be surprising indeed. And yet in the poems, superficially at least, the narrator conveys a feeling of directness and candour. Are we to conclude that this is a misleading impression? Do the fables in fact contain covert verdicts on the material, but so artfully incorporated that at first sight they give the illusion of being simplistic? Is the poet pretending to make simple points, but instead saying something much more complex? With these questions in mind, I want to examine the use of narrative voice in the *Fables*. I shall be looking first at the poet's standpoint in third-person narrative, and will then move on to the question of first-person narration, and of the identity of 'je' in these poems.

Let us start by looking at an example of an apparently straightforward fable, told in the third person, to see if there is more to the narrative voice than meets the eye.

VI 8 'Le Vieillard et l'Ane'
Un Vieillard sur son Ane aperçut en passant
Un pré plein d'herbe et fleurissant.
Il y lâche sa Bête, et le Grison se rue

Au travers de l'herbe menue,
5   Se vautrant, grattant, et frottant,
Gambadant, chantant et broutant,
Et faisant mainte place nette.
L'ennemi vient sur l'entrefaite.
Fuyons, dit alors le Vieillard.
10   Pourquoi? répondit le Paillard.
Me fera-t-on porter double bât, double charge?
Non pas, dit le Vieillard, qui prit d'abord le large.
Et que m'importe donc, dit l'Ane, à qui je sois?
Sauvez-vous, et me laissez paître:
15   Notre ennemi c'est notre maître:
Je vous le dis en bon françois.

*['The Old Man and the Donkey'. / An old man on his donkey noticed /
A grassy, flowery meadow as he rode past. / He unharnessed his beast,
and the donkey raced / Over the tender grass, / Flung himself down,
scratching and rubbing himself. / He gambolled, brayed and cropped
the grass, / Eating it away in several places. / During all this, the
enemy appeared. / Then the old man said: 'Let's run away.' / 'Why?'
said the Donkey. 'What difference does it make to me whom I belong
to? / Make your escape and leave me to graze. / Our enemy is our master; / I tell you so in good French.']*

This seems like a simple story, told without disguise: an old man
sees a lovely meadow and unharnesses his donkey so that the beast
can enjoy it. An enemy appears, and the old man suggests they run
away. But the donkey refuses on the grounds that one master is as
good as another. His refusal incorporates the moral. This moment
gives us our first inkling that the narrator's position is not entirely
straightforward: the moral is spoken by a character, not directly by
the poet.[193] Therefore the poem contains no overt authorial judgment. Instead, readers are manipulated to experience the events
from a particular point of view, which will colour their response.

Looking back over the narrative, other ambiguities become
apparent. First, we should note the difference in treatment between
the three characters. The enemy is portrayed as completely colourless – the poet makes sure that we waste no time thinking about
him. Indeed, so faceless is he that we have no idea whether the
word 'ennemi' is singular or collective, and we are obliged to resort

for elucidation to Chauveau's illustration, in which we see a distant army approaching.[194] The old man is also underemphasized: all we learn is that he is kind enough to allow his donkey freedom to graze. We are told in passing that he escapes the enemy in l.12, a fact which further contributes to making him unremarkable, since it prevents us from feeling interested in him as an unfortunate victim.

As for the donkey, the poet lavishes all his attention on building up this one character, but in doing so, achieves a very particular result. To begin with, the donkey is full of enthusiasm and vitality, but remains more animal than anthropomorphic. The description of his antics on being let loose in the field is so realistic that it gives the lie to those who maintain that La Fontaine's animal creations are invariably taken from literary tradition, not life.[195] This donkey scratches, brays, rolls, rubs himself, and grazes greedily. The string of verbs gives the impression of constant activity, conveying the animal's enthusiasm at his unexpected treat. The names the poet gives the donkey also make him seem like an ordinary, menial animal rather than an anthropomorphic cipher or an appropriate mentor for man. He is called 'bête' with its double meaning of animal and fool, and 'grison' (which gives the impression of a grey, dull figure, and also of a social inferior[196]). One should also note that the donkey's personality is brought to life well before it is revealed that he is a talking animal: his character as a dumb beast is established first.[197]

In l.10, the donkey speaks for the first time. After he has spoken just one word, 'Why?', the narrator steps in to add a new trait to his character portrait, with the only overtly judgmental comment in the poem. He calls the donkey a 'Paillard', which Furetière defines as 'un puissant coquin' *[a mighty scoundrel]*. The animal's impertinence at presuming to answer his master back and questioning the master's decision is indicated before he is allowed to explain his position.

So before the donkey can speak the epimythium of the fable, La Fontaine has built him up into a lively, cheeky, strikingly animal figure, whose reactions are graceless and instinctive. This character portrait has a considerable impact on the poem, affecting our attitude to the moral as spoken by the donkey.

The moral is voiced in the penultimate line: 'Notre ennemi c'est notre maître' *[our enemy is our master]*. It seems straightforward, the expression of an obvious truth. The donkey's speech is as crude and natural as his earlier behaviour. But it is in this line that the general moral comes out, and it becomes clear why the donkey has been portrayed as such a simple animal, so different from man. For this line, rejecting authority, has been described as one of the most outspokenly subversive in the whole of La Fontaine.[198] In a more anthropomorphic context, one in which the relevance of the fable to the human condition was at the forefront of the reader's mind, it would have stood out as shockingly forthright. As it is, the emphasis on the speaker's animality enables the line to be slipped in unobtrusively as a throwaway remark spoken by a simple beast of burden. Simultaneously, however, the poet draws our attention in this line to the fact that the statement is a general truth. The use of 'nous' makes it clear that the words no longer apply to the donkey alone. Further, the words themselves, though superficially self-evident, have a paradoxical, oxymoronic quality, 'ennemi' and 'maître' being treated as syntactically synonymous, with the implication that they are in fact opposites – although they are neither the one nor the other. So though unobtrusive, the line is complex, and on examination is revealed to have significant implications for the attentive reader.

The next and final line of the poem reinforces the relevance of the message to La Fontaine's contemporaries, when the donkey unexpectedly describes himself as speaking 'good French'. Though strictly speaking this simply means that he speaks without ambiguity, there is also an implicit association of the donkey with France. Few of the animal characters in the *Fables* are stated to be French.[199] The fables taken from classical sources most often preserve the atmosphere of the ancient world. In order to make this a Francophone donkey, La Fontaine has had to update his source, a Latin version by Phaedrus.[200] The French allusion is thus likely to attract the attention of the reader familiar with the *Fables*, and to seem more than a throwaway comment. Is the poet drawing our attention to the relevance of the donkey's message to contemporary Frenchmen?

La Fontaine is disingenuous in claiming, in his Preface, that his fables are straightforward. There is much more to narrative voice than this. In this poem it has become a complex element, characterized by artful suggestion rather than blatant obviousness. The poet has become far more than a mere story-teller: he has manipulated and subverted his material. The reader has had to work to keep up. However, this fable is slightly unusual in that it lacks the element of irony, which repeatedly subverts the moral of other fables, and gives the lie to the poet's claim to be writing simply and directly. It is self-evident that an ironic narrative voice will obfuscate the message of a fable and complicate the reader's response, since irony implies a double standpoint and directness a single one. Examples of this in the *Fables* are numerous indeed, but it is worth going into the process in some detail because it operates on a particularly subtle level.

We have already seen La Fontaine indicating his standpoint indirectly, through the mouth of a character, when he makes his donkey speak the moral. This technique readily lends itself to ironic treatment: if the author does not intervene, the character may seem inadequate, and the moral be subverted. This subversion can occur at other points in a fable. 'Le Berger et son Troupeau' *[The Shepherd and his Flock]* (IX 19) begins with a lament by a shepherd, Guillot, for Robin, his pet sheep, who has been carried off by the wolf.

> Quoi toujours il me manquera
> Quelqu'un de ce peuple imbécile!
> Toujours le Loup m'en gobera!
> J'aurai beau les compter: ils étaient plus de mille,
> Et m'ont laissé ravir notre pauvre Robin;
> Robin Mouton qui par la ville
> me suivait pour un peu de pain … (l.1–7)

[What? Must I always be missing / One of this imbecile race? / Must the wolf always keep gobbling them up? / It's no good my counting them. / There were more than a thousand of them, / But they let him snatch our poor Robin, / Robin Sheep, who used to follow me / Through the town for a piece of bread …]

This speech is touching in its heartfelt simplicity; but we cannot fail to notice that it is couched in prosaic, clumsy language. Despite our initial sympathy, we can already sense mockery at the speaker's expense. His vocabulary is crude ('imbecile', 'gobble'), his activities humdrum (counting sheep, feeding them bread), his expression muddled (with whom does Guillot associate himself when he says '*our* Robin'? The other sheep, unspecified fellow-shepherds, or his own family?). The shepherd's problems too seem mundane, as he repeatedly and anxiously counts his sheep and tries to control them. In this part of the poem, then, the speaker's clumsy tone, as quoted by the narrator, makes him seem a somewhat ridiculous figure, although he is taking himself entirely seriously.

As well as this banality, Guillot's speech also demonstrates a clumsy attempt to imitate a formal lament for the dead. Some of the tropes here could in fact be seen as ludicrous parodies of the rhetoric of a real funeral oration – for example the combination of hyperbole, ejaculation and repetition ('What? Always ... always'), or the general apostrophe which resolves into a personal lament. Hence the speech in all its crude simplicity may even contain a hint of mockery at the expense of the real orations which were by all accounts among the most extravagant literary occasions of the age.[201]

The narrative now continues in the third person, and the irony becomes more apparent, reinforcing the impression that there is more to Guillot's speech than simple pathos:

> Quand Guillot eut fini cette oraison funèbre,
> Et rendu de Robin la mémoire célèbre,
> Il harangua tout le troupeau,
> Les chefs, la multitude, et jusqu'au moindre agneau,
> les conjurant de tenir ferme ... (l.12–16)

[When Guillot had finished this funeral oration, / And caused Robin's memory to be celebrated, / He harangued the whole flock, / The leaders, the multitude, down to the smallest lamb, / Urging them to stand firm ...]

The poet's attitude to Guillot is conveyed through the irony in the tone. The first thing to note, in the light of my earlier comments, is that Guillot's little speech, in all its banality, is now openly called a 'funeral oration'. La Fontaine takes his scepticism a step further when he tells us that the memory of Robin Mouton has been preserved for posterity by Guillot's oration, since the reader knows that the silly little speech was delivered to nobody but a flock of sheep. These sheep are, however, described in inappropriately grandiose terms as a well-organized company with leaders ('les chefs') and common people ('la multitude') whom their master 'harangues' – could this even be a sly dig at Parisian society, which flocked like sheep to hear orations by the likes of Bossuet?

Overall, the tone of the narrative here is mocking and disparaging of Guillot. Yet beneath the irony the poet also preserves an element of indulgent, good-humoured affection for this simple rustic who takes life and its responsibilities so seriously. And all this is conveyed without a single overt value-judgment from the poet. So far, then, the author's assessment of Guillot's words has retrospectively clothed them with a veil of irony.

The greatest complications with this poem arise when we get to the epimythium. In giving the moral, the poet makes it clear that the fable is supposed to be an indictment of the weakness of the sheep, who, in spite of all Guillot's laudable efforts to rally them, fail to make a stand against the wolf. The fable concludes by spelling out the human implications:

> Haranguez les méchants soldats,
> Ils promettront de faire rage;
> Mais au moindre danger adieu tout leur courage:
> Votre exemple et vos cris ne les retiendront pas. (1.28–30)

[You can lecture bad soldiers, / And they will promise to do their worst; / But at the least whiff of danger, they'll bid their courage farewell. / Your example and your cries will not hold them back.]

At this stage, it becomes apparent that through the irony we have observed, La Fontaine has undermined the overt moral of his fable. If the poet has shown us the shepherd as an absurd figure, and his attempts to harangue the sheep as laughable, then how can we take the fabulist seriously when in the epimythium he censures the sheep for not obeying orders? In this example, there can be no doubt that the ironic narrative tone has complicated the situation so far as to change the message of the fable. The point of the fable is finally unclear; there may perhaps even be two contradictory messages. We remain uncertain even as to who is targeted, the unrealistic leader who tries ineffectually to control his subordinates, or his worthless inferiors who are too cowardly to obey him – with the possible addition, as I have suggested, of an implied criticism of the poet's contemporaries.

Even where the narrative voice is less subversive, the very presence of irony must of necessity devalue the moral of a fable, for the reason I have already given: the ironic narrator appears to have reservations about his own message. It does seem that the indulgent, light-hearted tone most often favoured by La Fontaine would be counterproductive if the poems were to be viewed purely as didactic fables. This can be demonstrated by taking a fable with a particularly straightforward narrative tone, one in which it seems at first sight that there is no ambivalence between the narrative voice and the message, and showing how even here the irony in the fable nevertheless clashes with the moral message. My example here is IX 5 'L'Ecolier, le Pédant et le Maître d'un jardin' *[The Schoolboy, the Pedant and the Owner of a garden]*, an attack on children and their teachers which on the surface seems unambiguous enough. The poet begins by openly expressing disapproval of the schoolboy (and his teacher) on two counts:

> Certain enfant qui sentait son collège,
> Doublement sot, et doublement fripon,
> Par le jeune âge, et par le privilège
> Qu'ont les Pédants de gâter la raison … (l.1–4)

[A certain child, a typical schoolboy, / Doubly stupid and doubly naughty / Because of his youth, and because of the privilege / That Pedants have of corrupting reason …]

The attack on both child and teacher is unequivocal here, and seems to represent an oft-rehearsed dislike on the poet's part. He will take up the cudgels again against both, later in the poem (and also against children in other late fables[202]). The fable tells of a child who climbs the trees in an orchard, whose owner complains to his schoolmaster. The schoolmaster then brings his pupils to the orchard to lecture them, but while he drones on his charges wreak havoc. The poet concludes:

> Je hais les pièces d'éloquence
> Hors de leur place, et qui n'ont point de fin;
>   Et ne sais bête au monde pire
> Que l'Ecolier, si ce n'est le Pédant.
> Le meilleur de ces deux pour voisin, à vrai dire,
>   Ne me plairait aucunement. (l.31–6)

[I hate eloquent set pieces / Which are not in their proper place, and which are never-ending; / I know no fool in the world worse / Than a schoolboy unless it is a Pedant. / To tell the truth, I would not be at all pleased / To have the better of the two for my neighbour.]

Here the double attack on the child and the teacher is repeated in more personal form. The passage shows the poet attacking the behaviour of the schoolmaster, whose ill-judged pedantry achieves the opposite of the desired effect. As for the child, his behaviour is beyond redemption – he is simply a 'bête' (which means 'fool' or 'beast'), who will never improve. The fable concludes with a pessimistic moral directed at the orchard's owner, who is implicitly blamed for trying to control the child and enlist the pedant's help: nothing can be done about such people, you just have to endure them. This final moral reinforces the unequivocal dislike of both pedant and child expressed in the poem, and both the fable's moral and the character portrayals appear entirely in accord with each other.

However, the above analysis presents a one-sided view of the poem. Although the poet voices his disapproval of the pedant and the child, the tone of the poem gives a very different impression. The story is told in a lively, witty manner (Sweetser detects echoes of Molière in it, 1 p.107), and the good-humoured narrative prevents the protagonists from seeming dislikeable, however deplorable their behaviour may be. To give a few instances, in the introductory lines quoted earlier, the way teachers destroy a child's natural good sense is described with witty irony as a 'privilege' (l.3). The lines describing the arrival of the teacher with the children are also tongue-in-cheek:

> Celui-ci vint suivi d'un cortège d'enfants.
> Voilà le verger plein de gens
> Pires que le premier. Le Pédant, de sa grâce,
> Accrut le mal en amenant
> Cette jeunesse mal instruite. (l.19–23)

[(The Teacher) came followed by a procession of children. / Now the orchard was full of people / Worse than the first. The Pedant, in his wisdom, / Made things worse by bringing along / These ill-educated youths.]

The 'cortège' of children follows in the wake of their master as though he were a monarch with his train. 'Cortège' is also associated with funerals, which gives a feeling both of ironic inappropriateness and appropriateness: it is inadmissible to use such a word to describe a rowdy gang of little ruffians; yet it seems admissible when we recall that they are following the funereal figure of the humourless old pedant. There is also a play on words which produces a similar dislocation when we are told 'Le Pédant, de sa grâce,/ Accrut le mal': 'de sa grâce' technically means simply 'on his own initiative', but 'grâce' has singularly inappropriate overtones for such an ill-judged and clumsy decision.

Throughout this poem, then, the strong disapproval expressed in the first person by the narrator is repeatedly undermined by the use of an inappropriate third-person narrative voice, and in particular of the sprightly, jocular tone. We are left unable to agree that children and teachers are the worst thing in the world, which is what we have been instructed to believe in the epimythium (l.33–4). Instead, the narrative voice has implied that they are the source of much amusement, not to be taken seriously as a disruptive element.

A further irony arises from the conclusion of the poem. As we have seen, La Fontaine singles out not the pedant himself but his wordy speech as his prime target (l.31). The pedant harangues his audience at length, but to no avail (as, incidentally, does Guillot the shepherd, capping his oration with a fruitless harangue). The discrepancy between the aims and the achievements of rhetoric as practised by incompetents is mocked in both these fables. In any case, the whole notion of ineffectual rhetoric is itself an absurdity, since rhetoric is supposed to be persuasive, not, as here, counterproductive. In order to enhance the absurdity of this, La Fontaine describes the events using an inappropriate register, further undermining the serious intent of the teacher's rhetoric by linguistic flippancy. Far from being a simple attack on teachers and children, then, this fable is in fact a complex work, in which the different ironies intertwine to subvert each other.[203]

The above examples suggest that the appropriate response to a La Fontaine fable may be suspicion. We cannot assume that the poet means us to take what he tells us at face value. By means of irony, he is constantly questioning, qualifying, subverting his own material. And yet, he also seems to speak from personal experience, an eye-witness to the events he describes. In the course of the third-person narration in my last example, he has intervened as 'je': we have seen him give as his own opinion that both teachers and children are loathsome, using the first person singular. This interpolation would tend to produce a very different impression. Whereas an ironic tone disguises the narrator beneath layers of indirectness, speaking in the first person makes a narrative seem authentic, the result of the author's own experience, the opposite of subversive, the opposite of ironic. Does the first-person narrative voice then counteract the ironic voice of the third-person narrator? What are we to make of the coexistence of the two seemingly contradictory elements, irony and first-person narration? Before addressing these questions, we must first sketch in the characteristics of La Fontaine's 'je' narrator.

In addition to the impression of honesty and directness, the first person appears to serve a number of functions in the *Fables*. Ostensibly, it seems to convey the poet's personality, in particular his modesty and self-deprecation; to establish a familiar rapport with the reader by the cosy, conversational tone; to enable the poet to share a joke with the reader. Generally, it conveys the impression that he is letting his own personality shine through, casting aside the formality of the fable genre to communicate directly with the reader. He seems to make his characters his own, referring to them with warm possessives: '*notre* Souriceau' *[our little mouse]*, VI 5; '*notre* Baudet' *[our Donkey]*, VIII 17; '*notre* maître ès arts' *[our master of arts]*, XI 5, etc. As Biard puts it, 'The voice of La Fontaine speaking *in propria persona* ... never fades out of the *Fables*, and its warm, cheerful, sensitive intonation is also heard in the narrative and descriptive passages' (Biard 1 p.87). But should we not also be suspicious of this voice?

* * *

Our first impression may well be that La Fontaine's first-person interpolations convey a feeling of cosy intimacy. This feeling is not necessarily to be trusted. Knowing the poet's oblique approach to his work, it is too simple to conclude that in his first-person interjections La Fontaine is making direct contact with the reader. He is rarely as obvious as this; indeed, his first-person narrative can actually play the paradoxical role of creating an impression of artificiality.

This alienation is only too apparent in the formal dedications, direct addresses to distinguished patrons or friends, which sometimes precede the apologue or fable proper.[204] Here the first person appears to be incorporated for reasons of convention, and does nothing to make the proceedings seem natural. As McGowan puts it, 'dans le contexte de l'éloge, c'était le rôle du poète de s'incorporer dans la facture de ses vers pour embellir ce qu'il avait à présenter' *[in the context of the eulogy, the poet's role was to include himself in the fabric of his verse to embellish what he had to present]* (McGowan 2 p.23). He dedicates his poems to a number of important people, ranging from the young princes of the ruling house ('A Monseigneur le Dauphin' which precedes Book I, XII 1 'Les Compagnons d'Ulysse, *A Monseigneur le Duc de Bourgogne*' and others) to influential friends like Mme Harvey, sister of the British Ambassador (XII 23 'Le Renard anglais'*[The English Fox]*), the French Ambassador Paul de Barrillon d'Amoncourt (VIII 4 'Le Pouvoir des Fables' *[The Power of Fables]*) or the Duc de la Rochefoucauld himself (I 11 'L'Homme et son image' *[The Man and his Image]*, X 14 'Discours a M. le duc de La Rochefoucauld'). These dedicatory verses tend to be artificial, elaborate affairs, the dedicatees often being given classical names. Mme de Montespan is Olympe in the poem that starts Book VII, Mme de la Sablière is Iris both in 'Discours à Mme de la Sablière' (Book IX, last fable) and in 'Le Corbeau, la Gazelle, la Tortue et le Rat' *[The Crow, the Gazelle, the Tortoise and the Rat]* (XII 15), which begins with an address to her by the poet in the language of classical hyperbole: 'Je vous gardais un temple dans mes vers: / Il n'eût fini qu'avecque l'univers' *[I was keeping a temple for you in my verse. / It would have ended only with the universe]*. Such opening lines situate the dedication firmly in the realms of neo-classical preciosity, an area where simple directness is out of the question. Here, then, the first person is associated with formality. The poet introduces himself in order to pay additional court to his dedicatees by personal flattery, performing an elaborate and insincere ritual.[205] So at the beginning of 'Les Compagnons d'Ulysse', he writes to the Duc de Bourgogne: 'Prince, l'unique objet du soin des Immortels,/ Souffrez que mon encens parfume vos autels' *[Prince, unique object of the Immortals' concern, / Suffer my incense to perfume your altars]* (XII 1 l.1–2), ostensibly bringing his own personal tribute to the young prince, yet simultaneously evoking ancient pagan religious beliefs and practices that have no relevance either to his dedicatee or to himself. It is surely not in such dedications that we will find the real La Fontaine.

However, such passages tend to be self-contained artefacts. Elsewhere, the poet seems to step in to introduce his material in a simpler manner. There are a number of first-person passages in which the poet is trying neither to impress important people, nor to make a serious or controversial point. This is the case with a number of apparently neutral first-person introductions to the poems, which take the form of matter-of-fact *entrées en matière*. Such introductions help to situate the poem or to present the material of the fable proper. Do they in addition provide us with an insight into the character of the narrator? Let us examine one such introduction, the beginning of ' Le Dépositaire infidèle' *[The fraudulent Banker]* (IX 1). In this case, the preamble is lent additional importance by the fact that it also forms the introduction to Book IX. The question we must consider is how the poet presents himself in the first few lines of this 40-line introduction:

> Grâce aux Filles de Mémoire,
> J'ai chanté des animaux
> Peut-être d'autres héros
> M'auraient acquis moins de gloire.
> Le Loup en langue des Dieux
> Parle au Chien dans mes ouvrages. (l.1–6)

[Thanks to the Daughters of Memory, / I have sung of animals. / Maybe other heroes/ Would have brought me less fame. / The Wolf in the language of the Gods / Talks to the Dog in my poems.]

The first sentence is an example of a seemingly informal 'je' interpolation. It apparently gives us a glimpse of a rare moment of unaffected and whimsical self-congratulation by the poet. He is endearingly delighted with his own success, yet humbly aware of his own shortcomings, an equally appealing trait. But that is the surface impression. On closer inspection, we can see that he both undermines his own self-praise by subtle self-mockery, and conversely counteracts his self-criticism by hints of self-approval. As Sweetser puts it talking of a similar introduction, 'Dans cet exorde se trouve un très savant dosage de fierté et de modestie' *[In this*

exordim we find a very skilful combination of pride and modesty]
(Sweetser 2 p.111).

He begins by explaining that by making his animals the subjects
of his poetry he has acquired fame. But already he is detracting
from this declaration of achievement: in his opening line he gives
all the credit not to his own gifts but to the Muses (the daughters
of Mnemosyne or Memory), then goes on to question whether his
talent would have been sufficient to bring him such renown if his
unusual characters had not captured the interest of the public. In
his next sentence (l.5–6) the poet appears still more modest. He
illustrates how intrinsically intriguing his animals are: a wolf who
can converse with a dog is likely to make the reader sit up and take
notice. The implication is that this would occur whatever the quality of the poet's input. In this self-deprecatory sentence, however,
he also slips in a sly hint of self-congratulation. He tells us that the
wolf speaks 'en langue des Dieux'. Technically, this simply means
that he talks in rhyme; but there is also the implication that his
language, as rendered by La Fontaine, is that of the gods themselves.

All this seems like a genuine, rather naive reproduction of the
mixed feelings with which a writer might greet success. The poet
wavers engagingly between pleasure at his own achievement and a
modest awareness that he does not deserve his fame. However, the
picture changes if we consider the impact of the passage on the
structure of the rest of the fable. We note that the poet has carefully avoided appearing either arrogant or complacent, while at the
same time hinting at his own worth. This prepares the reader for
the next section of the introduction, in which the author will go on
to list a series of character-types who form the *dramatis personae* of
the *Fables*. For these characters are described in terms of their faults
('Des Trompeurs, ... des Tyrans, et des Ingrats' *[Deceivers, ...
Tyrants and Ingrates]* etc, l.14–19). Character-portraits of this type
are bound to include an element of criticism or censure. So it has
been important, before revealing that he is a serious critic of man,
for the poet to present himself as of sufficient stature to be worthy
to tackle such material – without, of course, seeming over-earnest.
The first six lines of the poem, then, are carefully calculated to
present the fabulist in an appropriate light for what is to follow, as
a writer fitted both to 'instruct' and 'please'. What has seemed like
a spontaneous revelation is a calculated literary device.

It can be seen that in such first-person exordia the impression of any insight into the poet's personality is pure illusion. Such writing is strictly technical, designed to convey a message as effectively as possible. In passages like this, a first-person narrator has little if anything to tell us about the individual who was Jean de La Fontaine. The authenticity of the 'je' is spurious. And this conventional first-person voice is perfectly compatible with the dual standpoint of irony.

At the other end of the poem, it is customary for the fabulist to conclude with a direct address to the reader, or perhaps rather to the target of the epimythium. When La Fontaine does this, his first-person interventions take on a new character. He is speaking very much as the fabulist, rounding on perpetrators of error and rebuking them for their blindness. An examination of these passages soon reveals that yet again he is making no pretence of using his own authentic voice. For example:

> Petits Princes, vuidez vos débats entre vous.
> De recourir aux Rois vous seriez de grands fous.
> Il ne les faut jamais engager dans vos guerres,
> Ni les faire entrer sur vos terres.

[Minor princes, sort out your disagreements among yourselves. / You would be very rash to resort to Kings. / You must never involve them in your wars / Nor let them enter your lands.] (IV 4 'Le Jardinier et son Seigneur' *[The Gardener and his Lord]* l.58–61).

There can be no question of La Fontaine himself actually addressing his targets directly here. No commoner would have dared call a prince 'petit'. The poet is simply a mouthpiece for voicing a moral lesson. In this example, convention has it that Jean de La Fontaine, an insignificant man of letters without influence or breeding, should be allowed in his capacity as fabulist to mount an attack in print on great men, men so far above him that he would never in life address them on equal terms. These angry apostrophes are nothing but a literary artifice, and reveal nothing of the poet's situation.

Although the poet is not attempting to use his genuine voice in addressing his targets, this need not prevent him from expressing a view that he himself holds. In the above example, La Fontaine does not suggest that in life he could call princes 'very mad' to their faces; in this respect the verse does not correspond to reality. But we still sense that La Fontaine believes his message, which is that great kings are dangerous and should be avoided. Though artificial in one respect, such passages still give us a sense of at least partial sincerity.

The impression of veracity is conveyed rather differently when the first-person narrator, instead of giving us a clear opinion on his material, appears uncertain about it. He tells a tale, then seems unable to decide what it means: he adopts a stance that is the opposite of the omniscient narrator, humbles himself before his material, and in so doing lends it credence. For example, in 'Le Chat et les deux Moineaux' *[The Cat and the two Sparrows]* (XII 2) he tells the story of a cat brought up to be the friend of a sparrow. However, his diminutive companion is bullied by a visiting sparrow. Indignantly, the cat kills and consumes the passerine visitor; the taste is so delicious that he can't resist polishing off his own little friend too. When it comes to the epimythium, La Fontaine seems unable to decide what it is:

> Quelle morale puis-je inférer de ce fait?
> Sans cela toute fable est un oeuvre imparfait.
> J'en crois voir quelques traits; mais leur ombre m'abuse. (l.31–3)

[What moral can I deduce from this event? / Without one, every fable is an imperfect work. / I think I can see a few traits, but their shadow misleads me.]

This tentative approach cannot simply represent a genuine indecisiveness on the part of the poet. As Dandrey points out, he must be inferring the existence of a precise moral, since he claims that the fable would be inferior without one (Dandrey 1 p.43n). The context of his remarks may help to explain why he has couched it in this form. This fable is dedicated to the duc de Bourgogne. The poet goes on to end the poem by paying him a delicate compliment, telling him that with his superior intelligence he will work out the point of the fable. So the poet's admission of failure is more than simple statement – it is also a disingenuous means of pointing out his own inferiority to the brilliant young prince.

But there is a further nuance here. What exactly *is* the multiple 'moralité' that the poet pretends to perceive only dimly? As Rubin puts it, the most obvious moral 'is perfectly clear: nature is vastly more powerful than culture and will out' (Rubin 1 p.23). This accounts for the cat. But from the sparrows' point of view, the moral is rather different: the little birds are not on their guard against their feline friend, since he is such an old and trusted companion. This trust brings about their destruction, so the moral must be: don't put your faith in those stronger and more powerful than you, however well-intentioned they may seem. This moral is not one that the poet would wish to emphasize in a poem addressed to a royal prince.

Here the poet's adoption of a stance of apparent uncertainty enables him to put across a subversive moral without being tactless. And in general when he couches his material tentatively, pretending to be unable or unwilling to state his case baldly, it is worth asking oneself whether he is slipping in a home truth without rendering it too blatant. He may give us the feeling that he really does know what he thinks but is avoiding saying it for reasons of circumspection.

At other times this pretence of reticence seems very thin, scarcely more than a formality. For example, he concludes his fable 'Le Geai paré des plumes du Paon' [*The Jay decked out in the Peacock's feathers*] (IV 9) as follows:

> Il est assez de Geais à deux pieds comme lui,
> Qui se parent souvent des dépouilles d'autrui,
>   Et que l'on nomme plagiaires.
> Je m'en tais, et ne veux leur causer nul ennui:
>   Ce ne sont pas là mes affaires. (l.10–14)

[There are enough two-legged Jays like him, / Who often decorate themselves with other people's property, / And whom we call plagiarists. / I will say no more about them, I don't want to make trouble for them: / It's none of my business.]

His veiled attack on plagiarists strikes home every bit as powerfully as a more open onslaught could ever have done, as does his sniping at monks at the end of 'Le Rat qui s'est retiré du monde' [*The Rat who retired from the world*] (VII 3):

Qui désignai-je à votre avis,
Par ce Rat si peu secourable?
Un Moine? Non, mais un Dervis:
Je suppose qu'un Moine est toujours charitable. (l.32–5)

*[In your opinion, whom do I mean / By this rat who is so unhelpful? /
A Monk? No, but a Dervish: / I suppose a Monk is always charitable.]*

So far, none of the first-person demurrers examined here are
genuine expressions of the feelings of uncertainty, inadequacy or
discretion that they claim to be. Far from being unsure of his message, or unwilling to formulate it, he is using the pretence of tenta-
tiveness to slip in a comment that is so subversive that it cannot be
made openly. These comments are not an accurate reflection of the
poet's own views, but are as double-edged as any other aspect of his
writing.

There is an interesting group of fables in which the poet appears
to become so involved that he forgets that he is just the narrator,
and actually steps in and joins the debate. The illusion of directness
here is even more forceful. As he says at one point, 'je m'emporte
un peu trop' *[I'm getting a bit too carried away]* (II 13 l.43). A particularly telling example of this sort of first-person intervention is
repeated twice. In two separate fables, the poet steps in to comment on the evils of avarice, and both poems incorporate an element of debate between the poet and others. The first of this pair
of poems is 'Le Loup et le Chasseur' *[The Wolf and the Huntsman]*,
VIII 27. It begins as follows:

Fureur d'accumuler, monstre de qui les yeux
Regardent comme un point tous les bienfaits des Dieux,
Te combattrai-je en vain sans cesse en cet ouvrage?
Quel temps demandes-tu pour suivre mes leçons?
L'homme, sourd à ma voix comme à celle du sage,
Ne dira-t-il jamais: C'est assez, jouissons?
Hâte-toi, mon ami; tu n'as pas tant à vivre.
Je te rebats ce mot; car il vaut tout un livre.
Jouis. Je le ferai. mais quand donc? Dès demain.
Eh mon ami, la mort te peut prendre en chemin.
Jouis dès aujourd'hui: redoute un sort semblable
A celui du Chasseur et du Loup dans ma fable. (l.1–12)

*[Frenzied urge to accumulate, monster whose eyes / See all God's bene-
fits as a mere nothing, / Must I keep fighting you in this work? / How
long must it be before you learn from me? / Will man, deaf to my voice
as he is to words of wisdom, / Never say: 'Enough! Let us enjoy'? /
Hurry, my friend; you have not so long to live. / I won't go on about
this – what I say is worth a whole book. / 'Enjoy!' 'I will.' 'But when?'
'Tomorrow.' / 'But, my friend, death can take you on your way. / Enjoy
today: beware of suffering a fate / Like that of the Hunter and the Wolf
in my fable.']*

One crucial question here is whether the poet's claim that he
repeats this attack on acquisitiveness throughout his works is true –
if so, we should be able to take as equally true his insistence here
that this is one of the most important lessons to be learnt from the
Fables. Since this poem comes at the end of Book VIII, it would
seem reasonable to look at the fables that precede it in the second
Recueil, that is to say in Books VII and VIII.[206] If we look through
these two Books for attacks on the tendency to lay in store for the
future rather than enjoying the present, we find enough examples
to suggest that La Fontaine is indeed hammering this message
home – nine of the poems centre on this subject.[207] And in the
Book which immediately follows our poem, as we will shortly see,
we find a fable which begins in a manner almost identical to this
one, with an exasperated narrator pleading with a man to enjoy
what he has while he can. So it seems that here La Fontaine is
using a first-person narrator to convey a message that genuinely
concerns him.

The narrative technique reinforces the impression of strong feeling on the poet's part. He begins by apostrophizing the vice of
acquisitiveness in the strongest terms. The first word, 'fureur' *[fren-
zied urge]*, sets the tone. Acquisitiveness is a 'monster' who has to
be fought. The urgent rhetorical questions, addressed to this monster in l.3–4, reinforce the impression of violent emotion. Next, he
introduces man (l.5). He starts with a comment on mankind in
general, without addressing man directly, since man is deaf to what
he is trying to say, and doing so would be a waste of time. Then, in
exasperation at his failure to communicate, he speaks straight to
man in l.7, telling him that he has something important to say
(*'what I say is worth a whole book'*). His interlocutor now becomes a
particular man, with whom he can have a conversation. The tone

changes to a semblance of cordiality: the poet addresses the man as 'mon ami'. He embarks on a dialogue with this man, who is obsessed with saving up for the future. The poet points out the probable tragic consequences of his behaviour, and announces that he is going to tell him a fable as an object lesson (l.11–12). With this introduction, he launches into his fable.

These preliminary lines start on a very serious note, gradually shifting to a friendlier, more light-hearted tone, which corresponds more closely to that of the fable proper. La Fontaine makes a clear distinction between the introduction, in which he speaks directly, and the fable, which is, by contrast, one of his more far-fetched, unconvincing poems, in which a wolf tries to eat a bow-string (left strung by a hunter killed in mid-shot), and in so doing releases the arrow, which shoots him dead. Everything suggests that we are meant to regard the fable proper as pure artifice, but the introduction as a serious comment addressed to us by the author himself. Is he at last being straightforward here?

I said above that there was a later poem which conveyed a very similar message to that of 'Le Loup et le Chasseur', reinforcing the impression that La Fontaine's attack on acquisitiveness is a serious and heartfelt one. This second poem is 'L'Enfouisseur et son Compère' [*The Man who buried treasure and his Companion*] (X 4). The fable begins with a statement of fact: a miser is looking for a place to hide his money. La Fontaine continues as follows:

> ... En voici sa raison.
> L'objet tente; il faudra que ce monceau s'altère,
>   Si je le laisse à la maison:
> Moi-même de mon bien je serai le larron.
> Le larron: quoi, jouir, c'est se voler soi-même!
> Mon ami, j'ai pitié de ton erreur extrême;
>   Apprends de moi cette leçon:
> Le bien n'est bien qu'en tant que l'on s'en
>   peut défaire ... (l.6–13)

[This was the reason: / 'Objects are tempting; my pile will grow less / If I leave it at home. / I myself will become the thief of my own property.' / 'The thief: what? To enjoy is to steal from oneself? / My friend, I'm sorry for your terrible error; / Learn this lesson from me: / Property is only property if you can relieve yourself of it ... ']

The poet continues to upbraid the miser in this vein, for another four lines.

Here we are given the impression that the narratorial intervention has arisen spontaneously. In our extract we see the poet first entering the mind of the miser, allowing him to explain his reasoning in his own language; he lets him speak for three lines (l.7–9). But then, it appears, the poet cannot hold back his irritation, and interrupts the miser, confronting him directly. The outrage that prompts the poet's intervention is revealed in his indignant repetition of the miser's words 'the thief' (l.10). His desperate desire to convince his interlocutor is suggested by the ingratiating 'mon ami' (also used in ' Le Loup et le Chasseur'). After this first-person interruption, the poet resumes the third-person narrative, the miser goes off to bury his money, and the fable continues its course: so the poet's attempt to make the miser see sense has been ineffectual.

The impression of authenticity in this poem is similar to that in 'Le Loup et le Chasseur'. In both cases, the fact that the author addresses a character he has created makes this character seem more powerful and realistic. It also emphasizes the strength of the author's feelings: he is so carried away by his interlocutor's disgraceful reasoning that he forgets that the latter is a mere fictional creation. The condemnation of avarice, too, seems correspondingly stronger. We seem to see Jean de La Fontaine himself stepping onto the page to join his characters.

From another viewpoint, however, the situation in both fables is completely implausible. In the first place, what sort of intervention have we witnessed? was the protagonist aware that the author had suddenly intervened, or not? In the first example, the man seems to answer the poet directly. In the second, the miser does not react, so it would seem that he was probably unaware of being watched. Perhaps, like the man in 'Le Loup et le Chasseur', he is deaf to any suggestion that he should change his ways (indeed, it seems to be implicit in many a moral lesson that the object addressed remains deaf to it). More fundamentally, we may well ask ourselves how an author can invent a character, then disagree with what his own creation says, and think it appropriate to argue with him. The technique shows La Fontaine playing with the notion of fiction, authorial creation and reality in a lively manner. In fact, far from seeing the poet as personally involved in the proceedings, we are witnessing a literary artifice of considerable sophistication.

There is, interestingly, a fable in which La Fontaine rejects what he seems to be doing at this stage of 'L'Enfouisseur et son compère'. In 'Le Statuaire et la statue de Jupiter' *[The Sculptor and the statue of Jupiter]* (IX 6), the sculptor fashions a likeness of the god which then terrifies him. In this poem, the poet makes it clear that he deplores the failure to distinguish clearly between illusion and reality:

> Chacun tourne en réalités,
> Autant qu'il peu, ses propres songes:
> L'homme est de glace aux vérités;
> Il est de feu pour les mensonges. (l.33–6)

[Every man makes reality / Of his own dreams, as far as he can: / Man is like ice when faced with truth; / He is on fire when faced with lies.]

But the device of making his fiction seem real has been treated with great skill in my two examples, giving the impression that La Fontaine, far from being such a victim of his own fictional creation, is manipulating his narrative, putting words into the mouth of his narrator, bringing sparkle to his poem.

On close examination, then, the fiction that he is an active participant in the proceedings, far from making the narrator's input appear sincere and genuine, ultimately results in a contrived and artificial effect.

There is, however, one group of fables in which the poet begins with a promythium stating his standpoint in the clearest terms, in a general introduction to the reader. Can there be any ambiguity about such exordia? Let us examine an example. In 'Le Rieur et les Poissons' *[The Prankster and the Fish]* (VIII 8), he begins by stating a very clear position:

> On cherche les Rieurs; et moi je les évite.
> Cet art veut sur tout autre un suprême mérite.
> Dieu ne créa que pour les sots
> Les méchants diseurs de bons mots. (l.1–4)

[People seek out pranksters, and I avoid them / It is an art above all others that requires a supreme merit. / It was for fools alone that God created / Bad tellers of jokes.]

We are invited to share the fabulist's opinion, regarding the protagonist with contempt because of his predilection for *bons mots*. As Pascal says, 'Diseur de bons mots, mauvais caractère' *[A teller of jokes has a disagreeable disposition]*. So before the fable even begins, we may think we are already supposed to be clear about the poet's standpoint.

However, here too there is more to the introduction than meets the eye: the poet has also acknowledged that producing witticisms is an 'art' in l.2; he could be seen to be elevating wit by commenting that it is an art which requires 'un suprême mérite', suggesting by implication that it is accessible only to the finest minds. And the phrase 'bad tellers of jokes' is ambiguous. It could imply that all wags are 'bad', or refer merely to those wits whose efforts at jokes are incompetent (as *GEF* points out, 'méchant' carries no moral connotations here). In other words, the poet could here be castigating only those pranksters who are bunglers, while simultaneously acknowledging the supreme merit of skilful humorists. So we are already uncertain as to whether the poet is surreptitiously rehabilitating pranksters as a group even as he condemns the incompetents among them.

La Fontaine now proceeds to introduce his fable tentatively, leaving further room for doubt as to his precise meaning:

> J'en vais peut-être en une fable
> Introduire un [Rieur]; peut-être aussi
> Que quelqu'un trouvera que j'aurai réussi. (l.5–7)

[I may perhaps introduce (a prankster) / In a fable. And perhaps, too, / Someone will feel I have succeeded.]

He seems undecided as to whether he is actually going to tell the tale of the rieur ('perhaps') – although he does in fact begin it in the very next line. Moreover, he by no means rejects the notion of a successful fable about a wit, since he acknowledges that 'someone' from among his readers may feel that this one has made its mark. In a different sense, then, a witticism may be effective: the joke itself may be poor, but it may yet make a good story.

The prankster's witticism now forms the apologue of the fable. It is the story of a greedy wag who is served small fish at his patron's table. He pretends to interrogate the fish about the fate of a possibly shipwrecked friend, and asks to talk to a bigger fish who would have more knowledge and experience, and is rewarded with a very large fish indeed. When the poet has recounted this *bon mot*, he comments:

> De dire si la compagnie
> Prit goût à sa plaisanterie,
> J'en doute ... (l.24–6)

[I doubt if I can say / That the company enjoyed / The joke ...]

Here the poet appears to be reinforcing his initial censure of *bons mots*. However, even this apparent condemnation is in fact ambiguous: the eighteenth-century commentator Chamfort takes it to mean that the other guests found the prankster's make-believe unfunny; but Régnier suggests that they were annoyed at him for procuring the big fish for himself. Whatever the truth of this, La Fontaine goes on to point out that the joker's witticism was effective in one sense at least, since it achieved the result he intended.

It can be seen that the author's initial statement of opinion, apparently so straighforward, actually incorporates an unusual degree of ambiguity. In the first line the poet seems to be rejecting pranksters; thereafter he shifts from one approach and one attitude to another. At the very end of the poem, he sidesteps the issue altogether, concluding with a beautiful lyrical evocation of the drowned,

> ... chercheurs de mondes inconnus
> Qui n'en étaient pas revenus,
> Et que depuis cent ans sous l'abîme avaient vus
> Les anciens du vaste empire. (l.28–31)

[Seekers for unknown worlds / Who had never returned, / And who had spent a hundred years beneath the abyss, visiting / The ancient inhabitants of that vast empire.]

Again, commentators have been puzzled by these last lines. L'abbé Guillon has this to say:

> Arrivé au bout de sa narration, et peut-être assez peu satisfait de son conte, quoi qu'il en dise au commencement, le poète s'a-

muse à polir quatre beaux vers qui ne tiennent en rien à sa fable, mais qui reposent agréablement l'oreille, et font presque oublier au lecteur le *nescio quid* que le fabuliste ne s'est pas donné le temps de trouver.'[208]

[Having reached the end of his narrative, perhaps rather dissatisfied with his tale, whatever he may say at the beginning, the poet amused himself by polishing four beautiful lines of poetry, which have nothing to do with his fable, but which rest the ear in an agreeable manner, and almost make the reader forget the nescio quid that the author did not give himself the trouble to solve.]

Guillon's bewilderment at this strangely divergent ending seems only too understandable. The abrupt change of tone at the end confirms the impression conveyed throughout, that the poet is making every effort to make his fable seem confusing and inconsequential.

But perhaps the most puzzling aspect of this bizarre fable is that despite the poet's intervention at the start, we are left without a clear moral. The story appears to be based not on a true fable but on an historical (or at least apocryphal) anecdote. The Greek grammarian Athenaeus (c. A.D. 230), tells it about the much earlier poet and gourmet Philoxenus, said to have been a lover of fish. Fumaroli (II 342) convincingly interprets La Fontaine's poem as applying to his own position: the poet's reservations about pranksters reflect the problems he experienced in attempting to 'égayer' *[brighten up]* his fables, which he claims as his chief innovation in the 'Avertissement' to Book VII; his distinctly bitter attitude to the prankster's joke echoes his distaste for the self-abasement necessary for success in the world of letters; and his solemn final lines are a reminder of his own mortality, evoking as they do generations of the dead. We should note that Fumaroli's interpretation requires us to ignore the first-person narrator's ostensible rejection of the prankster and everything he stands for in the first lines of the poem, since the prankster is ultimately the poet himself.

What moral can one tease out of this fable? Probably a grudging acknowledgment that what matters is not self-respect, but effectiveness. By making himself ridiculous, the rieur has after all achieved his aim. The concluding lines could perhaps be seen as a vindication of the prankster-poet, who shows us first how poor entertainers such as he have to debase themselves to live off their wits, but then reveals that he too is capable of writing sublime verse. Whatever the truth here, the fact remains that the poem, introduced as the expression of a clear-cut individual opinion, emerges as one of the most enigmatic works in the collection, and the poet's personal intervention is seriously devalued as a result. For our purposes, we should note that in this fable the poet's initial statement of his position, far from giving us an insight into his personality, has been the prelude to a process during which, teasingly, the reader has been reduced to a state of unparalleled perplexity.

In examples like the above, the poet's whole stance is mocking and double-edged. His so-called personal opinion is lightly presented, not like a heartfelt and sincere statement of belief, so that it does not unnerve the reader when he seems to undermine his own views.

But what about those moments when he appears to strip off his mask, offering the reader an insight into what really seem to be the circumstances of his own life? There are a number of poems in which La Fontaine makes a point of urging on the reader his honesty and directness as a writer. The poet is apparently cutting through the conventions to speak straight to the reader. He may do so very forcefully. We must next look at these strongly personal interventions and consider what he is actually telling the reader about himself.

La Fontaine frequently bolsters the impression that a moral is genuinely felt by the way he phrases his conclusions. He begins the epimythium of 'Le Berger et la mer' *[The Shepherd and the sea]* (IV 2) with the words 'Ceci n'est pas un conte à plaisir inventé. / Je me sers de la vérité' *[This is not a tale gratuitously invented. / I am using the truth]* (l.21–2). The most extreme example of this technique is the note in prose placed at the end of 'Les Souris et le Chat-huant' *[The Mice and the Screech-Owl]* (XI 9). After telling an improbable tale about an owl who tweaks off the legs of the mice he catches, imprisons them and brings them food, he comments: 'Ceci n'est point une fable; et la chose, quoique merveilleuse et presque incroyable, est véritablement arrivée.' *[This is not a fable, and although the story seems fantastic and almost unbelievable, it really happened.]* This firm assertion that he is telling the truth makes it difficult for the reader to question his information. Interestingly, Collinet gives the source of the anecdote as Bernier, who himself had it from a thoroughly unreliable informant, a credulous cabalist called Gaffarel (Collinet, p.1272). It seems, though, that La Fontaine himself believed it to be true, and in this case, we feel justified in taking his remarks at face value. For the first time, we feel we may be hearing the authentic voice of the poet.

More significant, because more central to his preoccupations, are the few precious occasions when La Fontaine seems to cut through the conventions of his poem to express his sincerest feelings about an important subject that he cares about desperately. Interestingly, these heartfelt personal interventions are among the passages of La Fontaine that are best loved and best known. I am thinking for instance of his whimsical account of his daydreams in 'La Laitière et le Pot au lait' *[The Milkmaid and the Jug of Milk]*, where he disarmingly refers to himself by name as 'Gros-Jean' *[good old Jean]*; his passionate defence of solitude in 'Songe d'un habitant du Mogol' *[Dream of an Inhabitant of Mogul lands]*; or his wistful question 'Ai-je passé le temps d'aimer?' *[Have I passed beyond the time for love?]* in 'Les Deux Pigeons' *[The Two Pigeons]*. Can we deny the authenticity of such authorial interventions?

All three passages are placed at the end of a fable, as epilogues in which the narrator sets aside the fable proper in order to give us a personal, lyrical evocation of a poetic theme: love, daydreams and solitude respectively. I will examine one of them in detail, in an attempt to ascertain just how much of his own personality La Fontaine is actually prepared to reveal.

The first point to note is that such emotional outpourings, far from representing a bold rejection of convention, are in fact instances of a literary tradition. 'Les Deux Pigeons', which was discussed in detail in Chapter 4, illustrates this point very clearly. The lyrical epilogue to this poem is a moving evocation of the power of young love, followed by the poet's doubts as to whether he is now too old to experience it. The artificial flavour of the lines is apparent. The poet places his vision of love in an idyllic rural setting (he mentions woods and river-banks). The details of the lovers' behaviour are elevated but vague : 'Soyez-vous l'un à l'autre un monde toujours beau, / Toujours divers, toujours nouveau' *[Be a world to each other, one that is always beautiful, / Always different, always new]* (1.67–8). When he comes to his own early loves, he adopts the persona of a classical shepherd, describing his beloved as 'l'aimable et jeune bergère / Pour qui, sous le fils de Cythère, / Je servis' *[The charming young shepherdess, / Whom I served under the son / Of Cythera]* (l.75–7). The initial impression of literary artifice is much increased when we realize that many of the actual formulations are literary borrowings. This has been clearly proved by Collinet, who sees the whole poem as a mosaic of plagiarisms from earlier writers, and makes his point with the aid of detailed references.[209] Collinet quotes a number of sources for these lines, ranging from Epicurus to Molière. Some of La Fontaine's lines seem indeed to be direct imitations: for example, La Fontaine's 'j'ai quelquefois aimé' is also found in a play by Mme de Villedieu of 1665, *Le Favori*. However, Collinet also quotes from quite a different source, a letter written by La Fontaine to his friend the duchesse de Bouillon in 1671, when he had just turned fifty. Here he writes 'Pour moi le temps d'aimer est passé, je l'avoue'.[210] *[For me, the time for love is past, I admit.]* The more tentative 'ai-je passé le temps d'aimer?' *[Have I passed beyond the time for love?]* with which La Fontaine ends his poem exactly echoes these words, which represent the poet's authentic mood as conveyed to a close friend.

The appropriate response to the personal lines that end 'Les Deux Pigeons' is surely to view them as a complex mixture of literary artifice and genuine feeling. Yet again, it proves impossible to accept as entirely true the poet's assertion that he is talking of himself. Only the revelation of the private letter (and such corroboration is rare with our poet) allows us to glimpse La Fontaine himself for a fleeting moment. In my view this is the only undoubted sighting in all the examples I have given in this chapter.

'Le fabuliste est trop présent dans chaque vers de ses *Fables* pour qu'on s'y méprenne. Mais pas où, ni comme on le supposerait' *[The fabulist is too present in every line of his Fables to be missed; but not where or how one expects]*, writes Dandrey (1 p.117). Throughout this chapter, we have seen that the poet plays with the notion of narrative voice. In particular, he manipulates the illusion of spontaneity and directness implicit in first-person narrative. We have observed him conveying an impression of informality, bringing himself in to comment in apparently relaxed asides to the reader. But we have seen that, with very few exceptions, such informality is pure illusion. In actual fact, the poet is almost invariably using the first person to alter or subvert his message. The final impression is that La Fontaine is very willing to present us with 'the fabulist', an unreliable narrator whose illusory presence can imperceptibly influence the course of the narrative. What he will not do is to offer himself to the reader. Ultimately, as Collinet puts it, 'il...se montre discret sur sa propre vie' (6, p.177) *[he shows himself to be discreet about his own life]*. To find any trace of Jean de La Fontaine, we must read between the lines – our reward a mocking glimpse of the poet's elusive, disappearing form.

CHAPTER 10

Echoes and allusions –
creating a world

It is one thing to study La Fontaine's fables as individual poems; another to make sense of the *Fables* as a whole. And yet, the task is essential – it is obvious that the *Fables* form a unity. The poems are of course linked by the fact that they are all fables.[211] They are also consistent in one respect: they reflect an elusive authorial presence which has tantalized many critics into seeking, in La Fontaine the fabulist, La Fontaine the man.

This aspect has already been discussed. In an earlier chapter, the way the animal characters are built up from one poem to the next to create composite portraits has been examined. But this is only one type of link between the poems. Much critical attention has been paid in recent years to links of all kinds between the *Fables*. Many of the Books that make up the *Fables* have been examined in detail, and connections established between the poems, suggesting an overall structure to each individual Book.[212] The question of whether each Book has its own distinct theme has been addressed; and, more generally, critics have wondered how far the poet reveals his own personal philosophy, coherent despite its apparent inconsistencies, in the fables as a whole.

Discussion of these matters is problematical because of a fundamental uncertainty – La Fontaine never suggested that there was a coherent strucure, or 'architecture secrète' to the *Fables*. As a result, the evidence for the existence of patterning between the fables must be drawn from the poems alone, and must be absolutely conclusive. In this chapter, I will avoid general discussion of La Fontaine's philosophy, a topic well aired by many critics, and speculative rather than provable. Instead, I shall provide detailed and I believe convincing evidence of close and minute connections between the poems, which demonstrate that La Fontaine definitely saw a pattern in the collection.

Probably the most subtle means by which La Fontaine links his *Fables* is the creation of a network of echoes and correspondences. The overall impression is of a little world, which becomes steadily more familiar as we read on. The process is wide-ranging, embracing details of character portrayal, word patterns and indirect allusions. The technique is apparent from the beginning of the collection. For instance, the crow who drops his cheese in I 2 reappears in II 16; but this time, as he attempts to carry off a sheep, he has to admit that 'La moutonnière créature / Pesait plus qu'un fromage' *[The sheepish creature / Weighed more than a cheese]*– a transparent allusion to the earlier fable. (We will see more of this crow later.)

By the time La Fontaine reached the end of his collection, with Book XII, there was naturally much more scope for echoes and allusions to his own earlier works than in any of the previous books, since the poet had by then been working on his fables for more than a quarter of a century. So it is with the late poems that the full complexity and subtlety of the allusions to his own earlier work become apparent.

Apart from making the collection seem more of a piece, the Lafontainian reminiscences to be examined here also have implications for the late poems in which they occur. For their most direct impact will be on their immediate context. From this angle, it is in fact difficult to interpret their significance. Should we view them as proof of the poet's lack of vitality? An old man when he came to work on Book XII, did he no longer have the imagination and invention to create something completely new, falling back instead on his earlier, more fertile works for inspiration? Or are these echoes much more than mere 'borrowings' from earlier, more lively works: do they bring their own enrichment to the text? A close examination of their function and effects should help to answer these questions.

A second problem relates to the doubtful reputation of Book XII, the last Book of the *Fables*, in which many critics see little coherence, and from which the fables that I have chosen for my examples are drawn. The first edition of what is now Book XII was dated 1694 (though it actually appeared in late 1693), coming a full sixteen years after the second of the two *Recueils* that make up Books I–XI. In Book XII the poet collected together the fables that he had published separately in the intervening years, with very few new additions. Published shortly before his death, the final work of the poet's old age, the definitive version of Book XII has been described as an '"uneven" book of the twilight years, which, however, contains some outstanding, eloquent fables', as Sweetser puts it.[213] The question of the borrowings from earlier fables will play a crucial role in determining the status of Book XII. If it can be shown that they actually enrich their contexts, rather than merely demonstrating a lack of inspiration, then one of the apparent weaknesses of Book XII becomes one of its strengths.

I propose to examine two fables, the first of which is one that has struck critics as self-repetitive and lacking in inspiration, to see exactly what role is played by La Fontaine's self-imitations. The fable in question is 'Le Renard, les Mouches et le Hérisson' *[The Fox, the Flies and the Hedgehog]* (XII 13), one of the very last poems to appear during La Fontaine's lifetime (since, unlike most of the other poems in Book XII, it had not been published before it appeared in the 1693–4 edition). Collinet draws our attention to the large number of borrowings from earlier La Fontaine fables, commenting pertinently that in this fable 'son art ... tend à se scléroser, et son inspiration ne se renouvelle guère' *[his art ... tends to fossilize, and his inspiration is scarcely renewed]*. The references to early poems 'ne rendent pas un son bien neuf' *[do not sound very new]*.[214] The problem is how to interpret these borrowings. It may be worth looking beyond our initial disappointment at the poet's lack of new ideas, and asking ourselves if anything more positive can be discerned in the echoes and allusions in this poem.

The fable tells the story of a wounded fox who rails against the flies tormenting him. A hedgehog offers to catch them on his spikes, but the fox refuses: at least these flies have sated themselves on his flesh; if they were eliminated, a new, hungry swarm would appear to torment him even more.

The first 17 lines are germane to the issue I wish to discuss.

> Aux traces de son sang, un vieux hôte des bois,
>   Renard fin, subtil, et matois,
> Blessé par des Chasseurs, et tombé dans la fange,
> Autrefois attira ce Parasite ailé
>   Que nous avons mouche appelé.
> Il accusait les Dieux, et trouvait fort étrange
> Que le sort à tel point le voulût affliger,

Et le fît aux Mouches manger.
Quoi! se jeter sur moi, sur moi le plus habile
De tous les hôtes des forêts?
Depuis quand les Renards sont-ils un si bon mets?
Et que me sert ma queue? Est-ce un poids inutile?
Va! le Ciel te confonde, animal importun;
Que ne vis-tu sur le commun!
Un Hérisson du voisinage,
Dans mes vers nouveau personnage,
Voulut le délivrer …

[By the traces of his blood, an old dweller in the woods, / A cunning, subtle and crafty Fox, / Wounded by huntsmen, fallen in the mud, / Once upon a time attracted the winged parasite / That we have named 'fly'. / He reproached the Gods, / And found it very strange / That fate should wish to afflict him so deeply, / And have him eaten by flies. / 'What? To fling themselves on me, on me, the most skilful / Of all the dwellers in the forest? / Since when have Foxes been so good to eat? / And what use is my tail? Is it a useless dead weight? / Oh, may heaven confound you, importunate beast. / Why don't you live off common property?' / A neighbouring Hedgehog, / A new character in my verse, / Wanted to free him …]

The first link to note is the resemblance between the description of this fox and cunning predators in other fables. The fox here is described as 'un vieux hôte des bois, / Renard fin, subtil, et matois' *[an old dweller in the woods, / A cunning, subtle and crafty Fox]* (l.1–2). This has echoes in a number of other La Fontaine fables, so that we recognize that this fox fits into the customary mould. The closest similarity is with the cat of XII 8 l.34, 'Chat fin, subtil, et narquois' *[a cunning, subtle and sly Cat]* ('narquois' sounds so like 'matois' that the descriptions seem identical at first glance). But most of the antecedents are foxes: the fox of 'Le Loup et le Renard' (XI 6) excels in 'tours de matoiserie' *[cunning tricks]*; the hero of 'Le Renard ayant la queue coupée' *[The Fox whose tail was cut off]* (V 5) is 'Un vieux Renard, mais des plus fins' *[an old Fox but a very cunning one]*; that of 'le Fermier, le Chien et le Renard' *[The Farmer, the Dog and the Fox]* (XI 3) is also 'des plus fins' *[very cunning]*; though English foxes will later turn out to be even more crafty, 'plus fins' *[more cunning]* ('le Renard anglais' *[The English*

Fox], XII 23). From the start, then, the key words 'fin' and 'matois' provide an economical evocation of the typical cunning animal personality in the *Fables* (and indeed in fable literature in general). Moreover, the fact that they occur in the first line indicates the approach that La Fontaine is going to adopt throughout the poem – from the start the fox is linked to his counterparts in other poems.

This is a very simple and obvious type of link. The next echo is already more complex: when the fly comes in, it is introduced as 'ce Parasite ailé / Que nous avons mouche appelé' (l.4–5). 'Nous' could simply mean the poet and his contemporaries, and the phrase could simply be translated as 'That winged parasite whom we all call fly'. Other seventeenth-century writers also describe flies as 'parasites'. It seems indeed to have been almost a seventeenth-century cliché. Collinet quotes a line of Scarron: 'tous ces insectes ailés qu'on peut appeler parasites de l'air' *[all those winged insects who can be called parasites of the air]* (p.1201). However, a further dimension is added if we look at the antecedents of the whole phrase in the *Fables*, from which it becomes clear that when the poet uses the past: ' … que nous *avons* mouche appelé *[whom we have called fly]*, he means us to take the tense literally. For the line has precise echoes earlier in the *Fables*. The first poem in which it appears is 'La Mouche et la Fourmi' *[The Fly and the Ant]* (IV 3), in which the ant says rudely to the fly: 'Nomme-t-on pas aussi Mouches les parasites?' *[Does one not also call flies parasites?]*[215] The echo of the earlier poem prepares us for the moral of our fable, in which the importunate flies are likewise compared to human parasites. However, this is not the most obvious echo of an earlier poem. There is another linking reference, in which he uses exactly the same phrase 'ce Parasite ailé / Que nous avons mouche appelé'. For these same words also occur in 'L'Ours et l'Amateur des Jardins' *[The Bear and the Lover of Gardens]* (VIII 10 l.47). This fable has other close similarities with 'Le Renard, les Mouches et le Hérisson'. The story is of a bear who strikes up a friendship with an old man. While the old man is sleeping, the bear brushes away the flies in case they should bother him. He ends up inadvertently killing his friend by helpfully swatting a particularly troublesome fly off the old man's nose with a paving stone. This fable might indeed be regarded as forming a pair with our poem. Both show a naive animal trying to help his friend by ridding him of his flies. In both, it is made plain that such help is counterproductive. For any reader familiar with the *Fables* as a whole, the exact repetition of the words used in 'L'Ours et l'Amateur des Jardins' to describe a fly cannot but evoke this earlier poem. Once the earlier fable is recalled, the reader is likely to be reminded of its moral: 'Rien n'est si dangereux qu'un ignorant ami' *[Nothing is as dangerous as an ignorant friend]* (l.57). This moral is patently appropriate to our fable too, in which the hedgehog's proffered assistance is rejected because it would have adverse consequences that he has not foreseen. Yet this moral is not even hinted at in our fable. The only way we are likely to focus on it is through the echo of the other poem, which hence can be seen to add an important new dimension to our appreciation of the moral and message of our present fable. Thus the evocation of the past implied by the past tense 'avons' can legitimately be given its full force, and the line in our fable taken to mean 'That winged parasite to whom I gave the name of fly [on two previous occasions]', providing a clear case of self-reference. (It is worth noting that La Fontaine readily uses 'nous' for 'je' on other occasions. See, for instance, the way he flags his forthcoming moral in 'Le Loup et l'Agneau' *[The Wolf and the Lamb]*: 'Nous l'allons montrer tout à l'heure.' *[We will show it presently].*) As far as our poem is concerned, the allusion has added a new dimension which serves to undermine the friendliness of the hedgehog, a second 'dangereux ami'.

The next echo comes when the fox bewails the fact that he is unable to swish off the flies with his tail: 'Et que me sert ma queue? Est-ce un poids inutile?' (l.12). For readers familiar with the poems, this allusion to the fox's tail irresistibly recalls the fable 'Le Renard ayant la queue coupée' (V 5). In this earlier poem a fox who has lost his tail in an accident tries to persuade his fellows that tails are generally useless appendages:

> Que faisons-nous, dit-il, de ce poids inutile,
> Et qui va balayant tous les sentiers fangeux?
> Que nous sert cette queue? Il faut qu'on se la coupe.

['What are we doing?' said he, 'With these useless weights, / Which constantly sweep the muddy paths? What use are these tails? We must cut them off.']

In our fable too the tail is a 'useless weight'; and our fox says 'what use is my tail?' It may even be that the tail is the wounded part of our fox's anatomy as with his predecessor, since it is proving useless at brushing off the flies. Finally, in both fables there are references to the mud that incoveniences the fox. Our fox is 'tombé dans la fange' *[fallen in the mud]* (l.3), while the tailless fox claims that tails get dirty, 'balayant tous les sentiers fangeux' *[sweep the muddy paths]*. These are the only two occurrences in the *Fables* of 'fange', 'fangeux'.[216] Overall, the parallels with 'Le Renard ayant la queue coupée' are far too numerous to be coincidental, and both poems are variations on the theme of the mutilated fox. The fox in our fable is sadder and wiser than his tailless predecessor, and is also in pain (he asks to be left alone to suffer, whereas the tailless fox's sufferings were over before we met him); but the reminders of the more light-hearted earlier poem may prevent his plight from seeming too bleak, thereby lightening the tone.

The next line (l.13), while not a direct quotation from an earlier fable, nevertheless awakens echoes. The reminiscence here is of 'Le Lion et le Moucheron' *[The Lion and the Gnat]* (II 9). In both cases, the larger quadruped, unable to defend himself against the importunate insect, resorts to insults. The lion's invective is, however, more suited to his vast size and savage reputation: 'Va-t'en, chétif Insecte, excrément de la terre' *[Go away, puny insect, excrement of the earth]*, a memorable line, the more so because it is a parody of a famous vituperative line in Malherbe's 'Stance contre le maréchal d'Ancre' *[Stanzas against the Maréchal d'Ancre]*: 'Va-t'en à la malheure, excrément de la terre' *[Go to perdition, excrement of the earth]*.[217] The fox's 'Va! le Ciel te confonde, animal importun' *[heaven confound you, importunate beast]* (l.13) serves as an echo of the lion's words, but scaled down to suit a less majestic beast. Again, it emphasizes an aspect of the moral that is passed over in our fable, namely the fact that the importunate flies are small and insignificant, yet vanquish their prey. Recalling the point of 'Le Lion et le Moucheron' draws the reader's attention to it without the poet's needing to mention it. The notion that even great men are not invulnerable, found in other fables, is present too by implication here.

The final link in this poem is a line (l.16) which is self-referential, but in a paradoxical way. This is the singling out of the hedgehog as 'Dans mes vers nouveau personnage' (l.16). By drawing the reader's attention to the fact that the hedgehog has *not* been mentioned elsewhere in the Fables, La Fontaine differentiates between him and the other creatures, thereby implying that the same is not true of *them*. Thus he slyly underlines the existence of the echoes and links that I have picked out elsewhere in this poem.

Such evidence from the printed text already suggests that the echoes and allusions enhance the poem's content. But we can also bring to bear a different type of evidence. Uniquely for La Fontaine, we are able with this poem to analyse the process of composition. For there is in existence an earlier version of the poem, written in La Fontaine's own hand. This is the actual transcription[218]; the first seven lines are the relevant ones:

> Vn Renard tombé dans la fange,
> Et de mouches presque mangé,
> Trouuoit Iupiter fort étrange
> De soufrir qu'a ce poinct le sort l'eust outragé.
> Vn hérisson du voisinage,
> Dans mes vers nouveau personnage
> Voulut le délivrer ... (p.20)

[A Fox fallen in the mud, / And almost eaten by flies, / Found Jupiter very strange / To allow fate to abuse him to this extent. / A neighbouring hedgehog, / A new character in my verse, / Wanted to free him ...]

Looking back over the echoes I picked out earlier, how many of them are already present in this draft version of the poem? There is as yet no attempt to characterize the fox and make him cunning or sly, like his predecessors. The flies too are seen as neutral, not yet winged parasites. The fox does not yet mention his tail, and his indignant speech, reminiscent of the lion's, is omitted. We are left with the word 'fange' and the fact that the hedgehog is a 'new character'.

The existence of this earlier fable proves that La Fontaine did not unthinkingly incorporate allusions as he first composed his poem. He started with the bare bones of the text, and built it up afterwards. The process is clearly one of what La Fontaine himself called 'enrichissement' *[enrichment]*. In the 'Avertissement' to his second *Recueil* of fables (p.245), La Fontaine claimed that in composing his poems he was looking not for 'répétitions' but for 'enrichissements'. In this fable, then, we have a unique example of this process. We can see how seamlessly the new allusions are woven into the original story. This cannot be the careless writing of an uninvolved, ageing poet.

Instead, the echoes in this fable must surely be deliberate additions, included to build up a particular mood. Several of them serve to lighten the atmosphere. The poet adopts a teasing, merry tone, inviting the reader to establish the connections he has hinted at, and to share the joke. The story is made to seem comfortably familiar – we know this fox of old; moreover, the impression that the same fox's story has been told throughout the fables makes his present predicament seem less grim. He may be in trouble here, but we can expect him to pop up again, completely restored, in another fable (this is indeed what happens, since a 'madré' *[crafty]* fox and another 'des plus fins' *[as cunning as possible]* appear in later fables in Book XII[219]). We have also seen the grim implications of the present poem (Collinet draws attention to 'la tonalité de résignation lasse et désabusée qui donne à cette fable une coloration chagrine' *[the tone of tired, embittered resignation that colours this fable with gloom]*[220]), and we have observed how these are brightened by the echoes of more lighthearted earlier fables. So these references succeed in 'égayer' *[lighten]* the mood of the poem, an enterprise that was dear to the poet's heart.[221] Moreover, they lighten it on more than one level. They make the fable more entertaining by reminding us of other, witty poems, and in addition they enable the poet to describe the unrelenting suffering of a mutilated animal, and to put across a grim message, without seeming too distressing. These allusions also serve a more serious purpose. We have seen more than once that a mention of an earlier fable brings its moral to mind, and may thereby enrich the moral or the implications of its successor. Thus in this poem, the precariousness of friendship and of high rank are both hinted at purely through the echoes and allusions. Overall, La Fontaine's echoes in this poem both enhance the character portrayals, modify the tone, and add a further dimension to the moral.

* * *

Is this poem an isolated case, or do similar echoes in other fables fulfil an equally important function? We must resolve the question of the significance of this allusive technique before we can discuss it in the fables as a whole. To this end, let us examine a second late fable which also contains a number of self-referential echoes. It will become apparent that our conclusions have wider implications for the *Fables*.

My second late fable is 'Le Corbeau, la Gazelle, la Tortue et le Rat' *[The Crow, the Gazelle, the Tortoise and the Rat]* (XII 15). It is an unusually positive poem for La Fontaine, and outstanding as one of the most moving celebrations of friendship in the *Fables*. As such, the reader can expect a very different atmosphere from the pessimistic poem I have just discussed. In the course of its panegyric on friendship, our fable contains a number of allusions to earlier poems. As Marc Fumaroli puts it, it is as if 'La Fontaine tenait à faire apparaître le fil qui, tout au long des fables, nous attirait peu à peu vers cette révélation ultime, telle Isis à la fin de *L'Ane d'or*: l'amitié, l'entraide, *the milk of human kindness*' *[La Fontaine was anxious to bring out the thread which, throughout the fable, gradually drew us to that final revelation, like Isis at the end of* The Golden Ass: *friendship, mutual support, the milk of human kindness]*(vol II p.421). Fumaroli draws our attention to the echoes of fables such as 'Le Lion et le Rat' and 'La Colombe et la Fourmi' *[The Dove and the Ant]* (II 11 & 12), in both of which the protagonists come to each other's aid in a spirit of disinterested helpfulness. But there are also a number of references to other fables which fulfil a very different function.

With the animal portraits in this poem, these allusions build up their personalities, already familiar from earlier fables. Unlike 'Le Renard, les Mouches et le Hérisson', however, the echoes here do not build up a familiar picture. Instead, the characters in our fable bring new traits to the ones we know: a characteristic of this poem is its presentation of significant variations on well-known protagonists, settings and situations.

The fable tells the story of four loving friends, a crow, a gazelle, a tortoise and a rat, who cooperate to outwit a huntsman. The gazelle disappears, whereupon the other three creatures work together to save her. The crow flies off and finds her trapped in the huntsman's net. The rat gnaws through the net and frees her. Even the tortoise hastens to her aid, but is caught and put in a sack. The gazelle than lures the huntsman away to give the rat time to free the tortoise by gnawing through the sack.

The first of the four animals to appear, the gazelle, has not hitherto featured in the *Fables*, so will not be discussed here (though she is called 'la chèvrette' *[the little goat]* at various points in the poem, and could in fact be linked with earlier goat fables). The other three creatures remind us of the protagonists of earlier fables. Examining the implication of these reminiscences can enrich and modify our interpretation of the poem, and may even suggest a re-evaluation.

The most striking echo in this fable is the name of the rat, Rongemaille *[Netgnawer]*. There is only one other rat named Rongemaille in the *Fables*, the protagonist of 'Le Chat et le Rat' (VIII 22)[222], and on examination this earlier poem appears to have much in common with our fable. Both poems have four animals as protagonists. In each case the story is of how the creatures cooperate to outwit a huntsman; and in both the rat's talent for gnawing through a hunter's net, which has given him his name of Rongemaille ('le Rat eut à bon droit ce nom' *[the Rat had a good right to his name]*, writes La Fontaine in XII 15 l.102), is put to good use. There the resemblance ends, but there are also significant differences between the two poems. In 'Le Chat et le Rat' the four animals are enemies, and the rat agrees to help the trapped cat reluctantly, realizing that the two other creatures (an owl and a weasel, implacable predators both), present an even greater danger. In our poem, on the other hand, the four animals all help each other escape from danger with the greatest goodwill. This difference profoundly affects the respective moral messages of the two fables. With 'Le Chat et le Rat', the moral is that one cannot trust an enemy. With 'Le Corbeau, la Gazelle, la Tortue et le Rat', the moral is that with solidarity, and provided everyone plays his part, one can accomplish wonders. The earlier poem is pessimistic, the later one optimistic. The shared name of the rat, then, provides a striking link with another poem which treats a similar situation much more negatively. So the reminder of the earlier fable may make a difference to our response to the message of the later one, adding a new dimension: although we accept the later moral at face value, and although the alliance between 'Le Corbeau, la Gazelle, la Tortue et le Rat' is successful on this occasion, the reference to another fable reminds us that such alliances on other occasions are viewed with suspicion.

When the rat is first introduced, however, he reminds us of a different poem:

> ... Le Rat à l'heure du repas
> Dit aux amis restants: D'où vient que nous ne sommes
> Aujourd'hui que trois conviés? (l.66–8)

[The Rat, when mealtime came, / Said to the remaining friends: 'How is it that / There are only three guests today?]

The portrayal of this rat at table, eating meals at regular times, with a prearranged number of guests, echoes the strong association between rats and formal human meals in 'Le Rat de ville et le Rat des champs' *[The Town Rat and the Country Rat]* (I 9), in which the town rat invites his colleague to a ceremonious meal with game birds as the main dish. We merely glimpse the diners here, though the situation is similar in the two poems – in both, the rat's gourmet activities are interrupted by danger represented by man. This would appear to be a standard example of a self-referential echo, enabling the reader to recognize the character as a familiar figure, without adding further dimensions to the message. It may also, however, subtly serve the same purpose as the reference to Rongemaille, of casting a doubt on the positive message of our later fable. For in 'Le Rat de ville et le Rat des champs' the moral, as far as the rats are concerned, is that animals cannot hope to enjoy life if man is there to threaten them: 'fi du plaisir / Que la crainte peut corrompre' *[Down with pleasure / That is spoiled by fear]* (l.27–8). This pessimistic conclusion could cast a shadow over the ideal life of the four friends in our fable by reminding us of another occasion in which animals' lives are disrupted when man happens along.

The next animal to be introduced in our fable is the tortoise. She laments her lack of wings:

> ... Ah! si j'étais
> Comme un Corbeau d'ailes pourvue,
> Tout de ce pas je m'en irais
> Apprendre au moins quelle contrée,
> Quel accident tient arrêtée
> Notre compagne au pied léger ... (l.71–6)

[Ah! If I were / provided with wings like a Crow, / I would go off at once / To learn at least in what place, / What chance has delayed / Our lightfooted companion]

The tortoise's longing for wings and for distant travel recalls the fable 'la Tortue et les deux Canards' *[The Tortoise and the two Ducks]* (X 2):

> Une Tortue était, à la tête légère,
> Qui, lasse de son trou, voulut voir le pays.
> Volontiers on fait cas d'une terre étrangère … (l.1–3)

[A Tortoise there was, a light-headed one, / Who, wearied of her hole, wanted to see the world. / People willingly exaggerate the charms of distant lands …]

This earlier tortoise succeeds in flying, carried by two ducks.[223] The link between the two travelling tortoises is reinforced by the use of the word 'léger' *[light]* in both poems. In 'la Tortue et les deux Canards', indeed, 'léger' seems so inappropriate in a description of a ponderous tortoise that it stands out, and as a result, in our poem, placing 'tortue' and 'léger' close together seems to echo this earlier juxtaposition, although here 'léger' refers perfectly appropriately to the gazelle. Then too, the earlier poem presents a much more negative outcome in which the frivolous tortoise is horribly punished for her arrogance in thinking she could fly: 'Elle tombe, elle crève' *[She falls, she bursts]* (l.31). In our poem too, when the tortoise ventures forth, she is caught by the huntsman. This aspect of our fable is glossed over by the poet, who concentrates instead on the admirable solidarity of the four animal friends. And the tortoise is promptly rescued by Rongemaille and the gazelle. Nevertheless, our fable does demonstrate the dangers of ambition, though this aspect will become apparent only if the parallel with the flying tortoise is remembered. This particular echo links our optimistic fable to one of the poet's negative expressions of fear and dislike of the unknown, and warnings against enterprise.[224]

Later, in a much more explicit echo, the tortoise will call to mind another predecessor, the heroine of 'Le Lièvre et la Tortue' *[The Hare and the Tortoise]* (VI 10). In this earlier fable, the tortoise speaks the moral in a striking formulation: 'Moi l'emporter! et que serait-ce / Si vous portiez une maison?' *[Me, to win! What would it have been like / If you had been carrying a house?]* (l.34–5). This idea is echoed twice in our fable, first when the tortoise tries to go to

the help of the gazelle, 'Maudissant ses pieds courts avec juste raison, / Et la nécessité de porter sa maison' *[Rightly cursing her short
legs / And the fact that she had to carry her house]* (l.100–1). Later,
she is given the sobriquet 'Portemaison' *[Housecarrier]* (l.127).
Unlike 'Rongemaille', this name is not original to La Fontaine,[225]
but it nevertheless links the two fables. In our poem, the handicap
of the slow, heavily-burdened tortoise seems much worse than in
'Le Lièvre et la Tortue', in which, after all, the tortoise does win the
race. This introduces a hint of retrospective doubt to the suggestion in the earlier poem that an indomitable spirit will carry one
through in spite of all odds, and so contributes to the underlying
pessimism already apparent in these allusions. It is as though the
poet were reminding us of the fragility of the tortoise's victory over
the hare – on a later occasion, when she sets out once more, the
outcome will not be so happy.

The allusions to earlier tortoise fables should also be considered
as a pair, in which case they have a rather different impact. Taken
together they enable us to situate the later tortoise, who has the
staying power of the heroine of 'Le Lièvre et la Tortue', the original
'Portemaison', dauntlessly setting out on a mission to save the
gazelle, but lacks her predecessor's wisdom, and, like the empty-
headed heroine of 'La Tortue et les deux Canards' gets herself into a
scrape by unthinkingly courting danger.

The last of the characters in our fable is the crow. Again, he is
given the same name as a famous predecessor. Like the hero of 'le
Corbeau et le Renard' *[The Crow and the Fox]* (I 2 l.5) he is called
'Monsieur du Corbeau' in l.128. There is indeed a parallel between
his behaviour and that of the susceptible crow of I 2, whose weakness for flattery costs him his cheese. Just as the fox by his blandishments cajoles the crow into dropping his cheese, so in our fable
the tortoise persuades him into flying off in search of the missing
gazelle (though of course his behaviour in the present poem is
laudable and not ridiculous). He is also reminiscent of the hero of
'Le Corbeau voulant imiter l'Aigle' *[The Crow wanting to imitate
the Eagle]* (II 16) (which is itself linked to 'Le Corbeau et le
Renard', as we saw earlier). The link in our fable is a play on words.
'Le Corbeau voulant imiter l'Aigle' contains the striking line 'Mal
prend aux volereaux de faire des voleurs' *[Flutterers do not do well
when they try to fly (or, 'to steal')]* (l.24), which incorporates a
coinage, 'volereaux'. In 'Le Corbeau, la Gazelle, la Tortue et le Rat',

In the earlier fable, although the dogs were later shown killing the hare, the skill and intelligence of Miraut still shone through. But in our poem, the dog, who does no more than sniff a scent, is given no redeeming features. He is under attack simply because of his contact with man: it seems that the poet can no longer approve an ally of man. Comparing the two dogs reveals a new grimness in the poet's attitude to his fellow-men even in this most positive of fables.

The huntsman traps the gazelle, and the crow flies off to look for her. When he finds her, he flies straight back to warn the others, not wishing to ' … perdre en vains discours cet utile moment / Comme eût fait un Maître d'école.' *[waste this valuable moment in pointless speech / As a schoolmaster would have done]* (l.84–5). This is a transparent allusion to 'L'Enfant et le Maître d'école' *[The Child and the Schoolmaster]* (I 19), in which the schoolmaster does exactly what La Fontaine deplores, lecturing a drowning child before pulling him out of the water. It is the most straightforward evocation of another fable in this poem. Again, the reminiscence brings out a negative view of man, since the schoolmaster is here compared with a crow and found wanting.

My final parallel links our poem to other fables about animal loyalty. It is the description of how the gazelle tricks the huntsman into dropping the sack containing the captured tortoise. La Fontaine writes:

> [La Gazelle] quittant sa retraite
> Contrefait la boiteuse, et vient se présenter.
> L'homme de suivre, et de jeter
> Tout ce qui lui pesait … (l.114–7)

[(The Gazelle,) leaving her retreat, / Pretended to be lame, / And presented herself. / The man followed her, casting aside / Everything that weighed him down …]

This episode occurs in the Pilpay fable which served as La Fontaine's source[226]; so it might be argued that there is no self-referential significance in its inclusion here. Nevertheless, it is appropriate to note where in the *Fables* we find an earlier description of this behaviour. It comes in the 'Discours à Mme de la Sablière' (IX, last poem). There it is cited by the poet, not as an episode from a fictitious fable, but as a genuine example of a creature's devotion, based on the observations of naturalists and included to further the poet's thesis that animals are not unfeeling:

> Quand la Perdrix
> Voit ses petits
> En danger, et n'ayant qu'une plume nouvelle,
> Qui ne peut fuir encor par les airs le trépas,
> Elle fait la blessée, et va traînant l'aile,
> Attirant le Chasseur, et le Chien sur ses pas,
> Détourne le danger, sauve ainsi sa famille ... (1.82–8)

[When the Partridge / Sees her chicks / In danger, barely fledged, / And unable to flee death through the air, / She pretends to be wounded, and drags her wing along, / Attracting the Hunter and the Dog in her wake, / Draws danger away, and so saves her family.]

The parallel between this description and the behaviour of the gazelle in our fable becomes much more significant when we remember that 'Le Corbeau, la Gazelle, la Tortue et le Rat' is also dedicated to Mme de la Sablière, La Fontaine's admired friend and patron. The early part of our fable indeed takes the form of a compliment to Mme de la Sablière, incorporating much of the same material as the similar introduction to the 'Discours à Mme de la Sablière'. Both poems also contain a strong apology for friendship (though in our fable the poet focuses more directly on this subject, which featured only incidentally in the 'Discours'). Overall, then, there are three strong links between these two poems for Mme de la Sablière, suggesting that both should be seen as tributes to her: we must remember that La Fontaine composed our later fable in 1685 when she, and their friendship, were still alive.[227]

This loftiness of purpose suggests that the poem should be taken seriously overall. This view is reinforced by the tone of its conclusion. In his analysis of our fable, Collinet stresses this conclusion, in which the poet maintains that his subject is worthy of being turned into a Homeric epic (1.122–4). As Collinet points out (p.1292), the fable is 'digne de servir d'épilogue à sa geste de fabuliste' *[worthy of serving as an epilogue to his fabulist's chronicle]*, since here 'se regroupent quelques-unes de ses thèmes majeurs auparavant dispersés' *[several of his major themes, previously separated, are*

grouped together]. The reminiscences of earlier poems further reinforce the impression that this fable is a re-examination of the poet's
earlier ideas. It remains to determine the significance of this re-
evaluation.

Let us first sum up the different types of allusion here. It is
interesting to note that only one of them, the evocation of the
'Discours à Mme de la Sablière', reinforces the positive message of
our fable. The others have an opposite function. The evocation of
other tortoises and crows casts doubt on the friendship and altru-
ism that are overtly celebrated in the poem. Other echoes imply a
negative view of man, who spoils nature for those who live in it.

So it seems difficult to assess the reminiscences of earlier fables
as performing a consistent function in this poem. Instead, one
senses a dichotomy here between the poet's overt celebration of
friendship in praise of his patron, and an underlying pessimism,
implied by the echoes of other poems, which negates the value of
what he outwardly extols. It almost seems as if, through these
echoes, he is undermining his whole enterprise. Despite its
undoubted optimism, its celebration of loyalty and friendship,
most of the self-referential passages link this poem to the more pessimistic fables of Book XII. So the way is prepared for the message
of the final poem in the Book, which advocates turning one's back
on the world and on men, in favour of self-knowledge in solitude.

*   *   *

Characteristically, La Fontaine slips this element into his poems
imperceptibly. He ranges productively over his own past work,
picking out those details that on the one hand subtly modify and
enrich his new poems, and on the other hint at his final rejection
of the world of man. Taken as a whole, the allusions in my two
fables are so numerous and systematic as to create a strong meshing
effect between these poems and those of the other two *Recueils*. In
the other poems of Book XII there are equally obvious echoes of
other fables, far too numerous to examine in any detail.[228] In short,
in Book XII the fabulist is considering his fables as a whole, as
much or more than he did before.

What I am suggesting here is a rather particular and peculiarly
informal sort of 'architecture secrète' in the *Fables*. Normally, the
term suggests a systematic working out of a rigorous if concealed

connection. But this approach is inappropriate for the disorganized and subversive poet, whose bent was to call in question his own ideas – if there is to be a pattern of links in his work it is likely to be much less formalistic. The evidence of a close examination of individual fables, along the lines suggested in this chapter, reveals a network of allusions and echoes which enrich the poems in which they occur, and also increase each poem's significance for the collection. La Fontaine's reminiscences create a pattern that is latent, unclear, undisciplined: some allusions may escape the reader, or seem puzzling if they are noticed. For all that, they build up into a substantial sub-structure, a true microcosm.[229] They are enough to justify his vision of the *Fables* as 'Une ample comédie à cent actes divers, / Et dont la scène est l'univers' *[An ample comedy in a hundred different acts / Whose scene is set in the universe]* (V 1 l.27–8).

Epilogue

In one of his *Contes*, 'Le Tableau' *[The Painting]*, La Fontaine expresses his intention of including in the piece ' ... Nombre de traits nouveaux, piquants et délicats, / Qui disent et ne disent pas' *[A number of new, piquant and delicate traits, / Which are and are not said]* (l.5–6). He is about to embark on a description of an obscene painting, and hopes thus to achieve a convincing delineation without giving offence. Accordingly, he decides to disguise his account rather than giving it directly and crudely. He wants to allow the truth to emerge without having to dot the 'i's: 'Tout y sera voilé, mais de gaze' *[Everything will be veiled, but with gauze]* (l.20).[231]

Though the context here is one of sexual innuendo, his remark also suggests an important general principle. He is acutely aware of the value of suggestion, even insinuation, rather than bold statement. Later in the same poem, to his recipe for serving up a message in acceptable form, he adds a final, vital ingredient: craft. If a piece is well thought out and well expressed, controversial material can be included without giving offence:

> Qui pense finement et s'exprime avec grâce,
> Fait tout passer; car tout passe:
> Je l'ai cent fois éprouvé. (l.22–4)

[A writer whose thoughts are acute and gracefully expressed / Can do anything, for anything will do. / I've experienced this a hundred times.]

It cannot be said that, throughout his literary career, La Fontaine was uniformly successful in conveying potentially unacceptable material without arousing indignation. His outspokenness caused him trouble on many an occasion; in some respects he remained on the fringe of the literary establishment all his days; and his reception at the Académie Française, disgracefully near the end of his life, was fraught with difficulty. But though he sometimes failed to disguise his own subversiveness, the principle he stated in 'Le Tableau' governed his writing throughout much of his career, and underlies many of the points I have been making in this study.

I have indeed tried to show that in the *Fables* La Fontaine's thoughts are consistently presented in an oblique manner, and rendered with the help of a wealth of literary techniques and devices. I have also tried to demonstrate that his writing needs to be 'decoded' if its full impact is to be appreciated. Sometimes, as we have seen, the reasons for this obfuscation are readily apparent, as when he disguises criticisms of the king or other contemporaries, or otherwise introduces surreptitious political satire. In such cases he is acting to protect his own position. Elsewhere his oblique approach seems to be governed by a kind of shyness. He appears reluctant to expose his own authentic views, preferring to present them in disguised form – adopting his predecessors' fables, but subtly changing the message. Even more striking is the way that he systematically shrinks from allowing the reader any glimpse of the real Jean de La Fontaine beneath the persona of the poet/narrator. Not for nothing does he tell us that he sees his function as that of an entertainer: not hammering home a serious, heartfelt message, but telling a lively tale, enhanced by touches of 'gaieté'. This view of his purpose as a fabulist may also help to explain why he avoided discussing the overall architecture of the *Fables*, shunning an over-serious, theoretical approach which might make the 'papillon du Parnasse' *[the butterfly of Parnassus]* seem too like one of the pedants he mocks in his poems. As a result, it is left to us readers to hunt down the recurrent themes and allusions that build up into a structure for the collection and give it a framework. Finally, we may detect in La Fontaine's oblique approach a simple preference: he appears to favour complex, multi-layered effects so consistently that this must surely represent a personal predilection. This seems to be the case with some of the stylistic techniques I have singled out for discussion.

Whatever the reason, the final impact of the *Fables* is less transparent than is implied by La Fontaine's elegant conceit of the gauze veil which reveals everything that it pretends to conceal. Instead, La Fontaine's poetry is a densely-woven fabric. Many threads are worked into its underside, invisible at first glance. The reader may well find much to admire without ever perceiving these additional threads: for they cannot be detected without unpicking the finished work. On the surface, the poems may appear uncomplicated;

many of them can be enjoyed by small children. But in this book I
have tried to tease out some of the elements of an extremely subtle
process by which artistic and moral complexities are seamlessly
incorporated in a fable so that they may almost escape notice. My
chapter on hidden imagery illustrates one such effect.

The apparently easy, in reality difficult, poet is a rarity.
'Difficult' poets – Rimbaud, Mallarmé, Donne – tend to appear so
at first sight. La Fontaine seems easy but is not. In the Preface to
the *Fables* he draws our attention to the complexity of his verse,
though typically with a self-deprecating slant. Discussing his literary predecessors, he writes:

> La simplicité est magnifique chez ces grands hommes; moi, qui
> n'ai pas les perfections du langage comme ils les ont eues, je ne
> la puis élever à un si haut point. (p.7)

*[These great men's works are magnificent in their simplicity. But I,
who have not mastered language to perfection, as they have, cannot
raise it so high.]*

We must note that La Fontaine is saying two things here: firstly,
that he is inferior as a poet to Phaedrus or Terence; but secondly,
and much more importantly, that he himself has not attempted to
emulate his predecessors in their simplicity. By implication, he is
telling us that his own poetry is far from simple.

Odette de Mourgues claims that the difficulty of the *Fables* lies
in the fact that La Fontaine has omitted so much, leaving it to the
reader to fill in the gaps: 'a great deal of what constitutes the value
of each fable depends on things which are not there' (Mourgues 2
p.42). I would put it slightly differently: La Fontaine is a poet who
does not state, but instead suggests. He draws our attention to the
need for subtlety in narrative, though again he puts a misleading
slant on his remark. Writing of Aesop, he notes with approval:

> La lecture de son ouvrage répand insensiblement dans une âme
> les semences de la vertu, et lui apprend à se connaître sans
> qu'elle s'aperçoive de cette étude, et tandis qu'elle croit faire
> toute autre chose (*A Monseigneur le Dauphin*, p.3).

[Reading his work imperceptibly sows the seeds of virtue in a man's

soul, and teaches him to know himself, without his noticing that he has been learning, and while he believes he has been doing something quite different.]

The ostensible point here is that fables manage to instruct even as they entertain. But we should also note that La Fontaine is expressing admiration for a type of writing which insinuates ideas into the head of the reader, without the reader's being fully aware of what is happening.

La Fontaine not only admired such a technique, he also practised it. Oblique writing of this kind, found in his own *Fables*, is what this book is about.

Notes

INTRODUCTION

1. See Allott 2 p.240–1 for details.
2. See Biard 1 chapter 1 and Van Delft 1 for details.

CHAPTER 1. THE PRACTICAL CRAFTSMAN

3. Richard Danner, in Danner 1 Chapter III, has drawn our attention to the significance of the poems' closures. Their beginnings seem equally worthy of discussion.

4. 'Vieux mot qui se disait des flèches et des matras auxquels on mettait des plumes pour les mieux conduire dans l'air' *[Archaic word used for arrows and quarrels, which were feathered so as to drive them more accurately through the air]* (Richelet, quoted by Fumaroli).

5. Fumaroli agrees that La Fontaine is here introducing a personal view of this suppression of humanity in the wolf; he sees it as central to the poet's whole philosophy and moral world-picture. Couton, however, quotes several literary precedents for this tale of a vegetarian predator (p.519–20). Marcel Gutwirth, in Gutwirth 1 p.137, reminds us that the poet questions his own assertion that this is an exceptional wolf in an aside, 'S'il est de tels dans le monde' *[if such creatures exist in the world]* (l.2).

6. Thus Furetière gives impressive examples of the use of the word: 'Socrate, Platon, Aristophane estoient contemporains. La Reine Elizabeth & la Reine Marie Stuart estoient contemporaines.' *[Socrates, Plato, Aristophanes were contemporaries. Queen Elizabeth and Queen Mary Stuart were contemporaries.]*

7. The exception is, of course, popular verse, which, though much appreciated at the time, is only intermittently reflected in the sophisticated poems that make up the *Fables*.

8. Régnier quotes Hesiod as the source of this fable. His translation demonstrates how an overt simile makes the transition from promythium to apologue seem more ordinary: 'Les Dieux et les hommes s'indignent contre celui qui vit oisif, semblable aux bourdons ... ' *[Gods and men are indignant at those who live idle lives, like bumble bees.]* (*GEF*, I 120).

9. Collinet emphasizes the strong similarity between this poem and a child's fairy tale, and comments that the poet is subject to 'la logique propre au folklore de l'enfance' *[the logic proper to the folklore of childhood]* (Collinet 1, p.199).

10. 'Bique' is a Champagne dialect word, according to Richelet.

11. Collinet 1, p.199. Génetiot, in an analysis of the classical influence on La Fontaine, comments: 'L'oeuvre de La Fontaine est ...tout entière marquée par la tradition de la pastorale.' *[La Fontaine's work is influenced by the pastoral tradition throughout.]*

12. Régnier takes Taine to task for objecting to this brusque transition: he sees it as one more instance of La Fontaine's habitual 'mélange des moeurs et aptitudes des hommes avec celles des animaux' *[mingling of the customs and aptitudes of men with those of animals]* (*GEF* I 326–7).

13.   Sed temperatae suaves sunt argutiae,
             Immodicae offendunt (IV, Epilogue, l.3–4)

14. I de Benserade, *Fables d'Esope en quatrains*, 1678.

15. See Slater 3 for a discussion of La Fontaine's views on brevity.

16. Fumaroli gives a translation of Nevelet's version of the Aesop fable *Vulpes* which served as a starting-point for La Fontaine's fable: 'Le renard, ayant eu la queue écourtée par un piège, en était si honteux ...etc' *[The fox, whose tail was cut off in a trap, was so ashamed ...]* (I p.387).

17. A contemporary example is Mme d'Aulnoy's 'Le Nain jaune' *[The Yellow Dwarf]*. There is no mention in 'Le Chien qui porte de la viande' *[The Dog carrying a piece of meat]*, the Phaedrus fable on which La Fontaine based his version, of the water becoming rough. Régnier argues that the water becomes choppy 'du plongeon qu'y fait le chien' *[from the dog diving in]* (*GEF* II 56), which seems an improbable interpretation of La Fontaine's formulation.

18. In Mme d'Aulnoy's 'Le Roi mouton' *[The King Sheep]*, for instance, the princess's companions in the wood are a black girl, a monkey and a little dog.

19. See also Collinet p.1259, and Couton, who summarizes Poussines's version (p.526).

20. As in the two ugly sisters in Perrault's 'Cendrillon' *[Cinderella]*.

21. Couton gives a translation of the Abstemius fable on which La Fontaine's version is based. The relative status and qualities of the two men are indicated, but not emphasized by the style (p.493).

22. La Fontaine never specifies how great the expanse of water is. In the Chauveau illustration, it looks like a lake; but in his exegesis, commenting on the implications of the fable, La Fontaine remarks: 'Tout cela, c'est la mer à boire' *[All this is a sea to be drunk dry]* (l.38).

23. See Tyler p.228. Obvious examples are 'nuages' *[clouds]* which 'crevèrent' (XII 29) or an overfull storehouse which 'crève'(VII 5); a tortoise who falls from the sky shatters when she hits the ground: 'elle tombe, elle crève' *[she falls, she bursts]* (X 2); the frog who puffs herself up with air till she 'creva' (I 3) has a bursting death like the dogs overfilled with fluid. Furetière says that when 'crever' is used meaning 'to die', it is 'sur tout de mort violente' *[above all by a violent death]*.

24. Fumaroli translates the end of Nevelet's version, '*Culex et leo*', where the bathetic potential of the situation is entirely absent: 'Le cousin, victorieux, embouche la trompette et entonne un chant de triomphe et prend son essor. Mais voilà qu'il s'empêtre dans une toile d'araignée, et, sur le point d'être dévoré, il en était réduit à se lamenter, lui qui avait tenu tête aux plus puissants animaux, de périr dans les rets méprisables d'une araignée' *[The victorious midge put the trumpet to his lips, sounded a triumphal air and took wing. But lo! He became tangled up in a spider's web, and, on the point of being devoured, he was reduced to lamenting, he who*

had defied the most powerful beasts, that he must perish in the miserable net of a spider] (Fumaroli, I 369). Danner gives further details of the 'funny resonance' of La Fontaine's lines (Danner 1 p.101).

25. We must also remember that La Fontaine took his coincidence from his source, in this case Tabarin's *Baron de Grattelard* (quoted in *GEF* II 374).

26. Fumaroli sees this fable as an essential contribution to La Fontaine's ideas on Fortune: 'trésor et corde, ce pourrait être un rébus hiéroglyphique comme le fil et le soufflet dans le fou qui vend la sagesse. Ils résument en effet et la fable et le destin des avares. Ils révèlent aussi le langage chiffré et ironique que parle la Fortune, mais que le vulgaire ne sait pas lire'. *[The treasure and the rope... reveal the coded, ironic language which Fortune uses, and which common people cannot interpret].* Fumaroli II 373. Chamfort objects to this fable because of its tendency to 'faire jouer un trop grand rôle à la fortune' *[make fortune play too big a part]* (*GEF* II 435).

27. Fumaroli quotes the source, Gaulmin's *Le Livre des lumières*, 'D'un chasseur et d'un loup' *[Of a hunter and a wolf]*. In the Gaulmin text the hidden presence of the gods and fortune is entirely omitted except that the wolf calls finding the corpses 'cette bonne fortune' *[This good fortune].* II 356. However, in another source, the Indian *Hitopadesa*, 'la destinée' is mentioned, though much less subtly and systematically (see *GEF* II 509–10).

28. In the original Aesop fable (Nevelet's version) a lion and a man were travelling together and discussing statues of lions overthrown by men which they chanced to pass along their way.

29. In the original version, by Abstemius, there is only one young man, so that the coincidence is much less striking.

CHAPTER 2. CONJURING WITH STYLE

30. See my Chapter 5 for further discussion of this fable.

31. It is apparent that many of the phrases discussed in this section are taken by La Fontaine from earlier writers. Where I have come across probable sources, I will indicate this fact in a note. The importance of these paradoxes is in no way diminished by their not being original: the fact remains that the poet has chosen to put them in and give them prominence.

32. Richard Danner, in Danner 1 p.47, has an interesting discussion of the irony in this last example.

33. Collinet quotes *L'Astrée*, well known to be one of La Fontaine's favourite novels: 'Le blâme que l'on donne aux femmes peut être bien dû à quelques hommes' *[the blame attributed to women may well be deserved by some men]* (IV, Book IX, vol.IV, p.521) – which points the contrast but in a much less challenging manner (p.1196). Furetière comments: 'On dit aussi qu'un homme fait la femme lors qu'il est lasche, oisif & effeminé, qu'il se delicate trop.' *[We also say that a man plays the woman when he is cowardly, idle and effeminate, and shows himself to be too delicate.]*

34. This juxtaposition of 'fort' and 'faible' was common at the time. Furetière cites two proverbs, 'le fort portant le foible' *[the strong carrying the weak]* and 'Il en connoist le fort et le foible.' *[He knows the strong and the weak of it].*

35. Mme de Sévigné quotes this line in a letter of 8 January 1674.
36. CXV, v.6: 'Ils ont des oreilles et n'entendent pas' *[they have ears, but they hear not].*
37. Collinet (p.1126) quotes a number of versions of this formulation, which was apparently a popular *bon mot* of the time. The closest to La Fontaine's is Jean Bertaut's 'L'Avarice a changé mes biens en mon servage/ M'en rendant possédé plutôt que possesseur.' *[Avarice has transformed my property into my servitude, making me the possessed rather than the possessor].* None of the examples, however, is as pithy as La Fontaine's formulation, except possibly the Greek version of Bion the Borysthenite, which Régnier translates: 'Celui-ci ne possède pas son avoir, mais c'est son avoir qui le possède' *[That man does not possess his wealth, it is his wealth that possesses him] (GEF* I 345). Danner (p.47) has an interesting analysis of the line.
38. This is a favourite form of La Fontaine's, and echoed in less striking form in other lines such as 'Fortune aveugle suit aveugle hardiesse' *[Literally, 'Fortune blind follows blind boldness']* (X 13), or 'Mis beaucoup en plaisirs, en bâtiments beaucoup' *[Spent much on pleasures, on buildings much]* (VII 13).
39. Fumaroli (II 333) sees La Fontaine's pithy phrase as encapsulating his attitude to the whole art of interpreting the fable: 'un déchiffrement plus ou moins ingénieux de fables apparemment fictives ... ' *[a more or less ingenious deciphering of apparently fictitious fables].*
40. The idea is not new – Collinet gives a number of sources, such as Cicero's ' ... quam se ipse amans sine rivali'. La Fontaine's version is more slyly underplayed than his sources, though, which is what gives it its impact.
41. Gutwirth demonstrates this point with a close analysis of the versification of 'Le Chêne et le Roseau' *[The Oak and the Reed]* (Gutwirth 2). Gaudard gives a number of examples of La Fontaine's flexible versification, p.161.
42. It must however be acknowledged that an entire poem in a completely straightforward verse-form is exceptional in the *Fables*, and would seem to indicate that the tone is less ironic than usual. An example would be 'Le Vieillard et ses Enfants' *[The Old Man and his Children]* (IV 18), which is a serious poem told entirely in unexceptionable alexandrines.
43. *Georgics, I* l.383–7. See Couton's translation, p.434.
44. This would have been true in La Fontaine's time: the lines were centred in contemporary editions of the *Fables*. In the smaller 12mo contemporary versions in which all the poems were published, the lines often overran – there was just not enough space to fit them whole onto the page. If anything, this would emphasize the difference between this line and the others. I am grateful to T. Allott for this bibliographical information.
45. As Danner points out, the bathetic impact of 'Du vent' increases in that it is the closing line of the poem (Danner 1 p.69).
46. Danner (1 p.151) demonstrates the use of *enjambement* to similar effect in this poem.
47. The lines beneath the syllables indicate the strongest stresses. This is a much simplified version of the method of indicating stress used by Roy Lewis in *On Reading French Verse*, Oxford, Clarendon Press, 1982. He describes it as follows: 'Syllables may be indicated by placing a dot beneath the sounded vowel, this dot being doubled for a subsidiary stress and trebled for a major stress'. (p.xv).

48. See Collinet's edition and Biard 2 for details of Chauveau's illustrations.
49. Odette de Mourgues in Mourgues 1, p.122, makes the interesting observation that the irregularity of the seven-syllable line is ' … équilibré par le fait que ces vers se suivent régulièrement' *[balanced by the fact that these lines follow each other in regular sequence]*.
50. Added to this one could pick out purely linguistic effects which contribute to the impact, such as use of the ambiguous 'il' in l.9, which could be impersonal or could refer to the speaker, and so remind us that the pot is at once alive and inanimate. There is also word-play in 'débris', which is used to mean the ending of a life as well as the smashing of a pot.
51. Hence, according to Fumaroli, the sea is 'la métaphore non de la Cour seulement, mais du vaste monde séducteur et trompeur' *[The metaphor not only for the Court but also for the whole vast, seductive, duplicitous world]*. I 378. Couton sees these lines as alluding to the precarious financial situation at the time when they were written (1 p.71).
52. Furetière mentions the locution 'Il m'a promis monts & merveilles', so it must have been current at the time.

CHAPTER 3. IMAGERY: THE MAN IN THE ANIMAL

53. As Collinet points out (p.1279), there is an echo of Vergil here.
54. See the fable 'Le Loup, la Chèvre et le Chevreau' *[The Wolf, the Goat and the Kid]*, IV 15 l.20, where the kid insists that the wolf should show him his 'patte blanche', otherwise he will not believe that he is a goat.
55. In a detailed analysis of this poem and its moral, Gutwirth 1 pp.205–7.
56. I am grateful to Dr Roger Mettam for details of this historical event.
57. See Collinet 5.
58. Couton (p.537) draws our attention to a parallel with two other ladies, Mme de Beringhen and the Duchesse de Brissac, whose coaches met in a narrow alley. Neither lady would give way, and they remained there for five hours.
59. See VII 17 'Un Animal dans la Lune' *[An Animal in the Moon]* for a more explicit attack on Louis's belligerent foreign policy.
60. It is worth quoting the dialogue between the poet and an interlocutor, horrified at a merlin who, in 'Le Milan, le Roi et le Chasseur' *[The Merlin, the King and the Hunter]*, XII 12, presumes to land on the nose of a king, who, incidentally, has much in common with Louis XIV (See Collinet p.1287 for parallels):

> Quoi! sur le nez du Roi? Du Roi même en personne.
> Il n'avait donc alors ni sceptre ni couronne?
> Quand il en aurait eu, ç'aurait été tout un.
> Le nez royal fut pris comme un nez du commun. (l.44–7)

[What, on the nose of the King? Of the King in person. / Did he not have his sceptre or his crown? / If he had, it would have been just the same. / The royal nose was treated just like a common nose.]

61 'La Laitière et le Pot au lait' *[The Milkmaid and the Jug of Milk]* (VII 9 l.43). This is a characteristic La Fontaine message. See for example 'Le Mulet se

vantant de sa généalogie' *[The Mule boasting of his Genealogy]* or 'Le Rat et l'Eléphant' *[The Rat and the Elephant]*.

62. Furetière defines the term as follows: 'Utencile de cuisine qui a plusieurs pointes recourbées où on attache de la viande. Le croc d'un Juge de campagne est toûjours bien garny de volaille.' *[A cookery utensil with several curved hooks off which one hangs meat. A country judge's hook is always well hung with poultry.]*

63. In spite of his claim that 'Les Arbres et les Plantes / Sont devenus chez moi créatures parlantes' *[Trees and plants / Have become talking creatures in my work.]* (II 1 l.11–2) La Fontaine has few examples of actively participatory talking plants. Apart from this bush, the most obvious ones are in 'Le Chêne et le Roseau' (I 22), 'L'Homme et la Couleuvre' (X 1) and 'La Forêt et le Bûcheron' (XII 16).

64. For example, the shepherd in 'Le Berger et la Mer'(IV 2), the merchant in 'L'ingratitude et l'Injustice des Hommes envers la Fortune' (VII 13), and the four protagonists in 'le Marchand, le Gentilhomme, le Pâtre et le Fils du Roi' (X 15).

65. Furetière defines 'emplette' as 'achat de marchandises'*[purchase of merchandise]*, and adds: 'Il se dit particulierement de celles [i.e. ces achats] qui concernent les habits. Cette femme est allée faire des emplettes'. *[It is particularly said of purchases of clothes. This woman has gone to make some purchases]*.

66. 'Le Berger et le Roi' (X 9), 'L'Oiseleur, L'Autour et l'Alouette' (VI 15) and 'L'Ane portant des Reliques' (V 14) are examples. There are many others.

CHAPTER 4. HIDDEN IMAGES

67. This technique was popular among sixteenth-century Flemish and Italian painters; its two principal exponents are Joachim Patenier (d.1524) and Giuseppe Arcimboldo (1527–93). I have not been able to ascertain whether any of their works were in France, possibly in a royal collection, where La Fontaine might have seen them. However, he had seen human faces made out of shells in the grotto at Versailles. See Bibliothèque nationale Catalogue, p.59.

68. See Fumaroli 2 for a detailed analysis of the poet's view of the king.

69. A fuller account of this image and its implications was published as Slater 5.

70. I am grateful to Professor J.P. Collinet for drawing my attention to the human imagery here. Its existence is implied by other critics, for instance Jules Brody when he writes: 'le Chêne se présente comme le genre de personnage qui se sert du langage non pas pour communiquer sa pensée, mais pour traduire et souligner les différences qui semblent le séparer du commun des mortels' *[The Oak presents itself as the kind of character who uses language not in order to communicate its thought, but to translate and emphasize the differences which seem to set it apart from common mortals]*. Brody 1, p.17. Biard touches on it when he writes: 'It is not just mere chance that the verb "rider" and the time-old metaphor "la face de l'eau" occur in the same line (Biard 1 p.179). Odette de Mourgues comments briefly: 'Le chêne et le roseau sont personnifiés, mais discrètement, de façon ambiguë' *[The oak and the reed are personified, but discreetly, in an ambiguous manner]* (Mourgues 1 p.174).

71. See Jürgen Grimm, 'Modèles d'interprétation de la fable "le Chêne et le Roseau"' in Grimm 1 pp.16–31.

72. This is Horace's version too, though another tradition has it that he threw himself into the volcano so that his sudden disappearance should convince people that he was a god. But Etna flung out one of his bronze sandals, so the subterfuge was discovered.

73. In an interesting discussion of this fable, André Tournon points out that Empedocles was a dishonest philosopher, associated with the 'plus vaines ambitions du savoir, les leurres du langage' *[the vainest ambitions of knowledge, the trickery of language]*. So 'La Fontaine pouvait y soupçonner les leurres d'un imposteur ou les chimères d'un visionnaire, à joindre au vain projet de savoir universel dans une même dérision' (p.17) *[La Fontaine could suspect in him and deride in him at once the trickery of an impostor or the fantasies of a visionary, and also the vain project of acquiring universal knowledge]*.

74. We have already seen, in Chapter 2, the richness of the stylistic effects in this fable.

75. See *Quart livre* ch.LVII. It is perhaps significant that in Rabelais's version, Gaster the stomach-king is a horrific tyrant. La Fontaine purports to follow the traditional version, as found in Livy and Shakespeare's *Coriolanus*, in which the stomach (ie the ruler) is seen as essential for the welfare of the state; but his allusion to Rabelais might suggest that he has hidden reservations about the monarchy.

76. Although the chameleon was principally noted for its ability to change colour, an apt talent for a courtier, Furetière has the following entry: 'On dit …de celuy qui apparemment n'a pas de quoy vivre, que c'est un *cameleon*, qu'il vit de vent, à cause de la vieille erreur où on était que le cameleon en vivoit'. *[They say, of a man who seems to have nothing to live on, that he is a chameleon, that he lives off the wind, because of the ancient erroneous belief that that is what chameleons lived off.]*

77. There are minor examples of the same technique in l.16–21.

78. Furetière gives as the figurative definition of 'embarras': 'chagrins, inquiétudes de l'ame' *[sorrows, anxiety of the soul]*, and as an example: 'Le vice met les hommes dans un grand embarras d'esprit' *[vice produces in men a great anxiety of the mind]*.

79. In his article, Leo Spitzer tackles this same question. In his brief analysis, he notes instances of ambiguous language which could apply either to friendship or to love between the pigeons. In a later note, however, Spitzer modifies this view, asserting that the story of the pigeons is a tale of lovers, one male, one female. The fact that the two birds address each other as 'frère' he explains by suggesting that it is the fraternal, caring aspect of love that is depicted here. (pp.193–5). Gutwirth too is inclined to see the birds as 'un pigeon … une pigeonne?' (Gutwirth 1 p.127). Vincent, Chapter 4, agrees, basing his argument on the transformation of the travelling pigeon into a feminine entity with 'la volatile malheureuse'. However, this distribution of genders reverses the situation implied earlier in the poem, when the now 'male' partner was equated with Dido. Collinet, in Collinet 3 p.13, accounts for such discrepancies by suggesting that though the poet has changed the sex of the pigeon, this is 'une mutation que le fabuliste, pour plus de poésie, laisse volontairement dans le vague et la pénombre' *[a mutation which the*

fabulist, for greater poetic effect, leaves vague and twilit]. Sweetser suggests that each pigeon could be either male or female, having universal relevance (Sweetser 1 p.107). Rubin feels it is impossible to reconcile the story of the pigeons and the narrator's coda, suggesting that the relationship between the two parts 'is jarring in more ways than one' (Rubin 1 p.34).

80. Spitzer p.195, Collinet p.1222, Vincent p.58.

81. Furetière's dictionary gives us the example 'cette femme est pleine de charmes et d'appasts. La vie solitaire a ses appasts et ses charmes' *[this woman is full of charms and attractions. A solitary life has its attractions and its charms],* and tells us 'en ce sens on a accourci le mot, et dit appas, au lieu d'appasts'. If Furetière is to be believed, the spelling 'appas' is confined to the meaning 'charms'. Michael Vincent too sees this word as relating to erotic love in a literary context (p.61).

82. Jules Brody, however, offers a different, and delightful, explanation of 'le naturel': 'Pour qui a un peu vécu avec les chats, il est évident que La Fontaine traduit ici les attributs du 'naturel', sémiologiquement, en code félin.' *[To people who have lived with cats, it is obvious that La Fontaine is here translating the attributes of 'le naturel' semiologically, into a feline code.]* He goes on to explain that his own cat behaved exactly like 'le naturel' ('Lire la Fontaine', in Slater 1 p.21).

83. Quoted by Collinet, p.1092.

84. Jules Brody singles out the 'nombreuses occurrences de mots désignant la folie du monsieur en question' *[numerous instances of words designating the madness of the gentleman in question].* 'Lire La Fontaine', in Slater 1, p.19.

85. Significantly, in this passage La Fontaine has adapted, and masculinized, a quotation from Horace in which the protagonist is female: 'Naturam expelles furca, tamen usque recurret et male perrumpet furtim fastidia victrix' Horace, Epistles I, 10, l.24–5.

86. Furetière's dictionary definition is: 'Reveille-matin – Horloge qui a une sonnerie qui bat à l'heure précise sur laquelle on a mis l'aiguille, quand on l'a montée.' *[Reveille-matin – clock which rings at the precise moment to which the hand has been set when winding it up.]*

87. Odette de Mourgues comments 'cet agrandissement de l'huître rend plus acceptable la demi-personnification' (Mourgues 1 p.181) *[this enlargement of the oyster makes its demi-personification more acceptable].*

88. To modern readers this description might evoke the *rapprochement,* well-known to psycho-analysts, between shells and the female sexual organs.

89. See *GEF* II 396–8 for details of these references.

90. A shorter version of this chapter can be found in my article 'La Fontaine's Hidden Images', in *Seventeenth-Century French Studies,* vol 18, 1996, pp.91–101.

CHAPTER 5. ANIMAL CREATIONS

91. The talking deer San Cancil is the hero of many of Malaysia's traditional fables. Andrew Lang gives many traditional African tales of talking animals (see for instance *The Orange Fairy Book,* Longmans, 1922, pp.29–36 for a Mashona story about a talking rabbit and baboon). Of interest is a recent comparison by Joseph Nsengimana between a La Fontaine fable and a twentieth-century

Senegalese tale by Birago Diop, which features a talking toad and bee (Fablier 4, pp.43–8).

92. Preface to first *Recueil*, p.9. As Collinet points out, this is not actually the case (p.1052). La Fontaine, in his eagerness to give animals a high profile, has misrepresented Aristotle.

93. 'A Monseigneur le Dauphin', poem at beginning of First *Recueil*, p.29.

94. Letter to Monseigneur le duc de Bourgogne at the beginning of Book XII, p.449.

95. See Collinet 1 p.156 for an interesting discussion of La Fontaine's comments. Fumaroli, I, 36 remarks that ' … tout au long de ses *Fables*, La Fontaine fait voir et entendre les animaux comme un blason moral où ses personnages humains, et par ricochet son lecteur, peuvent apprendre à découvrir leur identité.' *[… throughout the Fables, La Fontaine shows us the animals like a moral blazon, in which his human characters, and by extension the reader, can learn to discover their identity.]*

96. See Fumaroli 1 for a detailed analysis of this point.

97. My analysis of 'Les Deux Chèvres' *[The two Goats]*, for example, demonstrates the number of levels on which the poet is operating in portraying his animals – and reveals a possible hidden satirical dimension to the poem. See Chapter 3.

98. One could cite numbers of other standard portraits: the timid hare, the vain peacock, the industrious ant, the garrulous frogs, the perfidious cat, and so on.

99. The problem of combining stereotype and individual in the animal portraits has bothered critics through the ages. Régnier's gloss to these lines reflects this unease: 'Lessing… critique [ces vers] comme un développement oiseux, contraire, dit-il, à la nature même de la fable, le nom seul du Renard suffisant pour éveiller en nous tout ce que contient cette description. Mais pourquoi, je le demande, cette règle étroite? De quel droit peut-on défendre au fabuliste de donner à ses personnages, outre les qualités du genre ou de l'espèce, un caractère individuel, qui peut être, par exemple, comme ici, de porter ces qualités au plus haut degré.' *[Lessing criticizes these lines as an idle development, contrary to the very nature of the fable, since the mere name of the Fox is enough to evoke in us everything contained in this description. But why should the rules be so narrow? What right has he to forbid the fabulist to give his characters not only the qualities common to the genre and their species, but also an individual personality, which could involve taking these qualities to the limit, as in this example?]* (*GEF*, I 378).

100. In Fablier 4, pp.11–17.

101. This is still a controversial topic. An article in *The Sunday Correspondent* by Robert Matthews, 15th April 1990, sums up recent thinking as follows: 'Stories about the rescue of drowning sailors by dolphins … appear to be true, but … the explanation is more prosaic than many would like to believe, say the experts … The rescues demonstrate the strong "epimeletic" instincts of dolphins – their urge to ensure the survival of their species by helping one another'. Incidentally, Collinet points out that La Fontaine's line is a precise imitation of a line from Scarron's *Virgile travesti*, which gives it an additional burlesque flavour (p.1115).

102. According to *GEF*, this belief, mentioned by Plutarch, probably arose because deer have a hollow under each eye.

103. Although this legend was common in the ancient world, it is not used by Aesop in the fable that inspired La Fontaine. In Aesop's 'The Swan and the Goose' the swan is a musical bird, bought by its owner 'for the sake of its song'. See Chapter 2 for a discussion of 'Le Cygne et le Cuisinier'.

104. Although I would stand by my interpretation of these final lines, there is more to La Fontaine's response than this if the poem as a whole is considered – see Fumaroli, II 339–40, for an analysis of the complex mix of irony and approval underlying the poet's attitude to puerile literature in this fable, and my analysis in Slater 4.

105. In Slater 7 pp.191–2, I discuss the complex case of 'Les Compagnons d'Ulysse' (XII 1). In this poem, La Fontaine seems to be denigrating animals, but on closer examination it becomes clear that he implies criticism of man instead. Richard Danner (pp.116–27) and David Rubin, in 'Dissolving Double Irony', Slater 1 pp.87–90, have perceptive analyses of this ambiguity.

106. Mme de Villedieu, *Fables et histoires allégoriques*, quoted by Collinet, p.1296. As a further refinement on the monkey as mimic, Fumaroli tells us that traditionally the monkey was pictured looking at himself in a mirror, and describes him as a kind of mirror-image of the poet (II 424).

107. See my article, Slater 6, pp.143–4 for more details on cats as religious hypocrites.

108. The exception might be the protagonist of 'Le Singe', but this monkey appears conscienceless rather than deliberately cruel.

109. In the original, the human side is far less detailed, so that the contrast between animal and human does not stand out. However, as Fumaroli points out (I 365), this fable is reminiscent of 'ce sous-genre de l'épigramme consacré à la *sollertia animalium* (l'ingéniosité animale)'*[that sub-group of epigrams dedicated to* sollertia animalium *(animal ingenuity)]*.

110. Compare also the use of 'gens' at the end of XII 1 'Les Compagnons d'Ulysse', where he uses the word to mean human beings as opposed to animals (l.113).

111. Génetiot has an interesting discussion of the irony in this passage (p.317–8). Fumaroli, however, argues that 'il s'agit moins ici de l'homme en général que des Grands' *[this is less about man in general than about the nobility]* (II 381).

112. La Fontaine's version is close to the original (see *GEF* I 246 for a translation). However, Fumaroli (I 376) gives a French translation of the nightingale's words in Aesop: 'Je refuse de raviver les souvenirs de mes anciens malheurs: voilà pourquoi j'habite au désert.' *[I refuse to reawaken the memories of my former misfortunes: that is why I live in the wilderness.]* The emphatic rejection of men is missing here.

113. Some of the arguments in this chapter and the next two chapters are developed from ideas presented in my article Slater 7.

CHAPTER 6. REASONING ANIMALS

114. Madeleine Defrenne, in her article 'Le Phénomène créateur chez La Fontaine: le poéte et le monde', *Australian Journal of French Studies*, 1975,

pp.119–67, argues convincingly that the poet made little attempt to present authentic animal portraits, instead relying on literary antecedents and anecdotes to present a conventional view.

115. VI 5 is taken by La Fontaine from Verdizotti, whose formulation he follows closely (Collinet, 1148). IV 3 is from Phaedrus, IV 25.

116. The narration of this fable is analysed in detail in Chapter 9.

117. In modern French: 'laissez-moi en paix'.

118. See Fumaroli for a French translation, I 360.

119. Fumaroli comments that the poet 'a transformé le canevas maussade et sec [d'Esope] en une scène de comédie brillante' *[has transformed the sullen and dry canvas (of Aesop) into a brilliant comic scene]*(I 379).

120. See Chapter 3 for a detailed analysis of this poem.

121. See Fumaroli for the original, I 387.

122. As Collinet points out, the footprint detective-work was not only in Aesop, but also 'proverbial dès l'antiquité' (p.1154). So the cunning behaviour of the animals here was far from original to La Fontaine. His version, however, is fuller.

123. Isaac-Nicolas Nevelet, *Mythologia Aesopica*, Frankfurt 1610 (includes Phaedrus's *Fabulae* and a Latin Aesop from an anonymous manuscript in the library of the Elector Palatine ['l'Anonyme de Nevelet'], also an Abstemius). Fumaroli postulates that La Fontaine knew and used this text, partly because it was the most complete collection of the antique fables, but also because Nevelet, like La Fontaine himself, was originally from Champagne. See Fumaroli, I 86–7, for an account of this version and its links with La Fontaine. The French translation given here is also by Fumaroli (I 368).

124. Collinet (p.1267) gives a number of possible sources for this, though none is systematically followed by La Fontaine. See also Fumaroli II 403, who comments that La Fontaine creates this fable 'dans sa nouvelle manière' *[in his new manner]*.

125. Préface, p.7.

CHAPTER 7. THE PRESENTATION OF TALKING ANIMALS

126. See the translation from the Prologue to Book I, l.5–7 in Collinet, p.1079. The original Latin is quoted by *GEF* I 130. Fumaroli makes the interesting point that in this poem La Fontaine includes animal characters in his examples of the epic and pastoral genres.

127. The fact that the animals talk in rhyme must however have a considerable impact on their speech. This is an important aspect which deserves investigation. Sweetser (1, p.96–7) touches on this in an interesting comment on how the rhyme enhances the speech in 'Les Animaux malades de la peste' *[The Animals sick of the plague]* (VII 1). Odette de Mourgues also examines this point (Mourgues 1, p.143–4).

128. This prankster's sense of humour will be discussed in Chapter 9.

129. See *GEF* I p.429–30 for the sources. Kohn (p.166) detects an echo of Rabelais in these words.

130. The film director Jean-Jacques Annaud, who was attacked by a bear when making his film *L'Ours* (1988), has described how he resorted to shamming dead in order to save his own life.

131. 'Vendre la peau de l'ours' *[selling the bear's skin]* was apparently a proverbial saying by the late seventeenth century. See Collinet, p.1143. Words were attributed to the bear in the version of Abstemius (*GEF* I 430).

132. This is a common technique when portraying animals. For example, Hergé's dog Milou, in the *Tintin* books, reflects on the situation in words which the reader can see, though Tintin remains unaware of them. Gillian Jondorf gives a lively account of the complexities of the situation (p.5).

133. Indeed, as Fumaroli points out (II p.381), much of their discourse imitates Vergil's *Georgics*.

134. Fumaroli (I 345) sees the sheep and the goat as exemplifying a naive form of Epicurean calm and resignation in the face of death, which the pig corrupts through fear. Dandrey, in a detailed philosophical and stylistic analysis of the poem (Dandrey 1 p.70–6), takes up this point, and links the underlying theme to the doctrines of Socrates and Montaigne (p.72).

135. I feel that it is perhaps an over-simplification to assert, as Odette de Mourgues does, that ' ... dans les fables de La Fontaine, les animaux ... parlent comme des hommes' *[in La Fontaine's fables, the animals ... talk like men]* (1, p.85).

136. As Collinet tells us, this means that he talks in rhyme (p.1220).

137. Haudent's earlier version contained the remark that the wolf 'de tuer a la nature, / Non de chanter' *[is a killer by nature, not a singer]*. See *GEF* I 212.

138. Fumaroli translates the Latin of Nevelet's version of Aesop: 'Le cousin, victorieux, embouche la trompette et entonne un chant de triomphe.' *[the victorious midge put his trumpet to his lips and blew a song of triumph]* (I 369). The witty image is missing, since the insect blows a real trumpet here. The original Aesop, quoted by *GEF* I 159, is closer to La Fontaine's version.

139. The sound effect comes across very clearly in the musical version of ths fable by the twentieth-century composer André Caplet.

140. Dandrey makes the subtle point that the donkeys' indignation works only if they are thinking of themselves as men, since if they are perceived as donkeys 'braire' is a technical term for their call, not an insult (Dandrey 1 p.253).

141. Preface, p.8. La Fontaine's early writings also include examples of what Dandrey calls 'le badinage des animaux parlants' *[the witty repartee of the talking animals]*(1, p.29), for instance the 'Aventure d'un Saumon et d'un Esturgeon' *[Adventure of a Salmon and a Sturgeon]* in *Le Songe de Vaux [The Dream of Vaux]*, OD p.95–7.

142. The original fable is in Aulus Gellius's, *Attic Nights* II 29, of which Fumaroli gives a French translation, I 384.

143. Biard gives many more examples (1, p.58–63). Odette de Mourgues, however, points out that 'ce n'est pas le langage parlé que nous donne La Fontaine, mais la stylisation du langage parlé' *[La Fontaine gives us not spoken language but a stylized form of spoken language]*: even if the characters appear to be simple rustics, poetic effects are achieved (1, p.126–7).

144. Of course, the implied moral is that curiosity can be deadly. However, Sweetser points out that this curiosity is not only fatal, but linked to speech, when

she comments: 'Intellectual curiosity, like the tongue, can be the best or worst thing' (1, p.105).

145. For further examples, see Danner's analysis of the frog's words in 'La Grenouille et le Rat' *[The Frog and the Rat]* (1, p.100–4).

146. See Chapter 3 for a discussion of the use of language in this fable.

147. From *Célinte*. See Collinet p.1112 for page reference.

148. This is how Couton 1 describes this oath (p.431).

149. Collinet has a detailed and illuminating analysis of this fable, and points out that the humour of the whole poem rests on a 'discrète résonance héroï-comique' *[discreet heroi-comic resonance]*, of which this is an instance (1, p.164–9).

150. For other examples see VIII 14 l.39–49, VII 6 l.30–2.

151. See *GEF* II 325.

152. Compare for instance Racine's lines: 'Il faut d'autres efforts pour rompre tant de noeuds' *[Other efforts are needed to break such knots]* (*Bérénice* V 7 l.1458), or 'Et je romps tous les noeuds qui m'attachent à vous.' *[And I break all the knots that bound me to you]* (*Iphigénie* IV 6 l.1416).

153. The cat's polished language and the contrast between the two animals' styles are absent from Poussines' version of this fable which inspired La Fontaine. Fumaroli (II 352–3) quotes Poussines, and comments that in his version, 'La Fontaine s'est livré à un travail de minutieuse orfèvrerie' *[La Fontaine undertook the labour of a meticulous goldsmith]*.

154. Chamfort commented on this fable: 'Ce qui en fait la beauté, c'est la vérité du dialogue' *[What makes it beauty is the truth of the dialogue]* (see Collinet, p.1067). Not all critics would entirely agree with my characterization of the wolf as brutal. Gutwirth puts forward a more positive view – for him the wolf is to some extent a rational being who seeks to square his actions with his conscience (1, p.134). Rubin, incidentally, argues convincingly that it is the lamb who is 'intellectually "le plus fort"' (1, pp.35–6).

155. I discuss the metre of these lines in more detail in Chapter 2.

156. *GEF* III 36 gives convincing parallels to Vergil, Pliny and Marot.

157. Gohin seems too disparaging when he dismisses the leopard's speech as 'emphatique, orgueilleux et maladroit' *[emphatic, arrogant and clumsy]*, p. 125.

158. See Biard 1 p.30–2 for a discussion of this latter term.

159. Daniel Bergez, *L'Explication de texte littéraire*, Paris, Bordas, 1989, p.111. The examination of this fable is on pp.100–16.

160. Rabelais, *Oeuvres complètes*, ed. Boulenger, Paris, Pléiade, 1959, p.99.

161.   At ille expirans: 'Fortes indigne tuli
             Mihi insultare: te, naturae dedecus,
             Quod ferre certe cogor, bis videor mori.'
Phaedrus I, Fable 21, l.10–2.

162. Despite the *GEF* punctuation, which turns the last line into an authorial comment, I would suggest that this line is spoken by the fox and not directly by the poet, since earlier in the poem we are told that it was the fox himself who applied his *bon mot* about the bust to aristocrats (l.7–8). Fumaroli comments that the 'pointe de critique sociale' *[nuance of social criticism]* is absent from the original version (I 382). See *GEF* I 325.

163. See *GEF* I 144 for the sources of this elegant speech. Wadsworth sees it and 'Le Lion devenu vieux' *[The Lion grown old]* as 'brief but serious poems which

seem like fragments of some mighty epic', and claims Vergil as La Fontaine's chief inspiration (p.52). See Chapter 1 for a detailed account of the beginning of this poem.

164. Incidentally, as Collinet points out (p.1088), La Fontaine departs from earlier versions of this fable in that he restricts himself to a single protagonist rather than a group of animals. This enables him to demonstrate how a single introspective animal might systematically follow through a train of thought through soliloquy.

165. Fumaroli, II 343–4, quotes the original.

166. Couton (p.424) quotes an emblem published by Guéroult in 1550 as the source for this fable. Guéroult's fox fails to sustain the fiction that all animals love each other to the end, and admits that he fears the hounds. The unremitting hypocrisy of both animals is thus La Fontaine's invention.

167. See Fumaroli I 392 for the original version.

168. A detailed examination of the moral implications of this fable can be found in Chapter 8.

169. Incidentally, La Fontaine's adaptation of this fable from Pilpay emphasizes the importance of language far more than the original. In Pilpay's version, the crayfish kills the cormorant, and the poem is about perfidy not going unpunished, not about how listening to blandishments can cause one's downfall. See Haddad pp.162–3.

170. A rare exception is 'La Chauve-Souris et les deux Belettes' *[The Bat and the two Weasels]*, II 5.

171. VIII 10 l.6.

CHAPTER 8. NEGLECTED PROTAGONISTS

172. See Rubin 4 pp.20–21, and Danner 1 pp.160–2 for discussion of this fable.

173. The importance of 'le voyage' as a Lafontainian theme is eloquently summarized by Van Delft (2 pp.186–8), and discussed more fully by Grimm (1 pp.84–91).

174. I am grateful to my student, Jane May, for drawing my attention to this.

175. In *Les Précieuses ridicules*, sc.ix, Magdelon orders her servant: 'vite, voiturez-nous les commodités de la conversation' *[quick, convey to us the commodities of conversation]*.

176. Biard comments that the word, which literally means 'the female pilgrim', carries two meanings, 'a popular pejorative meaning of shady, crack-brained' character and the more general meaning of traveller'. Biard 1 p.47.

177. See his 'Avertissement', p.245.

178. This circling movement is repeated elsewhere by La Fontaine: see II 16 'tourne autour du troupeau' *[circles round the flock]*.

179. Since during this war Apollo the sun-god supported the Trojans.

180. Vincent discusses the problems of this poem in an interesting chapter, pp.21–39.

181. See *GEF* II 342.

182. Perhaps literally the convolutions of a dissected brain (the Chauveau illustration shows a human head beside him on the ground), but also by implication the complexities of the human mind. Michael Vincent, in an interesting discussion of this word 'labyrinthe', points out that La Fontaine's source referred to dissected animals: Michael Vincent, *Figures of the Text: Reading and Writing (in) La Fontaine*, Amsterdam/Philadelphia, John Benjamins, 1992, p.31–3.

183. In two interesting reevaluations of this fable, Jürgen Grimm suggests that the the primary interest of the Abderites' words is as a defence of Democritus's philosophy ('La Fontaine, Lucrèce et l'Epicurisme, Grimm 1 pp.72–4), while Michael Vincent (p.24–7) sees in them the reflection of central ideas on reading and self-knowledge.

184. La Fontaine took their grief from the original apocryphal account of the letter they wrote to Hippocrates. See Fumaroli II 356 and *GEF, loc. cit.,* for details.

185. An idea that had been of interest to thinkers through the ages, and was to be explored by Fontenelle in his *Entretiens sur la pluralité des mondes* of 1686.

186. It has echoes of the Delphic 'know thyself', as Michael Vincent points out, p.25.

187. In particular, VIII 8. I 22, though much less trivial than VIII 8, resembles it in that the tone is suddenly much more grandiose at the end.

188. Jules Brody, in 'Lire La Fontaine: la méthode de Leo Spitzer', Slater 1 p.17, makes the interesting suggestion that this marriage of disparate styles represents a manifestation of what the poet called 'la discorde'.

189. See Collinet p.1184 and *GEF* II 187–91 for details.

190. See Chapter 7 for a discussion of this Cat's use of language.

191. For example, XII 3, XII 5 and VIII 22.

192. The discussions of fables X 2 and VIII 26 were published, with a slightly different slant, in my article 'Reading La Fontaine's Titles', in Slater 1 pp.23–33.

CHAPTER 9. THE POET'S VOICE

193. This donkey's use of language was examined in Chapter 6.

194. It will be remembered that, according to Perrault, La Fontaine discussed the illustrations of the first recueil with Chauveau (see Biard 2 and Bassy).

195. Although there is abundant evidence that many of the animal portraits are literary in origin, as Madeleine Defrenne demonstrates, I feel she overstates the position when she exhorts us: 'Ne revenons pas sur la question des "observations d'animaux"; il y a bien longtemps que Paul de Rémusat, Rémy de Gourmont et J.-H. Fabre ont prouvé qu'elles avaient été faites par un aveugle ou qu'elles n'avaient pas eu lieu.' Defrenne 1, p.129. *[Let us not return to the question of 'animal observations'. Paul de Rémusat, Rémy de Gourmont et J.-H. Fabre have long since proved that they were made by a blind man or that there weren't any].*

196. Furetière comments: 'un asne s'appelle absolument un grison, parce qu'il est ordinairement gris.' *[a donkey has to be called a 'grison' because it is normally grey.]* He adds: 'Se dit aussi par raillerie des laquais' *[it is also used as a joke term for lackeys],* because certain noblemen who wished to be discreet dressed their servants in donkey grey rather than in distinctive livery.

197. The combination of human and animal qualities in this donkey is discussed in Chapter 6.

198. Collinet tells us that a number of critics, writing after the French Revolution, saw in it an outspoken condemnation of the Ancien Régime. Interestingly, however, he also quotes Chamfort, in whose opinion La Fontaine's contemporaries failed to notice the implications of this potentially shocking line (Collinet, p.1150–1).

199. An exception is the Norman or Gascon fox of III 11.

200. Phaedrus I 15; see Fumaroli I 392 for Sacy's translation.

201. For example, see Jean-Michel Delacompté, *Madame, la cour, la mort*, Paris, Gallimard, 1992, for details of the flamboyantly ostentatious funeral service of Henriette d'Angleterre.

202. For example, in 'un fripon d'enfant, cet âge est sans pitié' *[a little devil of a child, they have no pity at that age]* ('Les Deux Pigeons', IX 2 1.54).

203. See Danner 1 pp.97–101 for an interesting discussion of intertwined ironies in 'Le Lion et le Moucheron'.

204. Sweetser describes these in a useful article, Sweetser 4.

205. Sweetser explains that in his formal first-person dedications La Fontaine is demonstrating the correct attitude to his patrons, particularly in the fables dedicated to royalty: Louis XIV's minister Colbert favoured high-sounding praise and classical allusions (Sweetser 2, p.105–6).

206. I am not, of course, implying that the fables in the second *Recueil* were written in the order in which they are printed; indeed, we know that La Fontaine re-ordered them for publication.

207. In Book VII we have fable 4 'Le Héron – La Fille', 5 'Les Souhaits', 9 'La Laitière et le Pot au lait', 10 'Le Curé et le Mort, and 11 'L'Homme qui court après la Fortune et l'Homme qui l'attend dans son lit'. In Book VIII we have 1 'La Mort et le mourant', 2 'Le Savetier et le Financier', 7 'Le Chien qui porte à son cou le dîner de son Maître', and 21 'Le Faucon et le Chapon'.

208. All commentators' views on this fable are from *GEF* II 250.

209. See Collinet p.1223–4, and also Collinet 3.

210. Collinet, p.1224. See also Collinet 7 pp.89–90 for a further discussion of the relationship between this line and other works by La Fontaine.

CHAPTER 10. ECHOES AND ALLUSIONS – CREATING A WORLD

211. Although some of the longer poems in Book XII might seem unsuited to the appelation.

212. Marcel Gutwirth gives a lucid account of the structure underlying Book II (pp.181–97). Nathan Gross makes a convincing case for a structure to Book VI, pp.78–90. I tackle the structure of Book VII in Slater 1. Jean Couton, in Couton 2, finds an Epicurean thread running through Book VIII. Richard Danner, in Danner 2, discovers a patterning in Book X (pp.90–99). Most critics do not go as far as Pierre Bornecque, who sees the *Fables* in its entirety as an elaborately structured edifice (Bornecque 2).

213. Sweetser 1, p.123. Dandrey, too, sees certain poems in the book as revealing 'la saturation du modèle de la fable' *[the saturation of the fable model]* (Dandrey 1, p.79). Sweetser, however, in interesting recent work on Book XII, has modified her view, and is now working on the convincing hypothesis that the book seems coherent if viewed as an instruction manual for the young Duc de Bourgogne (see 'Conseils d'un vieux Chat à une jeune Souris', Slater 1, pp.95–105, and *Le Fablier* 8). Jürgen Grimm, too, staunchly defends the structure of Book XII, finding a coherent philosophical line running through the poems, and seeing in it the poet's 'livre-testament'. In a recent article, he argues convincingly that there is a shape even to the final book, which he describes as seen by earlier critics as 'un salmigondis de dernière heure, produit d'une décrépitude sénile!' *[an eleventh-hour hotchpotch, the work of a senile, decrepit writer!]* (Grimm 3, p.67).

214. Collinet 4, p.231.

215. The characters' use of language in this fable is examined in Chapter 7.

216. See Tyler, p.402.

217. *OD*, p.142.

218. It is reproduced in Allott, 2, p.20. It can also be found in Collinet and *GEF*.

219. See fables 17 and 18.

220. In the article mentioned earlier.

221. He commented that this was one of his aims as a fabulist in the Preface to the first *Recueil* (p.7).

222. Although in modern editions the name is generally hyphenated in VIII 22 and not in XII 15, *GEF* comments that it was originally spelt as one word in both (II 324). Curiously, Raymond Josse mentions as a contact of La Fontaine's a certain Anthoine Rougemail, or Rougemaille, 'garde de la forêt de Wassy' *[a gamekeeper in the Forest of Wassy]*.

223. See discussion in Chapters 7 and 8.

224. There are many such fables, for example 'Le Pot de terre et le Pot de fer' (V 2) or 'Le Rat et l'Huître' (VIII 9).

225. See Collinet p.1293.

226. See *GEF* III p.404 for the relevant passage from Pilpay's *Livre des Lumières*.

227. See Collinet p.1292 for details.

228. See for example the name 'Raminagrobis' in XII 5, the personality of the monkey of XII 3, which complements and contrasts with that of other Lafontainian monkeys, the allusion to the Ligue in XII 10 which reminds us of II 5. There are links in every poem.

229. Louis Van Delft suggests that La Fontaine has drawn 'une mappemonde morale' *[a moral map of the world]* in the *Fables*, and reminds us of his ultimate message: 'apprendre à se connaître' *[learn to know oneself]* (Van Delft 1, p.108).

230. An earlier French version of this chapter, containing some of the same material but with a different slant, was published under the title 'La Fontaine imitateur de lui-même, les dernières fables' in *Fablier* 8, pp. 129–36.

231. See Lapp for an interesting discussion of these lines.

Bibliography

Note: Works cited in the text are there referred to by their author's name only. The Bibliography gives the full details, and, where appropriate, specifies the name used in the text. Where more than one work by an author is cited in the text, the name is followed by a number, with the corresponding number given in the Bibliography. Additional works which are of interest, though not mentioned in the text, are also included.

17TH-CENTURY DICTIONARY:

Furetière, A. *Le Dictionnaire universel*, 3 vols. [Paris, 1690], Paris: SNL Le Robert, 1978. ('**Furetière**').

EDITIONS OF THE *FABLES* USED:

La Fontaine, *Oeuvres complètes, I, Fables, contes et nouvelles*, J.-P. Collinet (ed), Paris: Pléiade, Gallimard, 1991. ('**Collinet**').

La Fontaine, *Fables choisies mises en vers*, G. Couton (ed), Paris: Garnier, 1961. ('**Couton**').

La Fontaine, *Fables*, M. Fumaroli (ed), Paris: Imprimerie nationale, 2 vols., 1985 ('**Fumaroli**').

(*Note:* the above edition has been reprinted in one volume: Paris, Livre de Poche, Classiques modernes, 1995).

La Fontaine, *Oeuvres*, H. Régnier (ed), Paris: Les Grands écrivains de la France, Hachette, vols. I–III, 1883–5. ('***GEF***').

EDITION OF OTHER LA FONTAINE WORKS CONSULTED

La Fontaine, *Oeuvres diverses*, P. Clarac (ed), Paris: Pléiade, 1948. ('***OD***').

OTHER FABULISTS CONSULTED:

Aesop, *The Fables of Aesop,* translated by S. Croxall and Sir Roger L'Estrange, London and New York: Frederick Warne (undated).

Aesop, *The Complete Fables,* translated by O. and R. Temple, London: Penguin, 1998.

Babrius and Phaedrus, translated by B.E. Perry, Cambridge MA: Harvard University Press and London: Heinemann (Loeb Classical Library no. 436), 1975.

OTHER BOOKS AND ARTICLES ON LA FONTAINE CITED:

Allott, T., 'Une Décennie d'éditions et de traductions des oeuvres de La Fontaine'. *Le Fablier*, numéro 3, 1991, pp.17–23.

Allott, T., 'La Fontaine éditeur de ses oeuvres', in *XVIIe siècle* no.187 (47e année, no.2), pp.239–54. ('**Allott 2**').

Bassy, A.-M., *Les Fables de La Fontaine. Quatre siècles d'illustration*, Paris: Promodis, 1986.

Bibliothèque nationale, *Jean de La Fontaine*, Paris, Bibliothèque nationale de France / Seuil, 1995 ('**Bibliothèque nationale Catalogue**').

Bornecque, P., *la Fontaine fabuliste*, Paris: SEDES, 1975.

Bornecque P., 'Thèmes et organisation des Fables', in *Europe* 515 (mars 1972), pp.39–52. ('**Bornecque 2**').

Biard, J.D., *The Style of La Fontaine's Fables*, Oxford: Blackwell, 1966. ('**Biard 1**').

Biard, J.D., Introduction to *Vignettes des Fables de La Fontaine* (1668) de François Chauveau. Exeter: Exeter University Press, 1977. ('**Biard 2**').

Bray, R., *Les Fables de La Fontaine*, Paris: Malfère, 1929.

Brody, J. *Lectures de La Fontaine*, Charlottesville, VA: Rookwood Press (EMF Monographs, I), 1995. ('**Brody 1**').

Brody, J., 'Lire La Fontaine', in Slater 1. ('**Brody 2**').

Collinet, J.-P., *Le Monde littéraire de La Fontaine*, Paris: P.U.F., 1970. ('**Collinet 1**')

Collinet, J.-P., *La Fontaine en amont et en aval*, Paris: Nizet, 1988.

Collinet, J.-P., 'La Fontaine mosaïste – une lecture des "Deux Pigeons"', in Fablier 5, pp.11–16. ('**Collinet 3**').

Collinet, J.-P., 'La Cigale et le Hérisson', in *Littératures classiques* 12, janvier 1990, pp.225–33. ('**Collinet 4**').

Collinet, J.-P., 'La Fontaine, "La Fille" et la grande Mademoiselle', in *Mélanges offerts à Georges Couton*, Lyon: Presses universitaires de Lyon, 1981, pp.359–71. ('**Collinet 5**').

Collinet, J.-P., *La Fontaine et quelques autres*, Genève: Droz, 1992.

Collinet, J.-P., 'Poésie pastorale et classicisme', in *Cahiers de l'Association internationale des études françaises*, no.39, mai 1987, pp.79–95. ('**Collinet 7**').

Couton, J., *La Politique de La Fontaine*, Paris: Les Belles lettres, 1959. ('**Couton 1**').

Couton, J., in 'Le Livre épicurien des Fables: Essai de lecture du livre VIII', *Travaux de linguistique et de littérature*, 13.2, 1975, pp.283–90. ('**Couton 2**').

Dandrey, P., *La Fabrique des 'Fables': Essai sur la poétique de La Fontaine*, Paris: Klincksieck, 1992. ('**Dandrey 1**').

Dandrey, P., 'Moralité', in *La Fontaine, Fables, livres VII à XII, Littératures classiques*, supplément au no.16, pp.29–47.

Danner, R., *Patterns of Irony in the 'Fables' of La Fontaine*, Athens, O.H.: Ohio University Press, & London, 1985. ('**Danner 1**').

Danner, R., 'La Fontaine's *Fables*, Book X: The Labyrinth Hypothesis' in *L'Esprit Créateur,* vol. XXI no.4, winter 1981, pp.90–9. ('**Danner 2**').

Defrenne, M., 'Le Phénomène créateur chez La Fontaine, le poète et le monde'. *Australian Journal of French Studies,* vol.XII no.2, May–August 1975, pp.119–67. ('**Defrenne 1**').

Duchêne, R., 'Les fables de La Fontaine sont-elles des contes?' (see *La Fontaine, Fables, livres VII à XII,* pp.85–97).

L'Esprit Créateur, vol. XXI no.4, winter 1981 (La Fontaine number).

Le Fablier, Revue des Amis de Jean de La Fontaine, Musée Jean de La Fontaine, Château-Thierry, nos. 1–7, 1989–96. ('**Fablier 1–8**').

Fumaroli, M., *Le Poète et le Roi: Jean de La Fontaine en son siècle,* Paris: Fallois, 1997. ('**Fumaroli 1**').

Gaudard, F-C., 'La Versification chez La Fontaine', *Champs du signe* 2, 1992, pp.149–80.

Génetiot, A., *Poétique du loisir mondain, de Voiture à La Fontaine,* Paris: Honoré Champion, 1997.

Grimm, J., *Le Pouvoir des fables – études lafontainiennes I,* Paris / Seattle / Tübingen: Biblio 17 (*Papers on French Seventeenth Century Literature*), 1994. ('**Grimm 1**').

Grimm, J., 'Jean de La Fontaine: "Malgré Jupiter même et les temps orageux". Pour une réévaluation du livre XII des *Fables*', *Oeuvres et Critiques* XVI, 2, 1991, pp.57–69.

Grimm, J., *Le Pouvoir des fables. Etudes lafontainiennes I,* Paris / Seattle / Tübingen: Biblio 17, 85, *PFSCL,* 1994. ('**Grimm 3**').

Grimm, J., *Le 'dire sans dire' et le dit, Etudes lafontainiennes II,* Paris / Seattle / Tübingen: Biblio 17, 93, *PFSCL,* 1996.

Gross, N., 'Order and Theme in La Fontaine's *Fables*, Book VI' (see *L'Esprit Créateur,* pp.78–90).

Gutwirth, M., *Un Merveilleux sans éclat: La Fontaine ou la Poésie exilée,* Genève: Droz, 1987. ('**Gutwirth 1**').

Gutwirth, M., 'Le Chêne et le Roseau, ou les cheminements de la mimésis', *The French Review,* vol XLVIII no.4, March 1975. ('**Gutwirth 2**').

Haddad, A., *Fables de La Fontaine d'origine orientale,* Paris: Société d'enseignement supérieur, 1984.

Heller, L.M. and Richmond I.M. (eds) *La Poétique des 'Fables' de La Fontaine,* University of Western Ontario, Mestengo Press, 1994. ('**Heller and Richmond**').

Josse, R., *Jehan de La Fontaine,* Château-Thierry, Société Historique et Archéologique de Château-Thierry, Maison Jean de La Fontaine, 1987.

Kohn, R., *Le Goût de La Fontaine,* Paris: P.U.F., 1962.

La Fontaine, Fables, livres VII à XII, Littératures classiques, supplément au no.16, Paris: Klincksieck, 1992.

Lapp, J.C., *The Aesthetics of Negligence,* Cambridge: Cambridge University Press, 1971.

McGowan, M., 'Moral Intention in the *Fables* of La Fontaine', *Journal of the Warburg and Courtauld Institute* 29, 1966, pp.246–82.

McGowan, M., 'L'Eloge et la discrétion: l'art de peindre chez La Fontaine', in Fablier 5, pp.23–9. ('**McGowan 2**').

de Mourgues, O., *O Muse fuyante proie …* , Paris: Corti, 1987. ('**Mourgues 1**').
de Mourgues, O., *La Fontaine*, London: Edward Arnold, 1960. ('**Mourgues 2**').
Rubin, D.L., *A Pact with Silence: Art and Thought in the Fables of Jean de La Fontaine*, Columbus: Ohio State University Press, 1991. ('**Rubin 1**').
Rubin, D.L., '[Dis]solving Double Irony: La Fontaine, Marianne Moore and Ulysses' Companions', in Slater 1, pp.87–94. ('**Rubin 2**').
Rubin, D.L., 'Four Modes of Double Irony in La Fontaine's *Fables*', in *The Equilibrium of Wit: Essays for Odette de Mourgues*, P. Bayley and D. Gabe Coleman (eds), Lexington KY: French Forum, 1982, pp.201–12.
Rubin, D.L., *Higher, Hidden Order – Design and Meaning in the Odes of Malherbe*, Chapel Hill, NC: University of North Carolina Press, 1972 ('**Rubin 4**').
Slater, M. (ed.), Actes du colloque La Fontaine de Londres, in *Papers on French Seventeenth Century Literature /Biblio 17*, vol. XXII no.44, 1996 ('**Slater 1**').
Slater, M., 'La Fontaine's Fables, Book VII: the Problem of Order' in *The Modern Language Review*, vol. 82 no.3, July 1987, pp.573–86 ('**Slater 2**').
Slater, M., 'La Fontaine and Brevity' in *French Studies* XLIV, no.2., 1990, pp.143–55 ('**Slater 3**').
Slater, M., 'la Fontaine et les Contes d'enfant' in *Actes du colloque de Montréal, Papers of French Seventeenth Century Literature*, 1997, pp.107–16 ('**Slater 4**').
Slater, M., 'La Fontaine and the Man in the Sun' in *French Studies Bulletin*, no.23, 1987. ('**Slater 5**').
Slater, M., 'La Fontaine's Christian Fables' in *Seventeenth-Century French Studies*, XI (1989), pp.136–45. ('**Slater 6**').
Slater, M., 'La Fontaine's view of Animals' in *Seventeenth-Century French Studies*, XIII, 1991, pp. 179–94. ('**Slater 7**').
Spitzer, L., 'The Art of Transition in La Fontaine', in *Essays on Seventeenth Century French Literature*, translated D. Bellos, Cambridge: Cambridge University Press, 1983.
Sweetser, M.-D., *La Fontaine*, Boston: Twayne, 1987. ('**Sweetser 1**').
Sweetser, M.-O., 'A la recherche d'une poétique dans le premier recueil des *Fables*', in Heller and Richmond, pp.105–17. ('**Sweetser 2**').
Sweetser, M.-O., 'Conseils d'un vieux Chat à une jeune Souris: les leçons du livre XII', in Slater 1 pp.95–103. ('**Sweetser 3**').
Sweetser, M.-O., 'Les épîtres dédicatoires des *Fables* ou La Fontaine et l'art de plaire', *Littératures classiques* 18, 1993, pp.267–85. ('**Sweetser 4**').
Tournon, A., 'Les Fables du Crétois,' in *Littératures classiques*, supplément 1992, janvier 1992, pp.7–27.
Tyler, J.A., *A Concordance to the Fables and Tales of Jean de La Fontaine*, Ithaca and London: Cornell University Press, 1974.
Van Delft, L., 'La Cartographie morale au XVIIe siècle', in *Etudes françaises* 21/2, 1985, pp.91–113 ('**Van Delft 1**').
Van Delft, L., *Le Moraliste classique, essai de définition et de typologie*, Genève: Droz, 1982. ('**Van Delft 2**').
Vincent, M., *Figures of the Text – Reading and Writing (in) La Fontaine*, Amsterdam/Philadelphia: John Benjamins, 1992.
Zuber, R., 'Les Animaux orateurs: quelques remarques sur la parole des *Fables*' in *Littératures classiques*, supplément 1992, janvier 1992, pp.49–60.

Index